Chronotopic Identity Work

ENCOUNTERS
Series Editors: Jan Blommaert, *Tilburg University, The Netherlands,* Ben Rampton, *Kings College London, UK,* Anna De Fina, *Georgetown University, USA,* Sirpa Leppänen, *University of Jyväskylä, Finland* and James Collins, *University at Albany/SUNY, USA*

The Encounters series sets out to explore diversity in language from a theoretical and an applied perspective. So the focus is both on the linguistic encounters, inequalities and struggles that characterise post-modern societies and on the development, within sociocultural linguistics, of theoretical instruments to explain them. The series welcomes work dealing with such topics as heterogeneity, mixing, creolization, bricolage, cross-over phenomena, polylingual and polycultural practices. Another high-priority area of study is the investigation of processes through which linguistic resources are negotiated, appropriated and controlled, and the mechanisms leading to the creation and maintenance of sociocultural differences. The series welcomes ethnographically oriented work in which contexts of communication are investigated rather than assumed, as well as research that shows a clear commitment to close analysis of local meaning making processes and the semiotic organisation of texts.

All books in this series are externally peer-reviewed.

Full details of all the books in this series and of all our other publications can be found on http://www.multilingual-matters.com, or by writing to Multilingual Matters, St Nicholas House, 31-34 High Street, Bristol BS1 2AW, UK.

ENCOUNTERS: 18

Chronotopic Identity Work

Sociolinguistic Analyses of Cultural and Linguistic Phenomena in Time and Space

Edited by
Sjaak Kroon and Jos Swanenberg

MULTILINGUAL MATTERS
Bristol • Blue Ridge Summit

DOI https://doi.org/10.21832/KROON6614
Library of Congress Cataloging in Publication Data
A catalog record for this book is available from the Library of Congress.

Library of Congress Control Number: 2019029667

British Library Cataloguing in Publication Data
A catalogue entry for this book is available from the British Library.

ISBN-13: 978-1-78892-661-4 (hbk)
ISBN-13: 978-1-78892-660-7 (pbk)

Multilingual Matters
UK: St Nicholas House, 31-34 High Street, Bristol BS1 2AW, UK.
USA: NBN, Blue Ridge Summit, PA, USA.

Website: www.multilingual-matters.com
Twitter: Multi_Ling_Mat
Facebook: https://www.facebook.com/multilingualmatters
Blog: www.channelviewpublications.wordpress.com

Copyright © 2020 Sjaak Kroon, Jos Swanenberg and the authors of individual chapters.

All rights reserved. No part of this work may be reproduced in any form or by any means without permission in writing from the publisher.

The policy of Multilingual Matters/Channel View Publications is to use papers that are natural, renewable and recyclable products, made from wood grown in sustainable forests. In the manufacturing process of our books, and to further support our policy, preference is given to printers that have FSC and PEFC Chain of Custody certification. The FSC and/or PEFC logos will appear on those books where full certification has been granted to the printer concerned.

Typeset by Riverside Publishing Solutions.

Contents

	Contributors	vii
1	Introducing Chronotopic Identity Work *Sjaak Kroon and Jos Swanenberg*	1
2	Are Chronotopes Helpful? *Jan Blommaert*	16
3	Inverted Youth Language in Mongolia as Macroscopic and Microscopic Chronotopes *Sender Dovchin*	25
4	The Care of the Selfie: Ludic Chronotopes of *Baifumei* in Online China *Kunming Li and Jan Blommaert*	49
5	The Mass Mediation of Chronotopic Identity in a Changing Indonesia *Zane Goebel*	67
6	Chronotopic Identities and Social Change in Yangshuo, China *Shuang Gao*	86
7	Chronotopes and Heritage Authenticity: The Case of the Tujia in China *Xuan Wang and Sjaak Kroon*	105

8	Languages and Regimes of Communication: Students' Struggles with Norms and Identities through Chronotopic Work *Martha Sif Karrebæk and Janus Spindler Møller*	128
9	Out of Order: Authenticity and Normativity in Communication at School *Jos Swanenberg*	153
10	The Moral Economy of Chronotopic Identities: A Case Study in a Polish Community in Antwerp *Malgorzata Szabla*	174
11	Insights and Challenges of Chronotopic Analysis for Sociolinguistics *Anna De Fina*	190
	Index	201

Contributors

Jan Blommaert is Professor of Language, Culture and Globalization and Director of the Babylon Center at Tilburg University, The Netherlands. He also holds appointments at Ghent University, Belgium and the University of the Western Cape, South Africa. Publications include *Durkheim and the Internet* (Bloomsbury, 2018), *Ethnography, Superdiversity and Linguistic Landscapes: Chronicles of Complexity* (Multilingual Matters, 2013), *The Sociolinguistics of Globalization* (Cambridge University Press, 2010), *Ethnographic Fieldwork: A Beginner's Guide* (Multilingual Matters, 2010), *Grassroots Literacy* (Routledge, 2008), *Discourse: A Critical Introduction* (Cambridge University Press, 2005).

Anna De Fina is Professor of Italian Language and Linguistics in the Italian Department and affiliated faculty with the Linguistics Department at Georgetown University. She holds a Master in Linguistics from Cambridge University and a PhD in Linguistics from Georgetown. Her interests and publications focus on discourse and migration, identity, narrative and super diversity. She has published widely on these topics. Among her publications are *Identity in Narrative: A Study of Immigrant Discourse* (John Benjamins, 2003), *Analyzing Narratives* with Alexandra Georgakopoulou (Cambridge University Press, 2012) and *Diversity and Superdiversity Sociocultural Linguistics Perspectives* with Wenger and Ikizoglu, (Georgetown University Press, 2017). She is one of the editors of the book series *Encounters* for Multilingual Matters and *Discourse, Narrative and Interaction* for Routledge.

Sender Dovchin is a Senior Research Fellow at the School of Education, Curtin University, Perth. She is a Discovery Early Career Research Awardee (DECRA) of 2018 by an Australian Research Council. Previously, she was an Associate Professor at the University of Aizu, Japan. She has authored numerous articles in international top-tier peer-reviewed journals. Her single-authored monograph *Language, Media and Globalization in the Periphery* was published in 2018 by Routledge. Her co-authored research monograph with Alastair Pennycook and Shaila Sultana, *Popular Culture,*

Voice, and Linguistic Diversity: Young Adults On- and Offline was published in 2017 by Palgrave-Macmillan.

Shuang Gao is a sociolinguist working at the Department of English, University of Liverpool, UK. Her research interests include language and identity, language ideology and globalization. Her publications have appeared in the key journals of the field and she is the author of *Aspiring to be Global: Language and Social Change in a Tourism Village in China* (Multilingual Matters, 2019).

Zane Goebel is an Associate Professor at the University of Queensland, Brisbane, where he teaches Indonesian and Applied Linguistics. Goebel works on language and social relations in Indonesia. He has extensive publications in this area, including *Language, Migration, and Identity: Neighbourhood Talk in Indonesia* (Cambridge University Press, 2010); *Language and Superdiversity: Indonesians Knowledging at Home and Abroad* (Oxford University Press, 2015). He also has four forthcoming books, including: *Global Leadership Talk* (Oxford University Press); *Reimagining Rapport* (Oxford University Press); *Rapport and the Discursive Co-construction of Social Relations in Fieldwork settings* (Mouton De Gruyter); and *Contact Talk* (with Deborah Cole and Howard Manns, Routledge).

Martha Sif Karrebæk, Associate Professor at University of Copenhagen, has worked with a broad range of topics in the field of multilingualism. Her PhD focused on peer group socialization and second language acquisition in pre-school, using Construction Grammar and Language Socialization. She subsequently studied how children become socialized into the role of students in a school with a student population characterized by diversity. She continued to focus on the use and non-use of different linguistic registers in the first grades. Karrebæk has led a project on Mother Tongue Education in Copenhagen, and is now starting a project on interpreting in the public sector in Denmark. Karrebæk is also well-known for her work on the intersections between food and language, and she has published on the intersection between (in)security and language.

Sjaak Kroon is Professor of Multilingualism in the Multicultural Society. He is a member of the Department of Culture Studies and Babylon, Center for the Study of Superdiversity at Tilburg University, The Netherlands. His main focus in research and teaching is on linguistic and cultural diversity, language policy, literacy and education in the context of globalization.

Kunming Li is lecturer of Sociolinguistics at Jiangnan University, China. He received a PhD degree from Tilburg University in 2018. His primary research areas are digital ethnography, multimodal discourse analysis and gender studies.

Janus Spindler Møller is Associate Professor at the Department of Nordic Studies and Linguistics (NorS) at the University of Copenhagen. He was awarded his PhD in 2009 for his thesis on longitudinal development of polylingual practices. His main fields of interest include languaging, interactional sociolinguistics, polylingualism, linguistic ethnography and language ideology, with current research projects including: The Everyday Languaging project (language use and ideology among students in a Copenhagen school), and SoMeFamily (a study of social media use in families). He has published in a range of journals including *International Journal of Multilingualism*, *Journal of Sociolinguistics*, *Applied Linguistics Review* and *Language in Society*.

Jos Swanenberg is Professor of Diversity in Language and Culture at the Department of Culture Studies and Babylon, Center for the Study of Superdiversity at Tilburg University, and adviser on heritage, language and culture at Erfgoed Brabant (Cultural Heritage Foundation) in 's-Hertogenbosch, the Netherlands. He is president of the board of Anéla, the Association of Applied Linguistics in The Netherlands and Belgium. He is co-editor with Sjaak Kroon of *Language and Culture on the Margins: Global/Local Interactions* (Routledge, 2018).

Malgorzata Szabla is a PhD Student at the Department of Culture Studies at Tilburg University, The Netherlands. Her research in the field of social anthropology and linguistic ethnography, conducted both online and offline, focuses on identity construction of Polish migrants in Belgium and the Netherlands in times of globalization and superdiversity.

Xuan Wang is a senior lecturer in Chinese Studies at the School of Modern Languages, Cardiff University, Wales, where she coordinates and teaches undergraduate courses of Chinese Studies. As a sociolinguist, her areas of interest and research cover language ideology, digital communication, heritage tourism, identity politics and peripheral globalization, with a focus on contemporary China and Chinese. She has released a number of publications with major publishers of journals and books. She is currently co-editing the book *Transnationalizing Chineseness: Language, Mobility and Diversity* (with Shuang Gao, Multilingual Matters).

1 Introducing Chronotopic Identity Work

Sjaak Kroon and Jos Swanenberg

Introduction

This introduction does not aim at introducing the reader to Mikhail Bakhtin's thinking in general nor does it intend to fully capture his thoughts on the concept of chronotopicity that is central in this volume. We merely want to introduce the content of this book that offers a collection of empirically grounded sociolinguistic studies that contribute to unraveling the intricate relationships between time and space in human interaction and identity work in times of mobility and superdiversity. We do so by first of all only very briefly introducing Bakhtin's concept of chronotopicity. According to Carr and Lempert (2016: 6) the rediscovery of Bakhtin's writings 'encouraged attention to the pervasive presence of other voices in what apparently single speakers say and made it difficult to maintain that speech is ever anchored in any one place and time' and showed 'how porous the spatial and temporal boundaries of communicative events can be' – for more about all of this the reader is referred to Jan Blommaert's chapter in this volume. After having introduced chronotopicity, we will connect this notion to recent developments in the study of language in society that, drawing on, among others, Wallerstein's (2006) world-systems analysis, Appadurai's (1996) analysis of the cultural dimensions of globalization, Castells' (1996) theorizing of a network society, and Vertovec's (2006) coinage of the concept 'super-diversity' a decade ago, have been termed by Blommaert (2010) as a sociolinguistics of globalization. We will finally present the various chapters in this book as dealing with a number of specific domains in which chronotopic identity work in a globalized society is of utmost relevance.

Chronotopicity in Language and Society

Little did Mikhail Bakhtin know that the *chronotope*, 'a concept that he initially developed for the analysis of space-time categories in literary texts' (Sandywell, 1998: 206; see also Bakhtin, 1981), like many other Bakhtinian tropes or neologisms posthumously would be met with such broad and positive, but according to Bell and Gardiner (1998: 7) also sometimes 'superficial', reception in different academic disciplines.

In their exploration of Bakhtin's 'legacy for the human sciences' Bell and Gardiner (1998: 5) claim that

> In highlighting the dialogical relations between different symbolic systems and practices that have generated the kinds of 'heteroglot' and composite cultural forms that we are becoming increasingly familiar with today in the wake of a pervasive globalization process, a Bakhtinian model holds considerable promises with respect to the theorization of such phenomena as the new media, popular cultural forms, 'hybridization' and multiculturalism, and the emergence of post-colonial discourses, just to name a few.

Still according to Bell and Gardiner (1998: 4), Bakhtin

> was at the forefront of the 'linguistic turn', perhaps the defining feature of twentieth-century social thought, in that he early identified communicative and symbolic practices as the *locus classicus of human life*. All sociocultural phenomena, according to Bakhtin, are constituted through the ongoing, dialogical relationship between individuals and groups, involving a multiplicity of different languages, discourses and symbolizing practices.

A case in point here is the recent adoption and gaining new currency of the concept of chronotopicity in the emerging theorizing of a sociolinguistics of globalization, i.e. 'a sociolinguistics of mobile resources, framed in terms of trans-contextual networks, flows and movements' in which language is considered 'as something intrinsically connected to processes of globalization' (Blommaert, 2010: 1, 2). This sociolinguistics of mobility presents itself as an alternative to the earlier Labovian or Fishmanian paradigm of a sociolinguistics of distribution or stability in which the people whose language repertoires are studied are dealt with as seemingly fixed in space and time (2010: 4). A sociolinguistics of globalization 'focuses not on language-in-place but on language-in-motion, with various spatiotemporal frames interacting with one another' (2010: 5).

In Bakhtin's work, the concept of chronotope refers to the 'the intrinsic connectedness of temporal and spatial relationships that are artistically expressed in literature' (Bakhtin, 1981: 84). It expresses 'the inseparability of space and time' (1981: 84) and is understood 'as a formally constitutive category of literature' (1981: 84) and as such 'determines to a significant degree the image of man in literature as well. The image of man is always intrinsically chronotopic' (1981: 85). Bakhtin, in other words, considered time and space as inseparable in constructing narratives and characters; they function as a fused, concrete whole – a chronotope – which is structured and encoded in specific ways, generating historical and semiotic conditions of meaning making. This conceptualization makes it possible to dissect and describe the multiple timespace configurations that co-occur, not only in literary texts, i.e. novelistic chronotopes through which readers can extract and connect multiple social meanings and agencies represented in a story, but also more generally, as cultural chronotopes, i.e. 'depiction[s] of place-time-and-personhood to which social interactants orient when they engage each other through discursive signs of any kind' (Agha, 2007: 320).

The cultural potential of chronotopes is formulated as 'invokable histories' in Blommaert's (2015: 110) attempt to use the notion of chronotope for addressing the complexity of language in society. Drawing on the central argument of discourse in history, Blommaert considers chronotope as an important aspect of contextualization in which 'meaning as value effects [is] derived from local enactments of historically loaded semiotic resources' (2015: 108). From this perspective, all interactive events can be seen as chronotopically organized: situated in timespace, occurring as here-and-now while indexing a myriad of 'historically configured and ordered tropes' (2015: 111). These tropes, or culturally recognizable systems of meanings and values, are applied and made understandable through genres, by means of ideologized, normative and enregistered features and styles that index and codify specific timespace relations. Each chronotope installs its own discursive frames and orders of indexicality (and of authenticity). Each invocation of timespace also constitutes ascription of specific genres, registers, indexicals and other chronotopically relevant norms, and, as such, enactment of specific intentions, behaviors and effects.

Globalization, Superdiversity and Chronotopic Identity Work

Referring to and elaborating on Bakhtin's work, Blommaert (2015), Blommaert and De Fina (2017) and Blommaert (this volume) among others proposed to include chronotopicity as a new way of looking at context and scale in studies of language, culture and identity (see also Carr & Lempert, 2016). In doing so they point out that the chronotopic nature of specific forms of identity is part of a common-sense understanding about the way in which certain groups and cultures function. Much the same way as Bakhtin (1981: 85) proposed that '[t]he image of man is always intrinsically chronotopic' Blommaert and others connect chronotopicity to identity work. Especially in times of globalization and superdiversity (Arnaut et al., 2016, 2017) people, affected by a multitude of macro-level influences, leave traditional structures of belonging and attachment such as fixed cultural, linguistic and ethnic communities behind and orient themselves on an ever growing number of micro-communities, often established online. This requires a totally new perspective on what it is to identify as a member of no longer one but rather a multitude of communities and what type of (cultural, linguistic and ethnic) identity work such memberships require, i.e. the timespace organization of who people want to be (Blommaert & De Fina, 2017).

The emphasis on chronotopicity in identity work is part of a sociolinguistic movement that no longer relies on fixed and stable concepts like community, competence and language but opts for more flexible, fluid and multilayered concepts like sites, activities and (trans)languaging (see e.g. the contributions in García et al., 2017). These new concepts explicitly do not intend to reduce or exclude complexity but rather take the increasing complexity of the contemporary, mobile, superdiverse, networked, on/offline global society as a starting point, as an *explanandum* rather than an *explanans*. A main characteristic of contemporary superdiverse societies is mobility of people, goods, ideas and languages (Arnaut et al., 2016). Mobility leads to contact and contact leads to change. This applies to more concrete things like languages, customs and rituals but also more intangible things like beliefs, identity or belonging. In superdiverse contexts people often have to re-imagine and re-establish things that used to be self-evident but became contested as a consequence of globalization induced mobility, migration and digitalization (Appadurai, 1996; Castells, 1996). This includes questions regarding who they are, where they belong to and how they make sense of their lives in an authentic way, how they do 'the right thing in the right way' (Blommaert & Varis, 2011, 2015).

This all basically boils down to the question of identity. Wang (2017) refers to the fact that the topic of identity has been one of the most fertile ones in sociolinguistic scholarship over the past two decades (cf. Bell, 2016) and states that '[t]here has been indeed a tremendous development of our conceptualization of identity and identity work based (inevitably) on the sociolinguistic and semiotic resources people deploy in social interaction with one another' (Wang, 2017: 6).

Taking this observation as a starting point, at the 2016 Sociolinguistics Symposium in Murcia, we made an attempt to bring together empirical work that gives some flesh on the bones of the rather abstract chronotopical theorizing as presented thus far in the field of sociolinguistics. Our main focus was on the discursive construction of chronotopic identities. The panel that we organized attracted many participants and instigated engaged discussions. From this, we gathered that it would be a good idea to prepare this edited volume on chronotopic identity work combining theoretical insights and empirical studies from contributions that were presented in Murcia as well as contributions that were invited for this book.

The authors in this collection explore forms of culture, language and identity work closely tied to specific timespace configurations. These can only legitimately be deployed in specific spaces and within specific temporary frames, and are in that sense 'scaled' phenomena. It is important to stress here that scales are not 'ontological givens' but rather the result of human action and therefore never ideologically neutral. As Carr and Lempert (2016: 4) put it, 'scale is process before it is product' and people 'develop scalar projects and perspectives that anchor and (re)orient themselves.' 'Youth language and culture' for example, would be a typical cultural formation of this sort, and whenever we refer to 'peripheries' or 'margins' we also locate cultural and linguistic phenomena in a certain space and time. Furthermore, various kinds of 'micro-hegemonies,' i.e. the norms regulating 'micro-groups' such as rappers, Ferrari or Saab drivers, hipsters, foodies, football fans and so forth, can be explored in such terms, and online 'light' communities such as Twitter followers and Facebook friends also operate within specific (online) timespace configurations.

In all these cases, identity work is bound to and compellingly (normatively) conditioned by immediate concrete contexts, defined by space and time, thus chronotopic. Chronotopicity points towards the inseparability of time and space in human social action and the effects of this inseparability on social action. Chronotopes involve specific forms of contextual agency when identity formation is at work: specific patterns of social behavior belong to particular timespace configurations, and when they 'fit' they respond to existing frames of recognizable identity, while when they don't fit, they are 'out of place', 'out of order' or transgressive (see Blommaert, 2015). These existing frames of recognizable identities follow from collectively shared categorizations and generalizations, the origins of stereotyping and prejudice.

Sociolinguistic and discursive features invariably emerge as important ordering indexicals of such chronotopic phenomena. The theoretical assumption driving this book is that most, if not all forms of identity and cultural formations are in fact chronotopic and in often uncomfortable ways relate to or, alternatively, resist 'hegemonic' and institutionalized standards imposed by for instance the scale-level of the nation-state and, for example, its educational system – with scale jumping or bending as a possible result.

The following chapters therefore provide us with meticulous analyses of microscopic behavior, fractal domains with specific subtle scripts and rules online and offline in a variety of contexts and societies. The different societies included here are Belgium, China, Denmark, Indonesia, Mongolia and the Netherlands. As far as the contexts or domains of identity work included, we can distinguish between online and offline, informal and institutional, central and peripheral, national and regional, micro and macro domains. We should however be aware that such domains are not monolithic and inseparable but can blend and mix depending on the concrete sociocultural, economic and geopolitical contexts in which they are located. The main domains the contributions in this book focus upon are the online-offline nexus in Mongolia, China and Indonesia, global peripheral tourism in China, and migration, more specifically education in a migration context, in Denmark, the Netherlands and Belgium.

Chronotopic Identity Work Online and Offline

In his book *Understanding Digital Culture*, Vincent Miller (2011) extensively deals with the issue of 'context (or lack of it)' (2011: 22) in digital culture. Starting from Walter Benjamin's (1969[1935]) claim in *The Work of Art in The Age of Mechanical Reproduction* that photography and mass reproduction in general create the potential for any object to be seen anywhere and as a consequence obliterate the contextual situation of the object, Miller leads the argument further and states that also digital culture is characterized by a 'lack of context'. He illustrates the 'horizonless, contextless world' of the internet as follows:

> Time and space are absent on YouTube, where one can just as easily watch episodes of a favourite television programme from childhood as watch the latest news events, upsetting the experience of memory, time and narrative biography. Digital music sites and MP3 culture pulverize bands, albums and genres into semi-anonymous files of singles embedded into endlessly diverse playlists that almost unreasonably span musical genres

and eras. Social networking profiles link friends from different periods of life, childhood, university, work, as well as family and brief acquaintances in a timeless and spaceless networked collection. In this environment, it seems quite reasonable to suggest that the accessibility created by the age of networked digital reproduction has accelerated the demise of the contextual link between cultural object, space and time. (Miller, 2011: 24)

Miller's argument about the lack of context in the digital world sounds like a critique. As if digitalization deprives culture of time and space and consequently makes it less meaningful. Or, to put it differently, as if culture, understood as the ways in which people give meaning to themselves and the world around them, as a consequence of digitalization becomes a virtual phenomenon that is not related to the so-called real world. We think that the chapters by Sender Dovchin, and Kunming Li and Jan Blommaert show that there is nothing virtual in the digital or online world. The often long hours that all people spend on the internet and the things they do there – surfing, lurking, reading, writing, posting, blogging, vlogging, gambling, dating, gaming, learning – is as real as the world around them. Against the claim that time and space are absent in the digital world, we propose that their chapters make clear that the internet provides its users an essentially chronotopic environment for being or becoming who they want to be, i.e. among others, declared members of all sorts of micro-communities with their own hegemonies and identities. It is notably on the internet that people establish, experiment and play with often multiple identities. It is for that reason that two chapters in this collection explicitly deal with identity work online.

Sender Dovchin analyzes mixed language practices on Facebook by young adults in contemporary Mongolia. She argues that these mixed and 'inverted' youth language practices should be understood as 'translingual', not only due to their varied recombination of linguistic and cultural resources, genres, modes, styles and repertoires, but also due to their direct subtextual connections with wider sociocultural, historical and ideological meanings. She also proposes that Facebook users metalinguistically claim authenticity in terms of their own translingual practices as opposed to other colliding language ideologies such as linguistic dystopia. How they relocalize the notion of authenticity, however, differs profoundly depending on their own often diverse criteria, identities, beliefs and ideas. Dovchin's analysis sheds light on various forms of chronotopic identities embedded within current cultural globalization where local and global resources are mixed. Inverted youth language becomes the crucial example, where global linguistic resources are blended with local linguistic repertoires and identities that perform the chronotopic condition of local youth in the peripheries.

Kunming Li and Jan Blommaert deal with identity play on the Chinese internet. As a consequence of the 'demotic' turn of celebrity culture, social media in China increasingly become an experimental field of fame-seeking identity plays governed by an 'attention economy'. Consequently, a myriad of web celebrities, more specifically 'micro-celebrities' emerge and form their fan bases. Against this background Li and Blommaert, using digital ethnography, describe the practices of young Chinese women who, as a so-called *baifumei* (white, rich, beautiful), engage in designing and marketing imageries of feminine beauty and attractiveness on social media platforms. Insisting that they are not what they are expected to be, is part of their identity work: becoming *baifumei* by refusing it. Within the ludic, frivolous and artful interactional work they perform online for their audience, economic transactions take place stimulated by competitive evaluations of the *baifumei*. Importantly, the presentation of the 'self' demands forms of knowledge and skill specific to the online chronotopes in which it is presented and performed. While describing these phenomena, they also sketch a conceptual framework for addressing such forms of online practice. The latter is necessary, for online social practices display features that may be similar to more common offline forms of social conduct but may still deviate in crucial ways.

Also Zane Goebel deals with chronotopicity in media. Instead of using data from online communicative practices he uses (the online edition of) a local Indonesian newspaper, *Suara Merdeka*, to investigate the formation or rather ascription of chronotopes of bureaucratic personhood in Indonesia. He examines the tensions between creating semiotically dense models of personhood (i.e. models that have more and more signs attached to them), and their subsequent reconfiguration and iconization through the use of deictics. His study draws on a database of over a thousand online newspaper stories between August and December 2003 and shows how multiple reported local practices that were formerly deictically anchored to specific people, places and times, are re-scaled and made to appear widespread through the use of universal select deictics and the erasure of particular selective deictics. The analyses are embedded within larger scale processes that include external pressure from the IMF and World Bank to implement good governance in return for aid in the mid to late 1990s, a regime change and reform agenda that imitated some of the IMF and World Bank agendas (1998–2002), an ongoing presidential election (2003–2004), and a loosening of media laws (1998 onwards) that allowed criticism of the bureaucracy for the first time in a decade.

Chronotopic Identity Work in Global Peripheral Tourism

Global travel in general and tourism in particular are central features of globalization. Not only has the growing amount of digitally available information on remote areas (read: destinations) and the increasing availability and accessibility of cheap flights to far away destinations contributed to the growth of mass tourism in general, it has also contributed to redefining hitherto rather exotic tourist destinations that were only visited by connoisseurs as 'the place to be' for enjoying the experience of an authentic and at first sight unspoiled world. A statistic of the fastest emerging tourism destinations worldwide for 2014 to 2024 has Namibia, Montenegro, Zambia, Angola, China, Gabon, Burma, Cambodia, Thailand and Cape Verde in its top ten (Statista, 2018). Tourists are of course only one side of the coin of global tourism, the other side being the 'natives' whose environments, cultures and customs are often almost overrun by the tourists in search for the ultimate authentic experience. Including a native or insider perspective in tourism studies means engaging 'with issues of power, inequality and development processes in tourism whilst acknowledging the significance of cultural diversities' (Bianchi, 2009: 484). Such a critical perspective includes dealing with the ways in which the people living in such newly discovered tourist areas respond to the challenge of being visited because of being culturally diverse and authentic, i.e. how they are forced or at least challenged to form a new material as well as psychological 'tourist identity' that fits both their own perspective on who they are and the outsiders' expectations of authenticity and exoticism. In the chapters by Shuang Gao, and Xuan Wang and Sjaak Kroon, we see how the commodification of cultural heritage actually helps shaping cultural identities and their accompanying language use.

Shuang Gao focuses on West Street in Yangshuo County, Southern China, that during the past three decades has turned from a traditional countryside neighborhood into a busy street of touristic entertainment, with bars, clubs, hostels, shops and restaurants. Tracing its demographic, semiotic and socioeconomic change, this chapter explores the changing dialectical relationships among signs, spatial practices and people, focusing in particular on the accumulative and disruptive effects socio-spatial change can have on people's self-positioning and everyday conduct in relation to new spatial orders, thereby revealing the dynamics and complexities among semiotic practice, spatiality and social behavior. Gao concludes that semiotic landscapes both reflect and contribute to the formation of new spatial orders, which in turn mediate people's spatial mobility, social behavior and interpersonal relationships. In this sense, the semiotic landscape constitutes one important perspective to explore power relations as it represents one key factor in producing socio-spatial differentiation via re-defining spatial functionalities and structures, and thereby changing the way people control, relate to and access space.

Xuan Wang and Sjaak Kroon focus on the ethnic minority group of the Tujia in Enshi, China, as an instance of geopolitical and sociocultural periphery, and examine the ways in which this community in the periphery engages with semiotic designing of cultural heritage as a complex project of authenticity in the context of globalization. In doing so, authenticity is taken as part of the chronotopic phenomena of identity making, namely, becoming authentic involves the interplay of multiple, nonrandom spatial-temporal frames of discourses and semiotic performances, which condition as well as offer new potentials to the meaning of authenticity. The chapter ethnographically observes how the Tujia in Enshi are confronted with the issue of authenticity as political and economic imperatives during different stages of China's modernization and globalization. For this community, authenticity, i.e. their Tujia minority status and ethnic heritage, was and is experienced as 'given' by the state, deriving from the hegemonic processes of nation-building and ethnic identification therein. This initially led to orthopractical activities, such as the local reiteration of the official discourses about who the Tujia themselves are and the chronotopically staged displays of certain Tujia 'characteristics', in which authenticity entailed a strong sense of ambiguity and ambivalence, for some even inauthenticity. However, the last decade of globalization and economic development in China has prompted active practices of designing the Tujia heritage in Enshi, such as designing their own ethnic attire, especially in the name of heritage tourism. What emerges from such practices, as the chapter illustrates, is a new collective voice, embracing not only the economic but also an identity opportunity in which the orthodoxy of authenticity is being internalized and strategically incorporated into the local narrative and semiotic representation of an authentic self. In this sense, the Tujia in Enshi chronotopically shift away from the periphery towards a new and reconfigured center of meaning-making, although this re-appropriation of authenticity still must be understood within the cunning scheme of cultural recognition, i.e. within the constraints of late modernity.

Chronotopic Identity Work in Migration

Mobility and migration are among the main drivers of globalization and superdiversity (Blommaert, 2010). At the same time ours is an information society in which large parts of information are produced and made available through online networks (Castells, 1996). Our smart phone contains more knowledge than the great library of Alexandria and the *Encyclopedia Britannica* and it is much more powerful than the computers from the 1980s. Online infrastructures have also found their ways into education as teaching and learning tools but at the same time there still is – and will always be – the direct interaction between teachers and their students in classrooms. In times of globalization, mobility and migration, classrooms of course have changed from linguistically and culturally rather homogeneous ensembles of students into superdiverse places where linguistic, cultural, ethnic, religious, etc. homogeneity is challenged instead of fostered (see the contributions in Arnaut *et al*., 2017). At the same time, education is still in charge of creating common ground or normativity as a basis for teaching-learning processes and a main element thereof is language. This resonates in the old adage 'a fatherland needs a mother tongue', i.e. a national standard language as a target language and medium of instruction at the same time. That is where not only in the nineteenth century (Kroon & Sturm, 1994) but also in our time and age education comes in and meets more and more problems because of the multilingual composition of the student body (Gogolin, 1994; Kroon, 2003; Spotti & Kroon, 2016). As has been extensively documented, such contexts of linguistic superdiversity in education might lead to processes of polylanguaging (Jørgensen, 2008; Jørgensen *et al*., 2016) or translanguaging (García & Li Wei, 2014) through which students attempt to construct and reconstruct their identities in everyday social interactions in the timespace of schooling. In the chapters by Martha Sif Karrebæk and Janus Spindler Møller, and Jos Swanenberg, we see how school situations, in and outside of the classroom, function as specific chronotopic settings for playing with language, culture and identity.

Karrebæk and Møller start from the observation that despite a relatively heterogeneous population of students, the Danish educational system mainly favors a monolingual, (standard) Danish dominant linguistic regime. However, the societal situation is far more complex linguistically, and individuals have varied linguistic and cultural life trajectories and experiences. Consequently, students are often left with the challenge of navigating the official system and integrating it with different communicative regimes of smaller or different scope and scale. Karrebæk and Møller explore how this navigation between regimes is carried out on a micro level of interaction and how viewing this as chronotopic identity work may help us understand the dynamics. They compare examples involving children from different age groups who all attend the same school in Copenhagen and carry out important communicative and identity-related work in a performance frame in which the linguistic form is on display and is given a metapragmatic evaluation. The analytical focus is on how configurations of time and space in representational universes, or chronotopes, are created. In such timespace envelopes, linguistic and other signs are attributed with meaning and indexical value, and they invite certain understandings and inferences. The chronotopes inform us of ideological understandings – of social personae, self, appropriate behavior, and the world in general – and the comparing of chronotopes invites alignment or disalignment with the ideologies and models represented in and through the chronotope. In the examples, all students orient to the institutionally preferred linguistic regime where Danish dominates, and simultaneously they demonstrate experience with linguistic and cultural diversity.

Jos Swanenberg asks the question how students deal with different language varieties and repertoires in different chronotopic contexts. In primary education, students and their teachers negotiate, either explicitly or implicitly, what language variety should be used in which situation. Standard Dutch obviously is the language for instruction, albeit regional accents and vocabulary may be part of that language during time spent at school. Local dialects can be used in specific situations, for comfort, corrective measures on undesired behavior and for specific clarification. Later in primary school, students seem aware of identity work through languaging, for instance when they refer to solidarity as the driving force in speaking vernacular. When they grow up and become adolescents, the diversity of the students' language use increases, especially in conversations outside the classroom. This chapter presents examples of such conversations from several case studies at institutions for secondary education. Interlocutors use language in a way that may be declined in other contexts as inauthentic and incorrect. Furthermore, their language practices are reflected upon, mocked, ridiculed and used for teasing. The speech samples show that language use in these cases is not a matter of shifting between languages or registers. It is constantly changing, and it draws upon a great variety of repertoires. On the other hand, interlocutors will correct each other when speaking the 'wrong' language variety in a certain context. This indicates that authenticity and normativity are differently and flexibly applied, according to chronotopic concrete contexts. In some instances even personal identities will be questioned. Not only language behavior but even a person may be 'out of order'. Heterogeneity and flexibility are the norm and it seems that the roles, identities and linguistic performances are constantly subject to change.

Just like Karrebæk and Møller, and Swanenberg, also Malgorzata Szabla deals with chronotopic identity work in an immigration context. In her chapter however, the focus is not on education but on the chronotopic whereabouts of a Polish immigrant community in Antwerp, Belgium. She illustrates how chronotopes include detailed moralized behavioral scripts. Most of the actual identity work performed by people in real social situations is organized chronotopically, i.e. the specific timespace configurations are connected to moral frameworks, preferred participant structures and specific types of social activity. This approach to identity avoids a priori generalizations about identity and helps us explain what is usually described as identity fragmentation or identity uncertainty as a more complex form of social identity organization, enabling more nuanced and more precise statements both on identities, moral 'indexical' orders and social structure.

The Usefulness of Chronotopes

As can be seen from the above overview, the chronotopic angle from which all chapters start provides us with an empirical tool for revisiting static models of social analysis and discussions of power and authenticity, by enabling a view of dynamic and mobile forms of (sub)culture engaging with equally dynamic (i.e. changing) hegemonic formations across scales. This enables us to make assumptions about the complexities and dynamics in society, about superdiversity and rapid social change, because it raises questions on how we organize actual situated meaningful behavior in relation to established identity categories such as ethnicity, religion, language and so on, as well as to newly emerging ones.

This collection is opened and concluded by Jan Blommaert and Anna De Fina, respectively. Blommaert contributes an introductory and more theoretically oriented chapter in which he asks the question what chronotopicity as a concept in the sociolinguistics of globalization is actually good for or, formulated a bit more provocatively, why we need another word for context. As one of the scholars who played an important role in introducing Bakhtin's concept of timespace in the study of language in society in order to give a new perspective to what hitherto was indeed mainly referred to as context, Blommaert is very well placed to ask this question. His answer is straightforward and simple: like all scholarly concepts, chronotopicity will have to be used, discussed and evaluated. If, in the end, the community of peers decides that 'context' is still more useful and valuable than 'chronotope', it will be a much more accurate, precise and analytically transparent notion of 'context' that will prevail, and 'chronotope' will have done its work. For arriving at this seemingly 'simple' answer, Blommaert meticulously dissects a number of sociolinguistic classics and as such creates a meaningful new perspective on aspects of context often dismissed or summarily taken into account in branches of scholarship, and to treat them with utmost precision as nonrandom elements of social situations that may account for much of how people make sense of social structure in actual moments of social action.

Anna De Fina, in her postscript to the contributions listed above, uncovers and discusses some of the insights and challenges that the application of the notion chronotope and the introduction of chronotopic analysis poses to a sociolinguistics globalization, especially where it aims at an in-depth ethnographic understanding of identity work in times that are characterized by ongoing processes of globalization and digitalization in a superdiverse world.

References

Agha, A. (2007) Recombinant selves in mass-mediated spacetime. *Language & Communication* 27, 320–337.
Appadurai, A. (1996) *Modernity at Large. Cultural Dimensions of Globalization.* Minneapolis, London: University of Minnesota Press.
Arnaut, K., Blommaert, J., Rampton, B. and Spotti, M. (eds) (2016) *Language and Superdiversity.* New York/London: Routledge.
Arnaut, K., Karrebæk, M.S., Spotti, M. and Blommaert, J. (eds) (2017) *Engaging Superdiversity: Recombining Spaces, Times and Language Practices.* Bristol: Multilingual Matters.
Bakhtin, M. (1981) *The Dialogic Imagination. Four Essays* (edited by M. Holquist; translated by C. Emerson and M. Holquist). Austin: University of Texas Press.
Bell, A. (2016) Succeeding waves: Seeking sociolinguistic theory for the twenty-first century. In N. Coupland (ed.) *Sociolinguistics: Theoretical Debates* (pp. 391–416). Cambridge: Cambridge University Press.
Bell, M.M. and Gardiner, M. (1998) Bakhtin and the Human Sciences: A brief introduction. In M.M. Bell and M. Gardiner (eds) *Bakhtin and the Human Sciences. No Last Words* (pp. 1–12). London, etc.: Sage Publications.
Benjamin, W. (1969) The *w*ork of art in the age of mechanical reproduction. In H. Ahrendt (ed.) *Illuminations: Essays and Reflections* (translated by Harry Zohn from the 1935 essay *Das Kunstwerk im Zeitalter seiner technischen Reproduzierbarkeit*) (pp. 217–252). New York: Schocken Books (original work published in 1935).
Bianchi, R.V. (2009) The 'critical turn' in Tourism Studies: A radical critique. *Tourism Geographies* 11 (4), 484–504.
Blommaert, J. (2010) *The Sociolinguistics of Globalization.* Cambridge: Cambridge University Press.
Blommaert, J. (2015) Chronotopes, scales and complexity in the study of language in society. *Annual Review of Anthropology* 44, 105–116.
Blommaert, J. and De Fina, A. (2017) Chronotopic identities: On the spacetime organization of who we are. In A. De Fina, D. Ikizoglu and J. Wegner (eds) *Diversity and Superdiversity: Sociocultural Linguistic Perspectives* (pp. 1–15). Washington: Georgetown University Press.

Blommaert, J. and Varis, P. (2011) Enough is enough: The heuristics of authenticity in superdiversity. *Working Papers in Urban Language and Literacies* 76.
Blommaert, J. and Varis, P. (2015) Enoughness, accent and light communities: Essays on contemporary identities. *Tilburg Papers in Culture Studies* 139.
Carr, E.S. and Lempert, M. (2016) Introduction – Pragmatics of scale. In E.S. Carr and M. Lempert (eds) *Scale. Discourse and Dimensions of Social Life* (pp. 1–21). Oakland, CA: University of California Press.
Castells, M. (1996) *The Rise of the Network Society*. London: Blackwell.
García, O. and Li Wei (2014) *Translanguaging: Language, Bilingualism and Education*. London: Palgrave MacMillan Pivot.
García, O., Flores, N. and Spotti, M. (eds) (2017) *The Oxford Handbook of Language and Society*. Oxford: Oxford Universiy Press.
Gogolin, I. (1994) *Der Monlinguale Habitus der Multilingualen Schule*. Münster, New York: Waxmann.
Jørgensen, J.N. (2008) Poly-lingual languaging around and among children and adolescents. *International Journal of Multilingualism* 5 (3), 161–176.
Jørgensen, J.N., Karrebæk, M.S., Madsen, L.M. and Møller, J.S. (2016) Polylanguaging in superdiversity. In K. Arnaut, J. Blommaert, B. Rampton and M. Spotti (eds) *Language and Superdiversity* (137–154). New York/London: Routledge.
Kroon, S. (2003) Mother tongue and mother tongue education. In J. Bourne and E. Reid (eds) *Language Education. World Yearbook of Education 2003* (pp. 35–48). London: Kogan Page.
Kroon, S. and Sturm, J. (1994) Das nationale Selbstverständnis im Unterricht der Nationalsprache: Der Fall der Niederlande. Eine Vorstudie. In I. Gogolin (ed.) *Das nationale Selbstverständnis der Bildung* (pp. 161–192). Münster: Waxmann.
Miller, V.A. (2011) *Understanding Digital Culture*. London: Sage.
Sandywell, B. (1998) The shock of the old: Mikhail Bakhtin's contributions to the theory of time and alterity. In M.M. Bell and M. Gardiner (eds) *Bakhtin and the Human Sciences. No Last Words* (pp. 196–213). London, etc.: Sage Publications.
Spotti, M. and Kroon, S. (2016) Multilingual classrooms in times of superdiversity. In S. May (ed.) *Encyclopedia of Language and Education, Volume 3, Discourse and Education* (pp. 97–109). Heidelberg: Springer.
Statista (2018) Fastest emerging tourism destinations worldwide for 2014 to 2024. Retrieved June 6, 2019, www.statista.com/statistics/303381/fastest-emerging-tourism-destinations-worldwide/
Vertovec, S. (2006) The emergence of super-diversity in Britain. Oxford University Centre on Migration, Policy and Society. Working Paper 25.
Wallerstein, I. (2004) *World-Systems Analysis. An Introduction*. Durham and London: Duke University Press.
Wang, X. (2017) Online and offline margins in China. Globalization, language and identity. PhD thesis, Tilburg University.

2 Are Chronotopes Helpful?

Jan Blommaert

Why Do We Need Another Word for Context?

'Why do we need another word for context?' I get this question repeatedly whenever I use the term 'chronotope': do we really, truly need yet another word for context? Don't the current terms we have do the job satisfactorily? What's *new* about chronotopes?[1]

I usually give not one but several answers to that question. One answer is general and refers to a practice that is at the core of scientific work. We need new terms, or renewed terms, often for no other reason than to check the validity of old ones. Neologisms, from that angle, are crucial critical *Gedankenspiele* that remind us of the duty of continuous quality control of our analytical vocabulary. And if the *Gedankenspiel* is played well, it often enables us to see how the existing concepts it critically interrogates have become flattened, turned into a *passe-partout* or a rather uninformative routine gesture in talk and writing. 'Chronotope' invites us to critically check the ways in which we use the term 'context' in a wide range of disciplines within the study of language in society. If, in the end, the community of peers in this discipline decide that 'context' is still more useful and valuable than 'chronotope', it will be a much more accurate, precise and analytically transparent notion of 'context' that will prevail, and 'chronotope' will have done its work.

A second answer is a disclaimer. One concept should never be expected to do *all* of the work in theory and analysis. It should do *a bit* of work, in conjunction with several others. And the point is to find the precise bit of work that can be done satisfactorily by that concept within a broader conceptual structure.

A third answer follows onto the previous one. It is of a different nature and also responds to the 'what's new' question. One should point out that the particular conceptualizations of context for which we can now use the term 'chronotope' are not new at all, and that, in fact, the use of 'chronotope' may help us to precisely capture *that particular trend* of studies of text-and-context. I could refer here to a large body of existing literature, but three clear instances can suffice: Aaron Cicourel's (1992) classic paper on the 'interpenetration' of contexts in medical encounters; Michael Silverstein's (1997) analysis of the 'improvisational' nature of real-time discursive practice; and Charles Goodwin's (2002) discussion of 'time in action', in which specific temporalities, real-time as well as invoked, pattern and co-organize the interactional work done by participants. What brings these examples together is:

- a view of context as a *specific* set of features both affecting and producing *specific modes of social action*;
- in which such features have very clear and empirically demonstrable timespace characteristics – the actual timespace constellation is the determining feature for understanding the actual text-context patterns we observe;
- in which some of these features can be carried over, so to speak, into different timespace constellations while others are non-exportable;
- and in which a precise understanding of timespace configurations is essential to account for a great deal of the sociocultural work performed in interaction.

I shall briefly elaborate this particular view of context in what follows, with special attention to how such views of context can affect work on identity construction and performance. Chronotope, I shall argue, can play a role within the broader conceptual structure developed within that tradition.

From Situation to Chronotope

It should not be hard to grasp the specific nature of the conceptualization of context I outlined above in contradistinction with several other trends of usage. In earlier work (Blommaert, 2005: Chapter 3), I surveyed some of the various ways in which context is used in analysis, pointing out flaws in mainstream usages of the notions in Conversation Analysis and Critical Discourse Analysis. Of the former, I argued that a conception of context reduced to the intra-interactional forms of demonstrable inference was untenable; of the latter I said that a priori statements about contextual 'influences' on discourse, for which discourse analysis would merely provide a symptomatic demonstration, would not do either. We can add to this that restrictions of context to purely cognitive universes for inference or to the inferential material that ensures text cohesion and coherence are equally inadequate (for discussions, see Duranti & Goodwin, 1992).

All of them, I would suggest, fail to take into account 'the situation' as defined in the linguistic-ethnographic tradition (for a classic statement, see Goffman, 1964; also Hymes, 1974; Scollon, 2001; Scollon & Scollon, 2004; Silverstein, 1992). Let us recall how Goffman stated the problem.

> A student interested in the properties of speech may find himself having to look at the physical setting in which the speaker performs his gestures, simply because you cannot describe a gesture fully without reference to the extra-bodily in which it occurs. And someone interested in the linguistic correlates of social structure may find that he must attend to the social occasion when someone of given social attributes makes his appearance before others. Both kinds of students must therefore look at what we vaguely call the social situation. And that is what has been neglected. (Goffman, 1964: 134)

Goffman connects two elements here, both of which appear as compelling *contextual* factors in analysis. First, there is the 'physical setting' within which interaction occurs – the actual timespace constellation within which people encounter each other, in other words.[2] Goffman adds to this a second element: 'the social occasion'. The latter is defined (with an oblique reference to Durkheim's 'social fact') as 'a reality *sui generis*' within any social system, and it stands for the rules of participation and communicative behavior that provide 'scripts' (if you wish) ordering concrete communicative events between people who carry 'given social attributes'. Both elements – note – are *coordinated* in actual interactional events. It is this dialectic of mutual influences between settings and social scripts that shapes the 'joint social orientation' characterizing social interaction, which enables Goffman to provide his own, interactional, definition of the social situation:

> I would define a social situation as an environment of mutual monitoring possibilities, anywhere within which an individual will find himself accessible to the naked senses of all others who are 'present' and similarly find them accessible to him. (Goffman, 1964: 135)

As we know, much of Goffman's work was focused on the precise description of *specific* social situations – think of the poker game in *Encounters* (1961) and the lecture in *Forms of Talk* (1981). In each of these situations, Goffman emphatically pointed to the ways in which situations came with sets of conditions on participation, rules of engagement and forms of communicative action. Concrete and socioculturally recognizable timespace configurations involve nonrandom modes of social action and lead to specific social effects – that is the major insight we can get from Goffman's oeuvre, and which resonates with the work of scholars inscribed in the same lines of inquiry (e.g. Garfinkel, 2002; Goodwin & Goodwin, 1992; Scollon & Scollon, 2004). It is this insight for which I believe chronotopes to be a helpful gloss.

Bakhtin's Chronotope

The concept of chronotope used here has, as we know, its origins in the work of Bakhtin (1981, 1986), and it is good to pause and consider some crucial aspects of the way in which Bakhtin designed it.[3]

A first observation, often overlooked, is that Bakhtin's chronotope is grounded in a profoundly *socio*linguistic concept of language: it is not an autonomous or separate object (as in mainstream linguistics), but entirely entangled with concrete aspects of the social world. Bakhtin sees language in its actual deployment (as e.g. in a novel) as a repository of 'internal stratification present in every language at any given moment of its historical existence' (Bakhtin, 1981: 263; see the discussion in Agha, 2007a). At any moment of performance, the language (or discourse, as Bakhtin qualifies it) actually used will enable a historical-sociological analysis of different 'voices' within the social stratigraphy of language of that moment: Bakhtin's key notion of heteroglossia – the delicate 'dialogical' interplay of socially (ideologically, we would now say) positioned voices in e.g. a novel – is the building block of a 'sociological stylistics' (Bakhtin, 1981: 300).

Two important points are attached to this. First, this sociological stylistics is necessarily *historical,* and note that the notion of 'historical' in Bakhtin's work is never a purely chronological one, but a timespace one. In actual analysis, the historical aspect operates via a principle of indexicality, in which a genre feature such as 'common language (…) is taken by the author precisely as the *common view*, as the verbal approach to people and things normal for a given sphere of society' (Bakhtin, 1981: 301; cf. also Rampton, 2003). Form is used to project socially stratified meaning ('verbal-ideological belief systems', Bakhtin, 1981: 311), and this indexical nexus creates what we call 'style', for it can be played out, always hybridized, in ways that shape recognizable meaning effects 'created by history and society' (Bakhtin, 1981: 323).

Second, this historical aspect is tied to what we can call 'valuation'. The historically specific heteroglossic structure of actual forms of language means that understanding them is never a linear 'parsing' process; it is an *evaluative* one. When Bakhtin talks about understanding, he speaks of 'integrated meaning that relates to value – to truth, beauty and so forth – and requires a *responsive* understanding, one that includes evaluation' (Bakhtin, 1986: 125). The dialogical principle evidently applies to uptake of speech as well, and such uptake involves the interlocutor's own historically specific 'verbal-ideological belief systems' and can only be done from within the interlocutor's own specific position in a stratified sociolinguistic system. Nothing, consequently, is neutral in this process – not even time and space, as his discussion of chronotope illustrates.

Bakhtin designed chronotope to express the inseparability of time and space in historical social action. The 'literary artistic chronotope', where 'spatial and temporal indicators are fused into one carefully thought-out, concrete whole', could be seen as 'a formally constitutive category of literature' (Bakhtin, 1981: 84), as the thing that could enable us to actually and precisely *understand* works of literature as sociohistorically situated acts of communication. Bakhtin saw chronotopes as an important aspect of the novel's heteroglossia, part of the different 'verbal-ideological belief systems' that were in dialogue in a novel and gave the novel the historical meaning potential with which readers had to engage.

Moralized Behavioral Scripts

We can now look at how Bakhtin's chronotope can assist us in giving a more precise analytical orientation to Goffman's social situation, in particular when we intend to address identity work. In what follows, I want to highlight two major points.

A first and obvious step forward is that we can see the social situation as intrinsically *historical* and therefore loaded with language-ideological affordances – 'orders of indexicality', we can say (Blommaert, 2005; Silverstein, 2003; also Scollon & Scollon, 2004). It is the historicity of situations that accounts for the defining trigger of communication: *recognizability* (cf. Garfinkel, 2002). It is when a situation emerges of which we can recognize (or believe to recognize) the sociocultural status that we can shift into the modes of interactional behavior that 'make sense' in and of such a situation. We do so, as e.g. Bourdieu (1991) and Hymes (1996) emphasized, under conditions and constraints generated by (equally historical) sociolinguistic inequalities – it is wise to remind ourselves of the fact that we rarely enter social situations as perfectly finished products of smooth socialization (cf. Blommaert, 2008).

A second advantage we can draw from Bakhtin's insights and add to Goffman's, is that understanding – 'making sense' of interaction in actual situations – is *evaluative* and refers not just to the linguistic codes of expression but to a broader complex of rules for social conduct, ultimately precipitated in identity judgments. In social situations, we make *evaluative judgments* of the participants (including ourselves); such judgments are *indexically* grounded and project *identities* onto concrete modes of conduct. Goffman's work is replete with such moments of situated identity judgment, in which an interactional move can be swiftly turned into a perception of awkwardness – which is a judgment of the *person* through the lens of his/her interactional conduct. Indexicality, we can see here, is entirely tied up with identity (a thing we already know: Agha, 2007b), and is entirely *moral* whenever it takes the shape of what is called 'appropriateness', 'felicity' or 'adequacy' in the literature on pragmatics (e.g. Austin, 1962).

We can now be far more precise and specific with respect to what Goffman called the social situation. Specific timespace configurations (think of Goffman's lecture hall) demand and impose specific *moralized behavioral scripts* offering affordances and imposing constraints on what can be recognized as 'meaningful' interaction in such situations. Scripts include participation frameworks – not everyone is a ratified participant in, e.g. a lecture, and the specific roles of participants are quite compellingly defined. They also sketch a plot or event structure, as well as the 'adequate' semiotic resources to be deployed in an order of indexicality we will recognize as 'appropriate' within the specific chronotope. A lecturer, thus, is expected to lecture in a lecture hall during a time slot defined as a 'lecture', and members of the audience are expected to attend in silence, listen, perhaps make notes or recordings, and react appropriately to discursive prompts given by the lecturer. As soon as the lecture is over, the entire script changes, identities and participant roles are redefined, and an entirely different set of rules for social conduct replaces that of the lecture.

Chronotopes and Social Life

I hope that I have given arguments demonstrating the usefulness of chronotope as a way of summarizing, and making more accurate, the tradition of approaching context sketched at the outset of this chapter. The notion of chronotope invites us to treat aspects of context often dismissed or summarily taken into account in branches of scholarship, and to treat them with utmost precision as nonrandom elements of social situations that may account for much of how people make sense of social structure in actual moments of social action (to paraphrase Cicourel's 1974: 46 words). Everyday social life can be seen, from this perspective, as a sequence of such chronotopically defined situations through which we continuously move, adapting and adjusting in the process our identities and modes of conduct in interaction with others.

A sequence, thus, of 'environments of mutual monitoring possibilities' as Goffman expressed it, each of which comes with specific sets of norms – the moralized behavioral scripts mentioned above. This is why a dinner table conversation has a particular character (e.g. Ochs & Shohet, 2006) fundamentally different from that of a social media interaction session (Tagg *et al.*, 2017), interactions in a hospital operation theater (Bezemer *et al.*, 2014), during a court hearing (Stygall, 1994) or during a session in which an archaeology instructor explains minute differences between kinds of soil to students (Goodwin, 1994). This is also why we can instantly shift from a quiet, withdrawn and 'mind-my-own-business' mode of conduct on a public bus into a chatty and engaged one when a friend gets on and sits next to us, and why we know that we cannot (or at least should not) talk to our children the way we talk to our colleagues at work. Each situation in which we find ourselves in everyday social life involves such shifts in normative-behavioral orientation. If we fail to make such shifts, we are swiftly categorized by others in categories ranging from 'awkward' to 'antisocial' or 'abnormal'.

So, yes indeed, I do think chronotope is helpful as a tool in our analytical toolkit. The least we can say is that it satisfies the first function of new terms, specified in the introductory part of this chapter: it provides a critical check of the validity and analytical power of the term 'context'. It allows us to observe the many superficial and inadequate ways in which that older term is being used, and to suggest more precise understandings of it. The latter may take the shape of a new collocation: 'chronotopic contexts'.

Notes

(1) I am grateful to Sjaak Kroon and Jos Swanenberg for stimulating discussions on this topic over the past number of years, and for asking me to contribute them to this book. Anna De Fina and Li Kunming greatly helped me in my attempts to formulate chronotopic context and its effects (see Blommaert & De Fina, 2017; Li & Blommaert, this volume).
(2) The 'physical setting' of interaction, one can note, is often relegated to the 'S' in disastrously simplistic usages of Hymes' SPEAKING framework for ethnographic-comparative description – 'Setting and Scene'. It is then confined to a quick-and-easy sketch of the material layout and physical circumstances under which interaction takes place, overlooking the 'scene' in Hymes' framework – the actual ways in which material environments *condition* and *enable* the forms of action occurring. Lots of examples could be given here; the reader can refer to those given in Blommaert (2005: Chapter 3). For a far more sophisticated discussion, see e.g. Bezemer *et al.*, (2014).
(3) The following paragraphs draw on Blommaert (2015), and I refer the reader to that paper for more extensive discussion. Blommaert (2018) adds to the discussion by focusing on cross-chronotope connections.

References

Agha, A. (2007a) Recombinant selves in mass-mediated spacetime. *Language & Communication* 27 (3), 320–335.
Agha, A. (2007b) *Language and Social Relations*. Cambridge: Cambridge University Press.
Austin, J.L. (1962) *How to Do Things with Words*. Oxford: Clarendon Press.
Bakhtin, M. (1981) *The Dialogic Imagination. Four Essays* (edited by M. Holquist; translated by C. Emerson and M. Holquist). Austin: University of Texas Press.
Bakhtin, M. (1986) *Speech Genres and Other Late Essays*. Austin: University of Texas Press.
Bezemer, J., Cope, A., Kress. G. and Kneebone, R. (2014) Holding the scalpel: Achieving surgical care in a learning environment. *Journal of Contemporary Ethnography* 43 (1), 38–63.
Blommaert, J. (2005) *Discourse: A Critical Introduction*. Cambridge: Cambridge University Press.
Blommaert, J. (2008) Bernstein and poetics revisited: Voice, globalization and education. *Discourse & Society* 19 (4), 421–447.
Blommaert, J. (2015) Chronotopes, scales and complexity in the study of language in society. *Annual Review of Anthropology* 44, 105–116.
Blommaert, J. (2018) Chronotopes, synchronization and formats. *Tilburg Papers in Culture Studies* 207.
Blommaert, J. and De Fina, A. (2017) Chronotopic identities: On the spacetime organization of who we are. In A. De Fina, D. Ikizoglu and J. Wegner (eds) *Diversity and Superdiversity: Sociocultural Linguistic Perspectives* (pp. 1–15). Washington: Georgetown University Press.
Bourdieu, P. (1991) *Language and Symbolic Power*. Cambridge: Polity.
Cicourel, A. (1974) *Cognitive Sociology: Language and Meaning in Social Interaction*. Harmondsworth: Penguin Education.
Cicourel, A. (1992) The interpenetration of communicative contexts: Examples from medical encounters. In A. Duranti and C. Goodwin (eds) *Rethinking Context* (pp. 291–310). Cambridge: Cambridge University Press.
Duranti, A. and Goodwin, C. (eds) (1992) *Rethinking Context*. Cambridge: Cambridge University Press.
Garfinkel, H. (2002) *Ethnomethodology's Program: Working out Durkheim's Aphorism*. Lanham: Rowman & Littlefield.
Goffman, E. (1961) *Encounters: Two Studies in the Sociology of Interaction*. New York: Bobbs-Merrill.
Goffman E. (1964) The neglected situation. *American Anthropologist* 66 (2, Part 2), 133–136.
Goffman, E. (1981) *Forms of Talk*. Philadelphia: University of Pennsylvania Press.
Goodwin, C. (1994) Professional Vision. *American Anthropologist* 96 (3), 606–633.
Goodwin, C. (2002) Time in action. *Current Anthropology* 43 (S4), S19–S35.
Goodwin, C. and Goodwin, M.H. (1992) Context, activity and participation. In P. Auer and A. Di Luzio (eds) *The Contextualization of Language* (pp. 77–99). Amsterdam: John Benjamins.
Hymes, D. (1974) *Foundations in Sociolinguistics: An Ethnographic Approach*. Philadelphia: University of Pennsylvania Press.
Hymes D. (1996) *Ethnography, Linguistics, Narrative Inequality: Toward an Understanding of Voice*. London: Taylor & Francis.

Ochs, E. and Shohet, M. (2006) The cultural structuring of mealtime socialization. *New Directions for Child and Adolescent Development* 111, 35–49.
Rampton B. (2003) Hegemony, social class and stylization. *Pragmatics* 13 (1), 49–83.
Scollon, R. (2001) *Mediated Discourse: The Nexus of Practice*. London: Routledge.
Scollon, R. and Scollon, S.W. (2004) *Nexus Analysis: Language and the Emerging Internet*. London: Routledge.
Silverstein, M. (1992) The indeterminacy of contextualization: When is enough enough? In P. Auer and A. Di Luzio (eds) *The Contextualization of Language* (pp. 55–76). Amsterdam: John Benjamins.
Silverstein, M. (1997) The improvisational performance of culture in realtime discursive practice. In K. Sawyer (ed.) *Creativity in Performance* (pp. 265–312). Greenwich CT: Ablex.
Silverstein, M. (2003) Indexical order and the dialectics of sociolinguistic life. *Language & Communication* 23 (3/4), 193–229.
Stygall, G. (1994) *Trial Language: Differential Discourse Processing and Discursive Formation*. Amsterdam: John Benjamins.
Tagg, C., Seargeant, P. and Brown, A. (2017) *Taking Offence on Social Media: Conviviality and Communication on Facebook*. London: Palgrave Pivot.

3 Inverted Youth Language in Mongolia as Macroscopic and Microscopic Chronotopes

Sender Dovchin

Introduction

This chapter investigates a very specific youth linguistic practice in a chronotopic environment that I call 'inverted youth language' in the Asian peripheral context of Mongolia. Its main feature is derived from inverting the syllables, letters and sounds in the unconventional linguistic structural sense of 'back-to-front' against the conventional sense of 'front-to-back', primarily used in non-institutional and daily lives of young Mongolians. 'Inverted youth language' also serves as an alternative social code for young Mongolians to achieve their multiple strategic communicative and identity practices. It is not just a random or spontaneous act, but rather a strategic and deliberate linguistic practice to make valid and intentional meanings and identities for many young people outside the hegemonic norms of Standard Mongolian language.

Recent interests in the studies of youth sociolinguistic creativity have mainly tended to concentrate on the contexts of hybridity and mixed linguistic practices among multi-ethnic and multilingual youth with migrant backgrounds and first or second-generation immigrants, mainly in post-industrial and multicultural contexts (Doran, 2004; Godin, 2006; Jørgensen *et al.*, 2011; Nørreby & Møller, 2015). Examples are seen in 'Rinkeby Swedish' (Godin, 2006), *straattaal* ('street language') in the Netherlands (Schoonen & Appel, 2005), *perker sprog* or 'integrated language' in Copenhagen (Jørgensen *et al.*, 2011), *illegaal spreken* ('speaking illegally') in Belgium (Jaspers, 2011), and Doran's (2004) discussion on youth street language *Verlan* in Paris.

In order to account for other chronotopic ways of explaining linguistic creativity, this chapter seeks to focus on youth identity issues from the global north to the global south. Much less attention has been paid to the sociolinguistic practices of non-migrant background, middle-class and fairly homogenous young speakers in a peripheral Asian country such as Mongolia, who have not been directly subject to migration and transnational mobility. As Bucholtz (2002: 539) points out, research on youth style and identity 'must look not only to the United States, Britain, and other post-industrial societies for evidence of youth cultural practice, but also to young people's cultural innovations in other locations around the world'.

Despite its non-exposure to transnational migration, young speakers in Mongolia illustrate strikingly similar linguistic traits to those observed in the contexts of migration (cf. Dovchin et al., 2015, 2017). This chapter, therefore, highlights the sociocultural chronotopes of linguistic practices in the post-socialist context of Mongolia, a nation very much underrepresented in the field of youth language studies in current globalization.

With access to internet and technology venues, entertainment and sports centers, shopping malls, karaoke bars, nightclubs and music festivals, which are proliferating all over Ulaanbaatar, the capital city of Mongolia, urban youth culture has become a progressively essential part of the modern lifestyle in Mongolia. Urban youth in Mongolia can distinguish themselves through their middle-class backgrounds including their fancy fashion choices, city style characteristic behaviors and mannerisms, busy daily activities and, of course, their linguistic practices. They mix linguistic resources at their disposal, creating new meanings and expressions through a variety of different sociolinguistic processes (Dovchin, 2017a, 2017b, 2017c, 2017d, 2018). The emergence of this new urban youth culture in Mongolia has been directly associated with globalization since 1990.

Prior to 1990, Mongolia was a socialist country with a communist regime and state-planned economy. In fact, Mongolia was under the heavy influence of the Soviet Union for 70 years until it was eventually transformed from a communist to a democratic nation with a market economy in 1990 (Marsh, 2009). There are still cultural and linguistic influences originating from Russia in modern day Mongolia since Cyrillic Mongolian is the standard Mongolian orthography, which dates back to the Soviet era when Mongolia replaced its classic script with Cyrillic (Rossabi, 2005). Many Russian-origin words and terms are used as part of the standard Mongolian language. A majority of Mongolians can (still) speak Russian due to their previous heavy exposure to the Russian language and culture (Billé, 2010). Mongolian food is also heavily influenced by Russian cuisine, as there are many culinary choices, which are considered to be local, but originated from Russia.

Beginning in 1990, Mongolia started integrating itself with the rest of the world, allowing diverse cultural, social, linguistic, financial and ideological flows into the country. Irreversibly, young Mongolians started learning foreign languages other than Russian, which had previously been the most desirable foreign language in socialist Mongolia, with English becoming one of the most popular foreign languages (Cohen, 2005).

Urban young people also started enjoying their freedom of experiencing new international media, popular culture, and technology. They began watching MTV, Western movies, surfing the web, playing computer games and so on – the experiences their parents could never have enjoyed during the communist regime (Dovchin, 2018). Not surprisingly, the language of young, urban and mainly middle-class Mongolians, who can afford to have easy access to media and technology, began transforming into something quite complex with diverse practices, due to their easy exposure and access to transnational linguistic and cultural resources. The complexity of youth language diversity and the performance of new identities and expressions have also started becoming evident thanks to the social and mass media outlets open to the public (Billé, 2010).

Microscopic and Macroscopic Chronotopes

In sociolinguistics, the notion of chronotope mainly refers to the ratio and characteristics of the temporal and spatial categories represented in certain language practices. Specific chronotopes are said to correspond to particular linguistic practices, genres, discourses or relatively stable ways of speaking, which themselves may represent particular identities. Blommaert and De Fina (2017: 5), in this light, point out that the chronotopic nature of specific forms of language and identity is part of common-sense understandings about the way certain groups and cultures function. In particular, understanding a phenomenon such as 'youth culture' in terms of its chronotopic conditions involves explaining certain things since it marks specific periods of life and all such periods must have their own forms of cultural and linguistic practices (Blommaert & De Fina, 2017: 5). Bakhtin (1981: 84–85) refers to 'chronotope' as the 'intrinsic connectedness of temporal and spatial relationships', drawing our attention towards the correlation and inseparability of time and space in human social action. As Bakthin (1981: 84) defines, 'chronotope' points to 'spatial and temporal indicators [that] are fused into one carefully thought-out, concrete whole'. Through chronotope, Bakhtin (1981) allows us to better understand the 'co-occurrence of events from different times and places' and the shifts of an entire range of new features and generated specific effects in discourses (Blommaert & De Fina, 2017: 3). The interplay of different chronotopes is significant because, on the one hand, every chronotope can be attributed to specific forms of identity, behavior, actions, and speech of certain characters, performed in specific timespace contexts. These specific timespace configurations may allow certain specific modes of speech acts as acceptable, disqualifying deviations from that order in negative terms. This may happen through the deployment of 'chronotopically relevant indexicals' that acquire a certain recognizable value when implemented within a certain time-space setting (Blommaert & De Fina, 2017: 3). Meanwhile, the incapability to recognize specific indexicals may point to communication failures – 'if they are invoked in different or unusual configurations', they may be considered 'incomprehensible', 'out of place', and/or 'transgressive' (Blommaert & De Fina, 2017: 3).

From this perspective, the rules of 'macroscopic' and 'microscopic' chronotopes are interactional and indexical, since every utterance signifies locally re-enacted packages of meaningful symbols – a set of sociohistorical linguistic, semiotic and cultural resources – orders of indexicality (Blommaert, 2010). Chronotopes underline a significant aspect of contextualization by which 'micro' circumstances of a particular dialogue may provoke larger 'macro' situations emerged in communicative practices (Blommaert, 2015). Orders of indexicality are recognized in certain chronotopic forms where discussants interact within the language-ideological aspects of 'chronotopes' that connect text and context to very local-specific 'micro' indexicals and broader socially structured 'macro' indexicals (Blommaert, 2015). From the perspectives of 'micro' chronotopes, this chapter, thus, sees youth linguistic creativity through the multiple co-presences of social indexicalities and semiotic codes, voices and repertoires, in which texts are meshed and meditated by diverse semiotic codes. Chronotopic language practices are not necessarily about one language at a time since they transcend individual languages and words that are in constant contact with each other. Language users integrate all available codes as a 'repertoire' in their everyday communication. Language is organically organized around miscellaneous semiotic resources, whilst operating in a discursively integrative universe. The youth chronotopic creativity in this chapter, therefore, is not seen as separate linguistic codes according to particular language systems, since the users are actively involved with the fusion of linguistic codes, modes, genres, repertoires and styles, i.e. the semiotic reconstructions that are becoming the lingua franca of the speakers' daily interaction.

Meanwhile, chronotopicity is further utilized in order to capture the 'macro' sociocultural frames and relations of power in understanding the language creativity of the younger generation, in which meanings are gathered through wider past and present contexts in their social, historical, local, discursive and interpretive elements (Sultana et al., 2015: 95). Not only does chronotopicity allow us to unlock the texts within a text, it also opens up the complex processes by which individuals use the texts to reflect their own personal, social and historical ideas (Dovchin et al., 2015). This also reminds us of Canagarajah's (2007: 927) view on youth linguistic creativity: 'Each participant brings his or her own language resources to find a strategic fit with the participants and purpose of a context'. As Leppänen and Piirainen-Marsh (2009: 279) suggest in terms of youth language creativity and identity: 'They can be mobilized for parodic and playful purposes, and they can be used in strategic ways to create aesthetically and culturally distinctive meanings, as well as to index identities – gendered, local, global – in particular ways'. Procházka (2018), in this regard, views that 'micro' acts of commenting on, for example, a Facebook post may reveal specific (mis)recognitions and their subsequent (in)validations in terms of 'vigilante' performance. Nevertheless, this, in turn, may also demonstrate the presently unfolding 'macro' conditions of the interaction – 'the coexistence and interplay of multiple chronotopes, their nested nature and hierarchy' (Procházka, 2018: 86). The social structure is never finished or final: 'vigilante' performances show that the economy of indexicals governing invocations of particular chronotopic conditions and their ratification points not only to established normative orders but also to emergent, ad-hoc norms defining modes of interaction at hand.

This chapter, thus, seeks to identify a phenomenon such as 'youth culture' in terms of its chronotopic mirco and macro sociolinguistic circumstances and qualifications. Micro chronotopes are about how individuals mobilize different semiotic resources and adopt different and chronotopic negotiation strategies depending on certain time and space configurations to make meanings across linguistic boundaries rather than focusing on fixed grammar forms and discrete language systems (Canagarajah, 2013). Individuals creatively mobilize different linguistic and cultural resources at their disposal and adopt deliberate communicative aims and tactics reliant on the specific context, time and space (Blommaert & De Fina, 2017).

Nevertheless, it is essential to understand micro chronotopes in relation to 'macro' chronotopes because micro sociolinguistic chronotopes are not necessarily random, spontaneous or fleeting linguistic behavior but rather strategic, powerful actions with macro multiple meanings (Dovchin, 2018). Speakers' repertoires should be considered from a broader indexical perspective, maintaining characters and associations shaped by one's complex life trajectories (Blommaert & Backus, 2013). With regards to the chronotopic repertoires, Blommaert and Backus (2013: 25), note that each of the resources is learned in the setting of the micro 'specific life spans', in 'specific social arenas' while leading to macro social tasks, needs and objectives. Youth culture, thereby, characteristically distinguishes itself by unconventional forms of argots, vernaculars, jargons, expressions, idioms, and slangs through the complex interaction of 'micro' and 'macro' chronotopic forms (Blommaert & De Fina, 2017). It seeks to expand knowledge in current youth sociolinguistic studies, in order to account for more complex ways of explaining chronotopic creativity by illustrating the practice of 'inverted youth language', a very specific youth identity performance in the Asian peripheral context of Mongolia.

Linguistic and Digital Ethnography

The data used in this chapter derive from a larger linguistic and digital ethnographic research, considering the fact that inverted youth language may occur in both online and offline contexts. Recent studies, including my own, in the debate of bi/multilingual speakers, have found that the methodological framework of 'linguistic ethnography' may constitute seeds of profound understanding about the sociolinguistic realities of language users (Copland & Creese, 2015; Dovchin, 2018). Linguistic ethnography is specifically characterized by the appropriation of both 'ethnographic' and 'linguistic' perspectives, where researchers are interested in understanding one's sociolinguistic experiences through ethnography. Linguistic ethnography allows for an improved explanatory warrant for statements about language and its actual connection with a real sociocultural context, focusing on people's daily social activities so as to derive their rationality from the local perspective, and on how speakers' linguistic actions at particular moments and in spaces are connected (Blommaert & Dong, 2010).

However, there is a strong evidence that linguistic ethnography on its own is inadequate to fully investigate youth daily sociolinguistic realities. It is equally important to look at the online language practices of youth since, as Stæhr (2015: 44) concludes, youth spoken and written discursive practices seem to be part of similar processes, 'because everyday language use on Facebook indicates that the normative orientations and value ascriptions to particular language forms correspond to those found in speech'. This study thus seeks to contribute to the existing methodological framework of linguistic ethnography by integrating the concept of 'digital ethnography' (Androutsopoulos, 2011; Varis, 2016). A cyber ethnographic analytic framework such as digital ethnography is often used to look at online youth linguistic behavior, employing a natural and unobtrusive manner. It is a qualitative research method devised specifically to investigate the multiple interactions and texts across virtual communities. It can be understood as a written account resulting from fieldwork, where both fieldworks and textual accounts are methodologically informed by the cyberspace (Varis, 2016). Linguistic ethnography thus is expanded through the integration of digital ethnography in this project.

I recruited young people based in Ulaanbaatar, Mongolia, who volunteered to participate in the study from July 2009 until December 2015. The majority of participants were students at the National University of Mongolia and their extended friends aged between 17 and 28. Overall, 50 young people participated in the research. As soon as the potential participants were identified, they were added to my own Facebook accounts. For the purpose of the present chapter, I will illustrate two extracts out of the hundreds of pages of examples, which were retrieved from the Facebook pages of my research participants. Clearly, these extracts cannot fully epitomize the overall space of online linguistic diversity, as only a limited number of young people participated in our ethnographic project. The Facebook account names and profile pictures of all participants in the extracts are pseudonyms to protect anonymity.

Meanwhile, following linguistic ethnographic methods, face-to-face offline interviews among students were conducted in order to understand this distinctive type of linguistic practice through the eyes of actual speakers. They provided me with their own metalinguistic interpretations about their language practices during our project. However, note also that the interviews were conducted through online correspondence (e.g. Facebook chat) sometimes when the participants were not available offline.

In addition, I also used linguistic ethnography to understand the extent of inverted youth language within some offline contexts. Here, I specifically looked at the linguistic practices of young popular music artists in Ulaanbaatar between 2009 and 2015, since popular music is one of the most linguistically complex youth contexts in Mongolia. I collected mainly the lyrics from pop music songs in Mongolia, resulting in dynamic selections for data analysis. During the (offline) linguistic ethnographic fieldwork trips in Ulaanbaatar, interviews with some representatives of popular music artists in Mongolia regarding their linguistic creativities were conducted. For this chapter, I use an extract to show the example of inverted language in the song lyrics of hip-hop musicians in Mongolia. Overall, all Mongolian texts used in the examples of this article were translated from Mongolian into English by the researcher. The interviews with the research participants were conducted in Mongolian and later translated into English by the researcher.

Chronotopic Conditions of Inverted Youth Language in Mongolia

In this section, I will analyze the forms of inverted youth language practiced by young Mongolians from online space to popular music sites. The examples are divided into three main subsections based on the macroscopic chronotopic conditions used to create the inverted language: inverted youth language 'as a secret code', 'as a euphemism' and 'as a pleasure', while also seeking to understand the microscopic chronotopic environments that lead to these grand chronotopes.

Inverted youth language as a secret code

Extract 1 shows how 'youth inverted language' can be locally formed and structured by microscopic chronotopes of youth Facebook engagements, while it can also be recognized as a macroscopic chronotope as a 'secret youth code' that is essentially defined as youth in-peer communicative practice. It has been noted in the literature that young speakers are engaged with linguistic creativity for the strategic purpose of creating a secret language incomprehensible to outsiders (Ag & Jørgensen, 2013; Dovchin, 2015; Kießling & Mous, 2004). Linguistic creativity gives young people an alternative space to have an exclusive way of speaking within in-group peer interactions – their own isolated language, serving its own communicative purposes. It is exclusive to inside audiences, strengthening the sense of ownership of the language, while totally incomprehensible to outsiders (Dovchin, 2015).

One of the most common macroscopic chronotopic conditions for using inverted language among young Mongolians is thus to create an exclusive and in-peer group secret linguistic code outside the norms of Standard Mongolian. Many of our research participants noted during the interviews that they opt for inverted language that is deliberately made unintelligible to outsiders so that they can communicate with one another. As Temir reiterates, 'We speak backward mainly as a secret code because people would not have a clue what we are talking about. If we use English, for example, people tend to understand what we are up to. So, it is much better if we just speak backward' (Interview Ulaanbaatar, Mongolia, 23 September 2010). It was also revealed that young people often use inverted language when they do not want outsiders, including, most specifically, their parents, grandparents, or some elder population, to find out their 'secret plans'. Secret plans can be anything from planning big parties, to get-togethers, and to dating and relationship issues. Let us examine Extract 1.

Extract 1 Facebook Interaction

Original

Translation (1) **Temir:** Quick! We need to invent a different super-secret language! Since Mongolian is now on Google Translate
(2) **Manlai:** Xaxa how about writing backward? You can do it!
(3) **Khosoo:** Don't be ridiculous!
(4) **Bayar:** You are overreacting! So are we going to call you a 'language' now then (since you are inventing a new language)? The new language called Хэѳѳѳл or something like that
(5) **Dori:** How about Kazakh?
(6) **Bileg:** we need to invent a language with lots of alphabets and letters
(7) **Temir:** or teach everyone Kazakh
(8) **Temir:** So they added the following languages
(9) **Temir:** Here's the full list:
Hausa (Harshen Hausa) – Nigeria and neighboring countries
Igbo (Asụsụ Igbo) – Nigeria
Yoruba (èdè Yorùbá) – Nigeria and neighboring countries
Somali (Af-Soomaali) – Somalia and other countries around the Horn of Africa
Zulu (isiZulu) spoken in South Africa and other south-western African countries
Mongolian (Монгол хэл) – Mongolia
Nepali (नेपाली) – Nepal and India
Punjabi language (ਪੰਜਾਬੀ) (Gurmukhi script) – India and Pakistan
Maori (Te Reo Māori) – New Zealand
(10) **Tulga:** honestly, when we look at people who are writing in Mongolian nowadays, it looks like a completely different language. There is almost no one who can write correctly, lol.

In Extract 1, we see the Facebook example authored by our research participant Temir. He is a recent undergraduate from the National University of Mongolia (NUM), and is most recently a postgraduate student in Japan, studying for his Master's degree. Temir is multilingual, fluent in Mongolian, Kazakh (his background is Mongolian Kazakh), Russian and English. His presence on Facebook is intense, largely composed of multilingual resources, including links and images of variable Western, Russian and Japanese popular music videos, ads and movie trailers. One of his most frequent linguistic resources integrated into his Facebook is a heavy incorporation of English. He uses sentences in exclusive or partial English to interact with his Facebook friends, or he uses a large amount of English-Mongolian mixed style terms and expressions. He learned English at a high school, and specialized in English and International Relations at NUM. However, Temir also acknowledges the importance of English cartoons, CNN news and MTV in acquiring his high proficiency in English. In terms of his heavy usage of English on his Facebook page, Temir explains, 'I use English most of the time on my FB because sometimes or most of the time it is easy to express things in English. The nuance is there and everyone understands English so you get more responses' (Facebook interview, 29 October 2014).

From the very specific and local perspective of microscopic chronotopic setting, Temir updates his FB wall post using exclusive English as part of his preferred FB linguistic choice. He urges his FB friends to invent a new language because the Google Translate program has just integrated the Mongolian language in its system. Later, Temir revealed that he was quite excited, in fact, proud, that the Mongolian language was finally integrated into Google Translate because he had never imagined that the Mongolian language with only three million speakers would be recognized in Google Translate. It was a quite a significant milestone for Mongolia according to Temir. Nevertheless, he expressed his excitement on FB in a sarcastic and tongue-in-cheek way, where he urged his FB friends to invent a new language so that Google Translate would not be able to keep up with the Mongolian language.

The reactions from his FB friends clearly show how inverted language is their very first linguistic choice for inventing a secret language. Using the standard Cyrillic Mongolian orthographic system, Manlai (line 2) suggests inventing a secret language, *тонгоргож бичвэл яасын* ('how about writing backward?'). Not only does Manlai suggest that they can invent a new secret language by writing backward, but also he demonstrates himself how to do it, by syllabically inverting the standard Mongolian form *чи чаднаа* into *ич дачнаа* ('you can do it!'). Here, *чи* ('you') has been written from back-to-front, while the middle syllable *да* in *чаднаа* ('can do it') has been placed as an initial syllable to form the reversed *дачнаа*.

In line 3, another FB friend of Temir, Khosoo teases his friend Temir for being silly about inventing a new language for Google Translate. Yet, Khosoo also shows his support for inverted language as a new secret code by inverting the original Cyrillic Mongolian form, *битгий шалчигана* into

Тибгий лашчигана ('Don't be ridiculous!'). Here, the initial syllable, *би* and the middle consonant '*т*' have been swapped to create *Тибгий*; while the consonant '*л*' in the middle of *шалчигана* has been placed at the beginning of *лашчигана*, placing the initial syllable *ша* backward. Note also that the inverted language seems to be executed through a syntactic level rather than lexical level here, as Khosoo writes his short sentence created by reversed vocabulary.

In line 4, Bayar uses an inverted language through the whole syntactic level: *Рүстэй саанан одоо мачайг гэтвэл хэл хэг үү Хээээл ртн* (see English translation in Extract 1). Here, Bayar teases Temir for overreacting about inventing a new language and asks him whether they should call the new invented language 'Temir' since it was invented by him. Alternatively, Bayar suggests coining some new and unconventional term like *Хээээл* for their invented language. *Рүстэй саанан* ('You are overreacting') is the inverted version of Standard Mongolian *сүртэй наасан* in which the initial syllable *сү-* is replaced by the middle letter '*р*' creating *Рүстэй*; and the last syllable *са* in *наасан* is forwarded into the front position, creating *саанан*.

In the next sentence, *одоо мачайг гэтвэл хэл хэг үү* ('so are we going to call you a "language" now then (since you are inventing a new language)?)', *чамайг* is inverted as *мачайг* ('you are') through the middle syllable *ма* forwarded at the start replacing *ча*; *тэгвэл* ('then') is inverted as *гэтвэл* through the middle consonant '*г*' forwarded at the start replacing the initial consonant '*т*'; the standard Mongolian word *гэх үү* ('so are we?') is inverted as *хэг үү*, through writing the word *гэх* from back to front as *хэг*.

Here, Bayar invents a new name for their new invented language *Хээээл* lengthening the Mongolian root word *Хэл* ('language'), followed by the phrase, *ртн* (shortened online version for the expression of 'something like that'). It is common for transnational online users to be engaged with multiple orthographic options, including one of the most common orthographic practices of shortening or abbreviating certain phrases and terms. To this end, by omitting the vowel 'e' from '*ene ter*' online users in Mongolia widely use *ntr*, meaning 'something like that' or 'for example' in English, unfamiliar to non-virtual space users (Dovchin *et al.*, 2015, 2016; Sultana *et al.*, 2013, 2015). Note that *ntr* is reversed from back to front here as *ртн*.

In line 5, typing in English, Dorj suggests using Kazakh since not so many people would not understand the language except Temir, who is a Kazakh-Mongolian – an ethnic minority group in Mongolia. In response to this suggestion, Temir offers to teach Kazakh to everyone instead of using it as a secret language. Kazakhs constitute 5% of the population, and they have been strongly encouraged to learn Mongolian in order to be accepted into Mongolian society and very few Mongolians speak Kazakh or engage with Kazakh cultural practices. Temir is very proud of his Kazakh heritage, as suggested in this FB extract when his friend offers to use Kazakh as a secret language, Temir opposes the idea through insisting the idea of teaching Kazakh to everyone instead. Temir clearly shows his desire that his fellow Mongolian friends should appreciate and take the Kazakh language seriously.

In line 6, using Roman Mongolian, Bileg proposes to invent a new language with many alphabets and letters; while in lines 8 and 9, Temir introduces the list of new languages that were added into the Google Translate application. In line 10, while using Roman Mongolian, Tulga refers to the common language ideology in Mongolian society, i.e. 'linguistic dystopia'. Tulga indicates that the Mongolian language looks like a foreign language anyway nowadays since no one uses it correctly. Thus, there is no need to invent a new language since the standard Mongolian has already been distorted anyway. In fact, some Mongolians have started vigorously questioning the role of English and other foreign languages in society. The hegemony of English and the Roman script is, for example, widely criticized as destructive, and American/Western consumer culture is often problematized by a well-known scholar and writer Lodongiin Tudev, referring to the Mongolian border security as not yet violated, but to its national language – Mongolian – as an already 'violated language' (Lodon, 2010). English and Mongolian mixing practices by young Mongolians are also referred to as 'an epidemic plague', which has 'infested the Mongolian language with lice', spearheaded by English as the sole imperialist language (Nyamjav, 2001: 68–69). Overall, young Mongolians are harshly criticized for distorting the Mongolian language and culture due to foreign influences and losing their own language and identity.

Overall, Extract 1 shows how 'youth inverted language' can be locally formed and structured by microscopic chronotopes of youth Facebook engagements, while it can also be recognized as a macroscopic chronotope as a 'secret youth code' that is essentially defined as youth in-peer communicative practice. Their inverted language is strategically used to keep information secret from outsiders. Temir and his friends informed that using inverted language as a secret code makes it relatively easy to communicate with their mates because they know the pertinent rules, while it is extremely difficult for outsiders to comprehend when they have no knowledge about the specific rules. While these linguistic repertoires might contain new elements that do not necessarily 'fit' into the social, cultural and linguistic order of the Mongolian society, they nevertheless can also be identified in the fixed macroscopic chronotopic frames.

Inverted youth language as a euphemism

In this section, 'inverted youth language as a euphemism' is viewed as a macroscopic chronotopic youth identity since it is quite accepted, recognized and fixed in the context of young popular music artists and their consumers in Mongolia. *Laajiishd* is, for example, a type of inverted language popular amongst hip-hop producers and consumers in Mongolia (Sultana *et al.*, 2013; Dovchin *et al.*, 2017), where the Mongolian word *aljiishd* transforms into *laajishd*. *Aljiishd* is a colloquial Mongolian word, widely used within the younger generation, indicating 'Rocking it!' or 'Nailing it!' It is an abridged form of the Mongolian lexicon *alj baina shuu dee* (someone is killing it), the present continuous simple form of the Mongolian verb root *alah*, meaning 'to kill'. Young Mongolians reduce the term *alj baina shuu dee* into a single word *aljiishd*, trading the last part *j baina shuu dee* with *jiishd*.

Previous studies in youth sociolinguistic practice illustrate that many speakers tend to engage with linguistic creativity to voice what is regarded as 'taboo' and 'disturbing' in the local society (Littlejohn & Putnam, 2010). Many local popular music artists in Asian countries such as South Korea and Japan, for example, tend to use English in their lyrics to exercise a freedom of expression or as a symbol of liberty as it can be used as an alternative resource for the performers to express what is regarded as distasteful, offensive and taboo in the local culture. For example, while the Korean lyrics often tend to emphasize the preciousness and innocence of love and relationship, the English lyrics seem to evoke images of explicit sexual encounters or more direct physical or sexual words and expressions (Lee, 2010). In general, popular music artists in Mongolia use inverted language for the strategic purpose of artistic and aesthetic euphemism. That is to say, they reverse the standard language features in order to form a generally innocuous word or expression used in place of one that may be found too offensive or one that suggests something taboo and unpleasant in the local society. My research participant B.A.T, a famous Mongolian rap artist, acknowledged in his interview that linguistic freedom is the most important aspect of his musical performances as he feels liberated and creative when he can play freely with words and expressions to express his philosophy to the audiences. However, B.A.T also notes that it is hard to please everyone because the elder, female or more educated population tend to harshly criticize his music due to his explicit lyrics and he feels the need to respect his audiences. From this point of view, he seeks to find an alternative way to express his music and inverting or distorting the lyrics sometimes may work out for him for this aesthetic reason. As B.A.T emphasizes,

> I can actually say what I want if I invert the language but in a more aesthetic and audience-friendly way to show my respect to my listeners. They will still understand what I am trying to say, which works out for me. My listeners do not need to feel offended or uncomfortable by what I have just said … (Interview Ulaanbaatar, Mongolia, 27 August 2010)

The song lyrics presented in Extract 2, meanwhile, will show how young Mongolians invert the language to create a euphemism under the microscopic chronotopic condition.

Extract 2 Hip-hop song lyrics

Mongolian original	*Translation*
1. Oh Hip Hop филисофи агуулж Rap дуулъя	1. Oh let's rap based on hip-hop philosophy
2. Нэр хүндээ өсгөж чамайг шархдуулъя	2. Let's hurt you by strengthening our reputation
3. Хоёр охинтой зэрэг явж гардуулъя	3. Let's date with girls at the same time
4. Хорвоогийн сайхан өгзөгнүүдийг магтан дуулъя	4. Let's praise the nice butts on earth
5. Ич тибгий духлаа шаа нааха айбна	5. You don't say bullshit! Where is yours?
6. Иб рээнээ рөөхөн сгөб рабьсан айбна	6. The way I'm touching a sexy ass!

The example presented in Extract 2 is retrieved from the hip-hop song lyrics called 'Freestyle', produced by the famous Mongolian hip-hop group, Lumino, which was established in 1996, with three members, MC Beatz, Baji and Cuthberth. Lumino is one of the most commercially successful Mongolian hip-hop bands, well known for its numerous chart-topping hits. The group is renowned for performing the first-ever live hip-hop concert in Ulaanbaatar and releasing Mongolia's first-ever independent hip-hop album. Lumino is also well known for incorporating varied international linguistic resources when they produce their songs, including English, French, Russian and Japanese (Dovchin, 2018).

'Freestyle' is one of those linguistically creative songs, which was released in 2005, as part of Lumino's commercially successful album, 'Lambaguain Nulims' ('Lama's Tear'). The song is one of Lumino's most popular songs of all time and considered as one of the Mongolian hip-hop classics. The song is about being young, modern and liberal, and it contains a heavy incorporation of English. However, English is mainly used as a hip-hop oriented repertoire, since Lumino freely uses African American Vernacular English and English hip-hop terms throughout the song. For example, in line 1, they rap, *Oh Hip Hop философи агуулж Rap дуулья* ('Oh let's rap based on hip-hop philosophy'), where they use 'Oh Hip Hop' and 'rap' inserted into the primary Mongolian sentence. These hip-hop oriented linguistic resources are repeatedly used throughout the song as an intro and during the chorus.

The song is about young Mongolian hip-hop artists exercising their freedom of expression as young people living in the new liberal society by voicing what is considered to be taboo and disturbing in the local culture. Clearly, as one of the first hip-hop groups in Mongolia, Lumino made an effort to break the taboo culture, which was heavily controlled by the communist party in the Soviet era. Meanwhile, Lumino uses the inverted language on a whole syntactic rather than the lexical level in order to avoid the cultural reference to excessively harsh or blunt sentiments that clearly indicate something unpleasant or embarrassing. According to Baji, one of the members of Lumino, they try to respect their audience by *downsizing* the harsh words and taboo sentiments in the local context. Baji reiterates the sentiment of B.A.T that it is much more aesthetically pleasing for the audience not to hear sexually or physically explicit words right into their ears because the Mongolian culture is quite traditional and conservative anyway. In the meantime, Lumino also stands for the hip-hop ideology of 'keepin' it real' – to stay true to hip-hop root and its philosophy, to speak freely what they want to express. From this point of view, in line 5, the whole sentence written in Standard Mongolian *Чи битгий худлаа шаа хаана байна?* has been inverted into *Ич духлаа шаа нааха айбна?*. *Чи* is written backward *Ич* ('you'); *битгий* is inverted as *тибгий* ('don't') with the initial consonant '*б*' and the middle consonant '*т*' are reversed; *худлаа* is transformed into *духлаа* ('lie') with the middle consonant '*д*' positioned into the front; *хаана* is transformed as *нааха* ('where') in which the middle syllable *на* is forwarded as the initial syllable; *байна?* is inverted as *айбна?* ('is?') with the middle syllable *ай*, forwarded into the front position. The word *шаа* ('to say bullshit') is left intact and the rest of the lexical elements in the sentence have been syllabically positioned in a reverse order.

Swear words are essential for young males to express their male aggressiveness, masculinity, anger and frustration. Young men find taboo expressions or swear words attractive because they allow them to challenge sociolinguistic conventions and intensify their emotional communication to a degree that non-taboo expressions are not able. Yet, swear words are also often considered as taboo, unpleasant and rude in the middle-class Mongolian society. In order to please and respect their middle-class audiences (since Lumino members are middle-class background youths anyway), Lumino uses the inverted language on a syntactic level because they are expressing a rude and offensive sentiment, attacking the other person for saying bullshit. Attacking people with a harsh tone through some strong swear words (*худлаа шаа*, 'say bullshit') has been thereby euphemized here, by inverting the whole sentence to soften their angry tone and rude sentiment.

Meanwhile, many taboos have developed around the topics of sexual and physical exposures in post-socialist Mongolia, since the topic of sex was strictly prohibited during the Soviet era. In particular, speaking about sex or sexualized body image is generally regarded as taboo in society. Following this tradition, in line 6, Lumino seeks to sound milder or more indirect when referring to what is regarded as a highly sexualized term in the local society. They employ the inverted sentence *Иб рээнээ рөөхөн сгөб рабьсан айбна*, which is derived from the standard Mongolian sentence *Би нээрээ хөөрхөн бөгс барьсан байна*. *Би* is written backward *Иб* ('I'); *нээрээ* is inverted as *рээнээ* ('by the way') with the middle consonant '*р*' shifted into front; *хөөрхөн* is transformed into *рөөхөн* ('cute') with the middle consonant '*р*' positioned into the front and the initial consonant '*х*' is omitted; *бөгс* is written from back-to-front as *сгөб* ('ass'); *барьсан* is inverted as *рабьсан* ('grabbed') where the middle consonant '*р*' is shifted into the front; *байна* is inverted as *айбна* ('am') with the middle syllable *ай* forwarded into the front position.

This sentence contains a sexually explicit expression, *хөөрхөн бөгс барьсан* ('grabbed sexy or cute ass'), which is considered to be extremely rude and distasteful in Mongolia. Here, Lumino seeks to praise the beauty of a woman's body but nevertheless decides to invert the whole sentence to euphemize the sexually explicit sentiment to express the taboo topic in the society through more aesthetic and audience-friendly, i.e. euphemized way. Overall, young Mongolians seem to perform their identities through the fixed chronotopic frames by euphemizing unaccepted and taboo discourses, engaging within the interaction of macroscopic and microscopic chronotopes.

Inverted youth language as a pleasure

Extract 3 shows how 'youth inverted language' can be formed and formulated by microscopic chronotopes of youth Facebook engagements, while it can also be recognized as a macroscopic chronotope as a 'pleasure of doing things differently' that is essentially defined as youth in-peer communicative practice. Pennycook (2007: 41–42) suggests that linguistic creativity is 'always connected with forms of pleasure and desire, and forms of pleasure and desire are dependent on transgression' and intricately intertwined with the 'pleasure of doing things differently'. It is thus important to account for both the playful and pleasurable language transgressions young speakers engage in. Creativity is often a source of humor as speakers manipulate the available resources offered by particular contexts to create opportunities for fun and enjoyment through building 'alignment verbally' and through 'embodied means' (Leppänen & Piirainen-Marsh, 2009: 270). Having fun, being humorous and youthful is an integral part of young people's social identity formation. They playfully combine, twist and mix linguistic elements to form certain types of inverted language and eventually find these inverted forms amusing, entertaining and funny. They enjoy the playful function of the language, usually used for making jokes, teasing or mocking each other.

On a macroscopic chronotopic level, young Mongolians thus produce inverted language simply to have fun, to tease each other and to create humor – they are involved with a pleasure of doing things differently. In Extract 3, I will show how young people invert the language for pleasure from a microscopic chronotopic framing. It is about being youthful, humorous and light-hearted, the characteristics that are negotiated through their linguistic creativity.

In Extract 3, unlike previous examples in which inverted language was mostly formed at the syntactic level, the examples are mostly created on the lexical level. That is to say, the inverted language is created on a word-by-word formation rather than at the whole sentence level. In lines 1 and 2, we can see how online users on Facebook produce hybrid forms of inverted language, using varied linguistic resources beyond Mongolian. The research participant Bayar updates his FB wall, posting a message about his long hard day, where he spent too many hours working on an MS Word document. This FB post is complemented by a picture created by Bayar, where he creatively used the famous Mongolian pop singer Bold's name and his standing image dressed in a traditional Mongolian outfit, a *deel*. In so doing, Bayar firstly refers to his long day, where he boldly (enthusiastically) started his day working on an MS word document, looking 'bold' just like the singer Bold in the image in the left half. However, at the end of the day, Bayar becomes very tired and confused, and this sentiment is expressed through the image in the right half, where Bold's 'bold' image becomes 'italics' as if he is about to collapse. He

Extract 3 Facebook Interaction

Original

Translation	(1) **Bayar**:	After working all day on MS Word document, this came to my mind haha [referring to the picture he has just posted]. Seems legit!
	(2) **Tungalag**:	Haha, why not? It is a cute creation
	(3) **Altan**:	You should have italicized the part '-*chin*' kk

(4) **Bayar:**		Yeah, I should have done that
(5) **Bayar:**		There you go haha
(6) **Altan:**		Haha

mocks the singer Bold's name and creatively reproduces his name as part of an MS word document writing features such as bold and italics.

In explaining his creation of the image, Bayar uses predominantly Cyrillic Mongolian, while incorporating an English-oriented technology-related term, 'MS Word'. This term, however, is never translated into Mongolian, as computer users in Mongolia simply use the English version, 'MS Word', to refer to a Microsoft Word document. Note, however, that the term 'MS Word' has been Mongolianized by the addition of the Mongolian suffix *дээр*, forming a local meaning of *MS Word дээр* ('working on MS word document').

In addition, we can spot the evidence of an inverted language form, *leems segit*, in which Bayar twisted English expression 'seems legit'. Here, unlike previous examples in Extracts 1 and 2, where the users inverted standard Mongolian, Bayar inverts Standard English terms. In order to achieve the inversion, Bayar swaps the positions of the initial syllable, 'se' in 'seems' and the initial syllable 'le' in 'legit', presenting a novel way of using inverted language, where the pair of words can be twisted and mixed into one another to achieve a meaning.

The use of inverted language, the image, and a FB post is, of course, related to the strategy of the pleasure of doing things differently where Bayar seeks to entertain his FB friends while having fun with words. Note that Bayar's post is light-hearted and complemented by a laughing emoticon. On many occasions, Bayar and his friends explained that creating something very funny and sharing it on FB with his friends make their days better because it is something to laugh about and enjoy. Clearly, Bayar's FB friends seem to find his post funny and cheeky as almost everyone who left their comments is laughing and obviously having fun. His friend Tungalag (line 2) laughs and acknowledges that the image was 'a cute creation'. The next friend, Altan (line 3) also finds the post funny as he laughs, '*kk*', but he also suggests that it would have been much funnier if the word *дуучин* ('singer') embedded within the center of the image and its last part *-чин* were italicized to synchronize with the sentiment of the picture. Bayar wholeheartedly agrees with his friend's idea (lines 4, 5), creating another revised picture, where the original bold *-чин* has been corrected into italicized *-чин*. Altan openly laughs at the new second version.

Conclusion

Drawing on data examples gathered from linguistic and digital ethnography among young Mongolians, this chapter seeks to point out the chronotopic nature of specific forms of sociolinguistic practice in youth culture. To be more specific, the study identifies one of the sociolinguistic conditions of youth culture, which characteristically distinguishes itself through the usage of chronotopic forms of linguistic creativity, called 'inverted youth language' in Mongolia. It is mainly formed and structured by 'interacting macroscopic and microscopic chronotopes'. I argue that the rules of 'macroscopic' and 'microscopic' chronotopes are interactional and indexical, since every utterance signifies locally re-enacted packages of meaningful symbols. Micro chronotopes underline a significant aspect of contextualization by which 'local' circumstances of a particular dialogue may provoke larger 'macro' situations emerged in communicative practices. From the perspectives of 'micro' chronotopes, this chapter, thus, sees youth linguistic creativity through the multiple co-presences of social indexicalities and semiotic codes, voices and repertoires, in which texts are meshed and meditated by diverse semiotic codes. Young Mongolians syllabically invert and reverse certain Standard Mongolian sentences (e.g. *Ич тибгий духлаа шаа наахa айбна*); single words and expressions (e.g. *laaji-ishd*). They change the positions of initial or middle syllables and letters or consonants. Some of the parts of vowels and consonants are omitted or lengthened, while the original or root words are completely transformed from back to front. They also create the mixed linguistic forms of inverted languages, in which they syllabically twist and turn some forms of English or Russian words and expressions, further mixing them with the Mongolian lexical and syntactic system. They swap the positions of initial syllables from a pair of words (e.g. 'leems segit'); change the syllables based on the standard local pronunciation (e.g. *tsabaan* instead of *пацан*); and omit or lengthen syllables and letters to show their emotions (*Eeesdaaa* instead of standard *пизда*).

Meanwhile, these microscopic chronotopes might contain new elements that do not necessarily 'fit' into the social, cultural and linguistic order of the Mongolian society, they nevertheless can also be detected in the macro chronotopic frames. As I discussed in the data sections, some examples of 'inverted youth language' become more fixed when they are supported by the strategic practices of these young language users. Thus 'inverted youth language' examples can also be based on relatively stable and macro chronotopically organized practices, identities and behaviors.

On the one hand, they form the inverted youth language as a secret code that is incomprehensible to outsiders, creating a kind of exclusive in-peer group language to keep the information secret or confidential within their own circle, and reversing the language, making it hard for outsiders who have no knowledge of the rule. On the other hand, they are further engaged with inverted language to create a euphemism in order to soften or downsize words or expressions that are too harsh and rude or to conceal something taboo and unpleasant. Moreover, young Mongolians seek to gain pleasure for doing things differently through having fun and entertaining themselves by inverting languages. They playfully combine, twist and turn the standard language system, and laugh at their creations. They are simply being youthful, fun, creative and light-hearted.

To sum up, the analysis of 'inverted youth language' practiced by young Mongolians seeks to shed light on the dynamics of macro and micro chronotopic identities embedded within current cultural globalization where local and global resources are mixed in sophisticated sets of indexically diverse modes. 'Inverted youth language' becomes the crucial example, where the global linguistic resources are blended with profound sociolinguistic locality – local linguistic repertoires – and identities that perform the chronotopic condition of local youths in the peripheries.

References

Ag, A. and Jørgensen, J.N. (2013) Ideologies, norms, and practices in youth poly-languaging. *International Journal of Bilingualism* 17 (4), 525–539.

Androutsopoulos, J. (2011) From variation to heteroglossia in the study of computer-mediated discourse. In C. Thurlow and K. Mroczek (eds) *Digital Discourse: Language in the New Media* (pp. 277–298). Oxford: Oxford University Press.

Bakhtin, M. (1981) *The Dialogic Imagination. Four Essays* (edited by M. Holquist; translated by C. Emerson and M. Holquist). Austin: University of Texas Press.

Billé, F. (2010) Sounds and scripts of modernity: Language ideologies and practices in contemporary Mongolia. *Inner Asia* 12 (2), 231–252.

Blommaert, J. (2010) *The Sociolinguistics of Globalization*. Cambridge: Cambridge University Press.

Blommaert, J. (2015) Chronotopes, scale and complexity in the study of language in society. *Annual Review of Anthropology* 44, 105–116.

Blommaert, J. and Backus, A. (2013) Superdiverse repertoires and the individual. In I. de Saint-Georges and J. Weber (eds) *Multilingualism and Multimodality. Current Challenges for Educational Studies* (pp. 11–32). Rotterdam, Boston, Taipei: Sense Publishers.

Blommaert, J. and De Fina, A. (2017) Chronotopic identities: On the timespace organization of who we are. In A. De Fina, D. Ikizoglu and J. Wegner (eds) *Diversity and Super-Diversity: Sociocultural Linguistic Perspectives* (pp. 1–15). Washington: Georgetown University Press.

Blommaert, J. and Dong, J. (2010) *Ethnographic Fieldwork: A Beginner's Guide* (1st edn). Bristol: Multilingual Matters.
Bucholtz, M. (2002) Youth and cultural practice. *Annual Review of Anthropology* 31 (1), 525–552.
Canagarajah, S. (2007) Lingua franca English, multilingual communities, and language acquisition. *The Modern Language Journal* 91 (1), 923–939.
Canagarajah, S. (2013) *Translingual Practice: Global Englishes and Cosmopolitan Relations*. New York: Routledge.
Cohen, R. (2005) English in Mongolia. *World Englishes* 24 (2), 203–216.
Copland, F. and Creese, A. (2015) *Linguistic Ethnography: Collecting, Analysing and Presenting Data*. London: Sage.
Doran, M. (2004) Negotiating between bourge and racaille: Verlan as youth identity practice in suburban Paris. In A. Pavlenko and A. Blackledge (eds) *Negotiation of Identities in Multilingual Contexts* (pp. 93–124). Clevedon: Multilingual Matters.
Dovchin, S. (2015) Language, multiple authenticities and social media: The online language practices of university students in Mongolia. *Journal of Sociolinguistics* 19 (4), 437–459.
Dovchin, S. (2017a) The ordinariness of youth linguascapes in Mongolia. *International Journal of Multilingualism* 14 (2), 144–159.
Dovchin, S. (2017b) The translocal English in the linguascape of popular music in Mongolia. *World Englishes* 36 (1), 2–19.
Dovchin, S. (2017c) The role of English on Mongolian Facebook users. *English Today* 33 (2), 16–24.
Dovchin, S. (2017d) The uneven circulation of resources in youth linguascapes of Mongolia. *Multilingua: Journal of Cross-Cultural and Interlanguage Communication* 36 (2), 147–179.
Dovchin, S. (2018) *Language, Media and Globalization in the Periphery* (Routledge Studies in Sociolinguistics). New York: Routledge.
Dovchin, S., Pennycook, A. and Sultana, S. (2017) *Popular Culture, Voice and Linguistic Diversity: Young Adults On- and Offline*. Basingstoke: Palgrave-Macmillan.
Dovchin, S., Sultana, S. and Pennycook, A. (2015) Relocalizing the translingual practices of young adults in Mongolia and Bangladesh. *Translation and Translanguaging in Multilingual Contexts* 1 (1), 4–26.
Dovchin, S., Sultana, S. and Pennycook, A. (2016) Unequal translingual Englishes in the Asian peripheries. *Asian Englishes* 18 (2), 92–108.
Godin, M. (2006) Urban youth language in multicultural Sweden. *Scandinavian-Canadian Journal/Études scandinaves au Canada* 16, 126–141.
Jaspers, J. (2011) Talking like a 'zerolingual': Ambiguous linguistic caricatures at an urban secondary school. *Journal of Pragmatics* 43 (5), 1264–1278.
Jørgensen, J.N., Karrebæk, M.S., Madsen, L.M. and Møller, J.S. (2011) Polylanguaging in superdiversity. *Diversities* 13 (2), 23–38.
Kießling, R. and M. Mous (2004) Urban youth languages in Africa. *Anthropological Linguistics* 46 (3), 303–341.
Lee, J.S. (2010) Glocalizing keepin' it real: South Korean Hip-Hop playas. In M. Terkourafi (ed.) *The Languages of Global Hip Hop* (pp. 139–162). London: Continuum.
Leppänen, S. and Piirainen-Marsh, A. (2009) Language policy in the making: An analysis of bilingual gaming activities. *Language Policy* 8 (3), 261–284.
Littlejohn, J.T. and Putnam, M.T. (2010) Empowerment through taboo: Probing the sociolinguistic parameters of German gangsta rap lyrics. In M. Terkourafi (ed.) *The Languages of Global Hip Hop* (pp. 120–139). London: Continuum.

Lodon, T. (2010) Хэлээр түрэмхийлэгчид хэн бэ? [Who are these language violators?]. Retrieved December 3, 2010, http://orch.blogspot.com.au/2010/10/3.html.
Marsh, P. (2009) *The Horse-Head Fiddle and the Cosmopolitan Reimagination of Tradition in Mongolia*. New York: Routledge.
Nørreby, T.R. and Møller, J.S. (2015) Ethnicity and social categorization in on-and offline interaction among Copenhagen adolescents. *Discourse, Context & Media* 8, 46–54.
Nyamjav, D. (2001) Undesnii ayulgui baidal ba soyol [National Security and Culture]. In National University of Mongolia & The Academy of Strategy Studies (eds) *Undesnii ayulgui baidliin uzel barimtlaliin shinjlekh ukhaanii undeslel* [Proceedings of the 2001 Conference on the scholarly basis of the national security concepts] (pp. 64–70). Ulaanbaatar: Ungut Hevlel.
Pennycook, A. (2007) *Global Englishes and Transcultural Flows*. London: Routledge.
Procházka, O. (2018) A chronotopic approach to identity performance in a Facebook meme page. *Discourse, Context & Media* 25 (1), 78–87.
Rossabi, M. (2005) *Modern Mongolia: From Khans to Commissars to Capitalists*. Berkeley: University of California Press.
Schoonen, R. and Appel, R. (2005) Street language: A multilingual youth register in the Netherlands. *Journal of Multilingual and Multicultural Development* 26 (2), 85–117.
Stæhr, A. (2015) Reflexivity in Facebook interaction-enregisterment across written and spoken language practices. *Discourse, Context & Media* 8, 30–45.
Sultana, S., Dovchin, S. and Pennycook, A. (2013) Styling the periphery: Linguistic and cultural take-up in Bangladesh and Mongolia. *Journal of Sociolinguistics* 17 (5), 687–710.
Sultana, S., Dovchin, S. and Pennycook, A. (2015) Transglossic language practices of young adults in Bangladesh and Mongolia. *International Journal of Multilingualism* 12 (1), 93–108.
Varis, P. (2016) Digital ethnography. In A. Georgakopoulou and T. Spilioti (eds) *The Routledge Handbook of Language and Digital Communication* (pp. 55–68). London: Routledge.

4 The Care of the Selfie: Ludic Chronotopes of *Baifumei* in Online China

Kunming Li and Jan Blommaert

Introduction: From the Self to the Selfie

In online-offline societies, both zones of social life offer specific affordances, some of which are compatible or complementary, and some of which are overlapping and conflictual.[1] Theorizing this new kind of social system is a task that still awaits the full efforts of a large scholarly community; consequently, much of the theory currently used for addressing new social phenomena draws on mainstream views designed to cope with pre-internet societies (but see Appadurai, 1996; Blommaert, 2018; Castells, 1996; Van Dijck, 2013). In this chapter, we intend to document the ways in which online infrastructures in China offer affordances for chronotopic identity work that are not available in offline contexts. More specifically, we shall describe the practices of young Chinese women designing and marketing imageries of feminine beauty and attractiveness on social media. While describing these phenomena, we also intend to sketch a conceptual framework for addressing such forms of online practice. The latter, we believe, is of great importance for studying online social practices, which display features that may be similar to more common offline forms of social conduct but may still deviate in crucial ways. It is such deviations that enable online technological infrastructures to offer specific, complementary affordances to internet users, and these affordances need to be described in a conceptual vocabulary that does not reduce online forms of social action to their offline near-equivalents.

The key issue in what follows is that of *identity*, broadly taken. There has been, and still is, a strong tendency, both in expert and lay discourse, to describe online identity work as 'virtual' (with connotations of 'fake') and as opposed to offline 'real' identity work (see e.g. Indalecia, 2010;

also Adrian, 2008). The point we must take on board right from the start is that identity work in online context is as 'real' as the work we observe in offline contexts, and that we need to be far more precise and specific in describing the peculiarities of online identity work. We can follow the tradition of Mead (1934) here, who emphasized that every social context demands specific forms of organization of the self, and add the fundamental insight of Erving Goffman (1959) that *any* form of identity is an outcome of 'dramaturgical' performance work and is thus, in a sense, 'ludic' (Blommaert, 2017). Thus, what we encounter in the Chinese online contexts we will examine, is as 'real' a performance as any other, and we should focus on the specific nature of that kind of performance and the conditions under which it can happen.

These conditions are, as we know, determined by the technological infrastructure that defines the online world. Conditions for online social interaction do not allow for the physical co-presence as in a closed and synchronized timespace arrangement characterizing, for instance, ordinary offline conversations. In that sense, these conditions exclude direct physical (tactile) contact between interlocutors, as well as the mutual monitoring access to the interlocutors' bodies – that crucial reservoir of knowledge of the self and the other in interaction, on which Goffman focused so much of his attention.[2] In return, technologically mediated interactions such as the kinds we shall discuss offer a number of very different affordances. The specific set of affordances we shall discuss here revolve around the design and construction of an artefactualized, technologically mediated representation of the self. As a shorthand for these affordances, and paraphrasing Foucault (1986), we shall use 'the care of the selfie': an elaborate complex of 'ludic' practices aimed at constructing and performing a *specifically online* (and more specifically small-screen) 'image of personality' in which usually three different elements have to be carefully created and maintained:[3]

- an *avatar*: an online name often containing significant clues as to the particular image of personality offered in interaction;
- carefully doctored *pictures or video-streamed images* of the selfie;
- specific online *interactional scripts* to be observed in contacts with audiences.

We shall see that when such rules are observed, a specific chronotopic environment emerges within which highly sophisticated forms of identity work can be interactionally performed, in ways that have no equivalent in the Chinese offline social spheres. Let us now turn to the case itself.

Becoming *Baifumei* By Refusing It

Li (2018) addressed a number of ways in which feminine beauty increasingly becomes a commodity to be traded in new, largely informal online economic contexts in China. A central feature of this new market is *baifumei*. The term *baifumei* has over the past number of years evolved from an online slang into a very widespread term in Chinese popular and media culture, pointing towards a particular 'type' of Chinese woman (Li et al., 2014).

The compound *baifumei* (白富美) was coined by internet users out of three Chinese lexemes, namely *bai* 白, *fu* 富 and *mei* 美. Each of these three constituent lexemes has a range of related meanings and discursive figures, grounded in Chinese tradition (as shown in Table 4.1). When used to describe people, especially women, *bai* primarily refers to the whiteness of one's skin; *fu* to a great amount of wealth in one's possession; and *mei* to one's attractive appearance.

Thus, *baifumei* identifies a woman who is attractive in a highly specific way (the white skin is critical) and who is, in addition, financially well-off. The connection between beauty and wealth brings a degree of moral ambivalence to the label due to the suggestion of prostitution or related forms of conversion of female attractiveness into money. In addition, the label is easily associated with an extravagant, luxurious and mercenary lifestyle. The caricature in Figure 4.1 features a stereotypic *baifumei*: a beautiful woman with a slim figure, fair skin, the feminine curve and an elaborate hairstyle, who cares obsessively about her looks and indulges in shopping sprees.

Despite the potential ambivalence, *baifumei* has been adopted by large numbers of Chinese women as a *model* of self-presentation in online contexts. It has become, in other words, a model for the care of the selfie, approximations of which may result in 'authentic' *baifumei* membership. This authenticity needs to be 'designed' (in the sense of Kress, 2010) by drawing on the available resources, perceived as contributing to that kind of authenticity, and in very precise and particular ways specific to the online contexts in which it must be performed.[5] According to Blommaert and Varis (2015: 5), identity practices are 'discursive orientations towards

Table 4.1 Meanings of the three lexemes of baifumei[4]

Lexemes	Meanings
Bai 白	White; pure; blank; in vain; waste efforts; free of charge
Fu 富	Rich; wealthy; abundant
Mei 美	Beauty; beautiful; good; beauteousness; prettily

Figure 4.1 A caricature of a *baifumei* girl (source: www.china.org.cn/china/2013-12/27/content_31022201.htm, last accessed in January 2014)

sets of features that are (or can be) seen as emblematic'. In this sense, to be considered as an authentic *baifumei*, one has to comply with the semiotic array of features and discursive practices that leads to 'enough' *baifumei* identity features – not too little and not too much. To get close to such level of enoughness and with that of authenticity, one needs to have a good control on the dose of 'enoughness' that ought to be perpetually adjusted, reinvented and amended (Blommaert & Varis, 2011). Put into the local context, women aspiring to the *baifumei* label need to use specific online contexts for testing, developing and improving their identity performances.

One such online context, and a quite popular one, for identity practices of *baifumei* is the 'Baifumei Bar' forum on the online platform Baidu Tieba (see Li, 2018; Li *et al.*, 2014). On this Baifumei Bar forum, *baifumei* authenticity needs to be played out visibly and is constantly subject to its audience's (both male and female) interactional assessment of the performed 'selfie'. The selfie, as we have seen, consists of a stage name, a doctored visual image, and carefully scripted interactional behavior. The latter is achieved by balancing two major categories of discursive moves: 'affiliating acts' and 'distancing acts'. The performance of *baifumei* often begins with a *distancing* act and a self-denial as a *baifumei* person. However, underneath this initial and also subsequent distancing moves, affiliating acts creep in. A concrete example will show this.

We shall look at the profile of a woman called *Fang;[6] in September 2014, Li (2018) noticed her top-ranked post in the Baifumei Bar, with 6578 replies up to the time of this contribution.[7] The post was headlined as follows:

Example 1[8]

Original	*Translation*
*Fang: 不是白富美，只是喜欢爆照而已	I'm not a *baifumei* but a girl who enjoys posting selfies online.

As we can see, *Fang straightforwardly denies being a *baifumei*, explaining she is just a lover of selfie-posting. The headline is followed by three photos, A, B and C, as shown in Figure 4.2:[9]

The choice and the visual architecture of the pictures are seemingly deliberate. Photo A in Figure 4.2 is a screenshot of *Fang's iPhone lock screen, backgrounded by a close-up photo of her. Compared with the selfie in a dim-lit bedroom in photo C, *Fang's skin tone in A is much paler. While different from the half-length portrait in A, *Fang in C displays her sartorial skills: a red blouse is matched with patterned shorts, a bracelet and red high-heel shoes. B is a photo taken in a BMW car, a stereotypical emblem of wealth. Observe that the driver in photo B is a man: *Fang's boyfriend and the owner of the car, as later confessed by *Fang. It is noted that the photos are *designed* in a well-ordered sequence from A to C, in which the attributes of being *bai* ('fair-skinned'), *fu* ('wealthy')

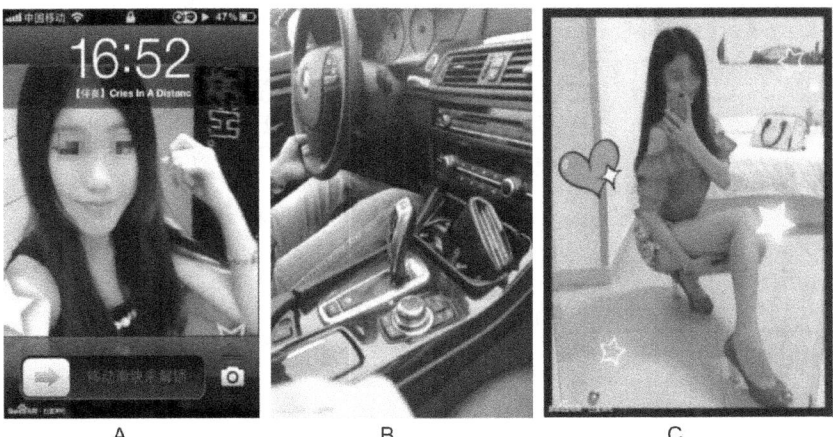

Figure 4.2 Three photos posted by *Fang (source: https://tieba.baidu.com/f?kw=白富美, last accessed on 10 August 2015)

and *mei* ('beautiful') are highlighted one after another. This clue unveils *Fang's 'backstage preparation' (in Goffman's words) towards *baifumei* authentication. Observe also how the self-disqualification of *baifumei* in her opening line is instantly contradicted by the 'grammar of visual design' of her three photos (Kress & Van Leeuwen, 2001).

Example 2 On the second étage of her post,[10] *Fang wrote the following:

	Original	*Translation*
*Fang:	我发帖没说让别人评论，我说了我长期更贴，我的生活是怎样我就跟大家分享的是怎样，不存在什么其他的，所以要讨论或者说我坏话的人省省	You are not in any way obliged to comment on my post. As was said before, I will continuously update my life status in this post and show you what my life is really like without any other intentions. So, those who are ready to judge me or speak ill of me are kindly asked to leave for the sake of your time and energy.

With a departure from the *baifumei*-affiliating act in Figure 4.2, *Fang here disclaims her intention of wanting to be a *baifumei*: her updates should be merely seen as a realistic documentary of her daily life. She suggests potential challengers to save their malicious remarks and leave her profile space. This, if interpreted in Goffman's terms, is an example of *dramaturgical circumspection*, in which a prior warning serves as a defensive measure and a safeguard. In the above two examples, *Fang's stance toward *baifumei* develops from the initial pronounced 'distancing' to a covert graphical 'affiliating' and then to the 'distancing' again. The orderly and multimodal stance pattern can be understood as the 'line', as used by Goffman (1967), to address the pattern of verbal and nonverbal acts that a person takes in a communicative event. The line is dynamic and, as in *Fang's case, is maneuvered constantly and strategically for appropriate impression management.

After the opening post in Example 2, the post threading proceeded among both positive and negative comments. *Fang often dismissed compliments and found a way out of the less commonplace challenges. On the 97th étage, a man (called Male A here) interacted with *Fang as follows:

Example 3

	Original	*Translation*
Male A:	我要逆袭白富美。	(As a loser) I wanna procure you, the *baifumei* girl.

*Fang:	(emoticon)	(A sweating face).
Male A:	嘿嘿，行不？	Lol, is that ok?
*Fang:	应该不行，哈哈	Honestly, it's not ok. Lol

In this example, by using the online catchphrase '逆袭 (ni xi)',[11] Male A shows his aspiration to procure a *baifumei* girlfriend and marry her. This aspiration obviously refers to *Fang, and we can see that Male A identified *Fang as a *baifumei*, in spite of *Fang's antecedent disclaimers. *Fang replies with a sweating-face emoticon which allows her to avoid a direct positioning: *Fang could have either felt overwhelmed or embarrassed by Male A's words. Then Male A repeats his request and gets refused. The refusal is a reply made to Male A's befriending (or marriage) request but does not directly rebuts his allusion to *Fang's *baifumei* identity. We see the play of affiliating and distancing acts at work here: disguised as a refusal, *Fang tacitly got confirmed as a *baifumei* girl.

Then on the 348th étage, the following communication happened between *Fang and another man (called Male B here):

Example 4

	Original	Translation
Male B:	就是白富美	You're a baifumei
*Fang:	…	…
Male B @*Fang:	难道不是	Aren't you?
*Fang @Male B:	我不觉得	I don't think so
Male B @*Fang:	我们就是穷屌丝	We are undoubtedly *diaosi*
*Fang @Male B:	我也是	Me, too
Male B:	哈哈~ 握爪	Lol…A hand shake with you

On this étage, *Fang identifies with Male B as a *diaosi* (屌丝, literally 'penis hair' and figuratively 'loser'),[12] distancing herself from the covert *baifumei* identity established on the 97th étage. However, *Fang's self-identification with *diaosi* fluctuates and she once became outraged at a boy who had described her similarly as a *diaosi* under another post of *Fang. Hence, *Fang's self-identification with *diaosi* is, to a large extent, a tactic aimed to establish a *rapport* with Male B. It is a form of self-belittling in Goffman's terms, in which one's own positive qualities are deliberately underplayed: 'if a person knows that his modesty will be answered by others' praise of him, he can fish for compliments' (Goffman, 1967: 24).

Seen from the above examples, *Fang's 'line' is context-adaptive and changes from the initial distancing in the headline to the affiliating in her photo arrangement, and then to distancing once more, with another affiliating act following. However, the line *Fang takes is not necessarily a consecutive distancing-affiliating sequence. What emerges prominently and importantly from the data is that *Fang never makes her affiliating acts obvious, overt and pronounced. By contrast, she shows her distancing in a clear and assertive way. Although *Fang did sometimes face questions about her true motives from critical participants, her dramaturgical circumspections and performed modesty helped her win a widely ratified *baifumei* identity, as attributed *by men*. It is an interactional achievement, resulting from highly skilled and flexible, 'ludic' performance practices.

The Ludic Economy of *Baifumei*

The practices performed by *Fang are entirely conditioned by the technological infrastructure in which she performs them: an online forum explicitly designed for and devoted to *baifumei* identity work. They are, in that infrastructure, entirely 'normal' – an expected behavioral script that demands careful performance, and in which participants draw on available cultural and technological resources for adequate outcomes. Such practices are, consequently, chronotopic in the full sense of the term (Blommaert & De Fina, 2017; Blommaert & Varis, 2015). The chronotope, however, is not a closed timespace constellation: it draws on cultural materials that have their origins in older traditions and organize conduct in a variety of social spheres.

The careful play of distancing and affiliating acts by *Fang is a case in point. Modesty is highly valued as a traditional virtue of China. 'Virtue' is called *mei de* (美德, literally beautiful moral) in Chinese. With the same *mei* (美) ('beautiful') as in *baifumei* (白富美), *mei de* indexes the general beauty of a person. Chinese people are, in many contexts, expected to understate their personal accomplishments rather than speak highly of their own merits. So, a woman's modesty, if recognized, relates to the Chinese virtue and adds weight to the 'enoughness' of the *baifumei* identity.

A very similar interplay between cultural tradition and new online technological affordances can be observed in the second case we examine here: the performance of *baifumei* on *Zhibo* (直播, literally online livestreaming). By June 2016, there were about 325 million livestreaming users in China, accounting for nearly a half of the Chinese total netizen's population (CNNIC, 2016). Across about 200 livestreaming platforms (iiMedia Research, 2016), there are 4 million participants (both hosts and watchers) simultaneously present in about 3000 livestreaming rooms at peak times. And one extraordinarily popular form of live-streaming involves *baifumei* women performing forms of online flirting and intimacy with male audiences, who, in return, donate 'gifts'. In contrast with the static images and texts we observed in the Baifumei Bar, we are facing moving real-time images and interactions here.

The livestreaming performances occur within a technologically circumscribed arena, enabling certain forms of interaction while constraining or excluding others. Almost all major internet companies in China have launched such livestreaming services, and the actual shapes of the interfaces are quite similar. Yizhibo (一直播), Yingke (映客) and Momo (陌陌), three of the most influential livestreaming platforms in China, look alike in their user interface layouts, as can be seen in Figure 4.3.

All of Yizhibo, Yingke and Momo have the status zone (marked as No. 1 in Figure 4.3) at the top, the hostesses' performing zone at the center (No. 2) with a display of her received gifts in the form of animated stickers (No. 3), the threading of viewers' comments at the left lower part (No. 4) and the viewers' operation zone at the bottom (No. 5). Such homogeneous interface designs along with similar livestreaming technological frameworks have resulted in severe competition between different service providers in China.

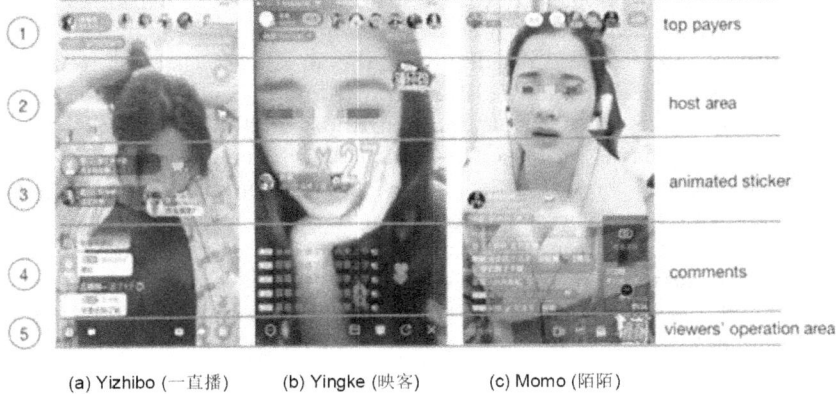

Figure 4.3 User interfaces of Yizhibo, Yingke and Momo (source: yizhibo.com; yingke.com; momo.com, last accessed on 14 December 2016)

*Wuxue (*污雪) is a top-ranking 'talk show' hostess on Yizhibo. As mentioned earlier, the avatar or screen name used in selfie performances is of importance, so let us first examine the name. *Wu* (污), a Chinese adjective which literally means 'polluted' and 'dirty' is put in juxtaposition with *xue* (雪), the 'snow', which is generally attached to purity (as it is white) in Chinese culture. As a screen name, '*Wuxue' offers layers of inferential meaning and suggests a sense of cynicism and dark humor of the name bearer. These characteristics contribute to *Wuxue's success. At the time of data collection on 11 December 2016, *Wuxue had already harvested 79,000 followers and earned 37,059,600 credits on Yizhibo, which amounts to 370,596 RMB (approximately 47,269 Euros) through 53 broadcasts within 46 days.[13] *Wuxue's income is about 54 times the average Chinese national income per capita, by which standard she is a highly successful *baifumei* entrepreneur.

The interface of Yizhibo, as seen in Figure 4.3(a), is characterized by a multimodal design, which encourages multilateral interaction and is responsive to ongoing communications during livestreaming. The essential structure is: a female hostess interacts with an online (male) audience, members of which can send messages and offer 'gifts' to the hostess, all of which is publicly visible. These gifts are shown as symbols on the screen but, converted by the platform, represent real money income for the hostesses. First, let us have a close look at the interface design of Yizhibo as illustrated in Figure 4.4.

We now begin to investigate the features of the specific chronotope of livestreaming female-male interactions. With all those multimodal elements in motion and interaction with each other, the message flow in the livestreaming is dialogical and responsive to ongoing communications. When new messages pop up, previous messages will immediately move up on the user interface and recede out of the audience's vision. Given that online livestreaming rooms are often crowded with viewers, new messages from viewers constantly appear, move up and then disappear – all at great speed. But the relative prominence of particular audience members (within the parameters of the system) is made visible. As shown in Figure 4.4, the top-five spenders among the viewers are listed on the top right on the users' interface, and their prominence is immediately visible to all viewers. The system also features an interactional asymmetry: *Wuxue as the hostess runs a continuous livestreamed performance in front of an audience, while the audience can only communicate with *Wuxue through text messages and gifting. The audience has no acoustic or visible presence. Given this exposure discrepancy, gifting, along with text messages, constitutes an important tool for an audience to interact with *Wuxue.

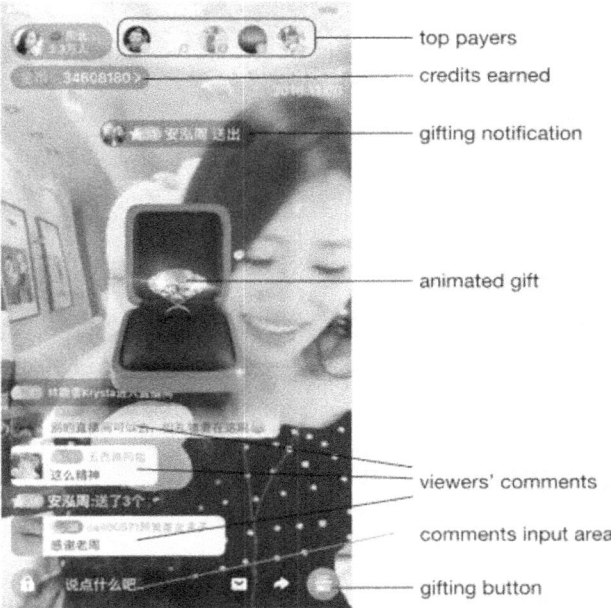

Figure 4.4 The Yizhibo livestreaming interface design for *Wuxue (source: Yizhibo iOS application, last accessed on 9 January 2017)[14]

Gifts occupy a large and central space in the interface design, the very epicenter of the stage, as with the glittering diamond in Figure 4.4. Gifts are further technologically glorified by triggering an array of enlivening animate effects. With much gratitude, *Wuxue tends to publicly address gift senders, especially those sending expensive items, in friendly and intimate ways. Each time after receiving the gift of 'love', which costs 10 RMB (approximately 1 Euro), *Wuxue immediately shows her 'love' by air kissing and playing a piece of love music that has been popularized by *Feicheng Wurao* (非诚勿扰, literally 'If you are the one'), a famous Chinese dating program hosted by Jiangsu Satellite TV. Figure 4.5 just features *Wuxue expressing her gratitude for a gift through air kisses while depicting a heart-shaped gesture for 'I love you' (我爱你). This immediate expression of appreciation is orchestrated to a large number of viewers, amplifying the importance of generous gifts and the prominence of those who offer them.

The gesturing and facial expressions of joy and gratitude are evident. But as we have seen, the system also allows the hostess to directly talk to her audience, while audience members can only respond through

Figure 4.5 *Wuxue's gestural response to a 'love' gift (source: Yizhibo iOS application, last accessed on 9 January 2017)

text messages. Discursively, such moments of affection are expressed as follows:

Example 5

An episode of interaction between *Wuxue and *Re, a viewer of her livestreaming, who sent her virtual gifts (Retrieved on 13 November 2016 from Yizhibo iOS application); *Yilai and *Gangwan are *Wuxue's showroom assistants; *Wuxue is bantering with *Minuo, a viewer in her showroom.

	Original	*Translation*
*Re:	[Send out 11 lollipops (gift)]	
*Yilai:	Thank you, Re (an abbreviated addressing of *Re).	
*Wuxue:	感谢热	Thank you, Re.
*Minuo:	我的妈	*Oh my God.*
*Wuxue:	我的妈我的妈	(Reading out *Minuo's comment) Oh my God. Oh my God.
	开玩笑的	I'm just kidding.
*Hushou:	我来了，我是黑粉	I'm coming. I'm one of your anti-fans.
*Wuxue:	我来了我是黑粉	(Reading out a *Hushou's comment) I'm coming. I'm one of your anti-fans. Hahaha… (Big laughter)

	(…)	
*Re:	[Send out a love (gift)]	
*Wuxue:	谢谢我热送的I love you哦	Thank you, my Re (still addressing *Re for short). Love you, ó (a sentence-final particle that conveys intimacy)
*Gangwan:	谢谢热	*Thanks, Re.*
*Yilai:	谢谢热*love*	*Thanks for Re's love (gift).*
*Wuxue:	[(action) Sketching out the heart shape for 'love' in front of the camera]	
*Wuxue:	Mwah [Giving out a 'pronounced' air kiss to *Re]	
*Wuxue:	I love you 哟 [Still keep the shape of 'love']	I love you, yó (a particle that serves to soften the expression before it)
	谢谢热啊	Thank you ā (an exclamation particle to emphasize what comes before it), Re.

As seen in Example 5, each time *Re sends in his gifts, *Wuxue focuses her attention on *Re. Although without entirely cutting herself off from interaction with other participants, *Wuxue treats *Re to repeated and emphatic verbal and nonverbal expressions of love and intimacy. Such moments of direct address in interaction shape the kind of ludic 'imagined togetherness' (Mortensen, 2017), a key feature of online flirting that is much coveted by male audience members. All of this evolves in the highly specific contours of the online livestreaming chronotope, in which such ludic roles, relationships and practices can be enacted as features of 'normal' interactional conduct.

With a slim figure, well-developed breasts and long hair, white-skinned *Wuxue embodies the *baifumei* model of feminine 'selfie' beauty. She is often scantily clad and is good at drawing male audience's attention as a good joke teller (more specifically, an excellent teller of *risqué* jokes). Being energetic, optimistic and talkative, *Wuxue has demonstrated excellent social skills to maintain a nice *rapport* with her audience through various acts of 'imagined closeness'. The 'selfie' she presents online is a virtuoso one that draws on a vast repertoire of identity features and is characterized by superbly executed performances. An important part of this revolves around her strategic reception of the gifts from the male audience.

Different from traditional business and mercantile practices, economic transactions in livestreaming undergo a semiotic 'romanticization' process, where the audience's money spent in showrooms is sugar-coated by a dazzling array of virtual gifts, which serve as cultural proxies that navigate the aforementioned ambivalence between beauty and wealth, and reduce the risk of moral condemnations and allegations of prostitution. The semiotic representation of the gifts, in particular, avoids the connotation of 'payment-for-sex' by calling on established Chinese traditions of courtesy and hospitality in a 'ludic' way. In China, which is characterized by collectivism and *Guanxi* (private and business networking), gifting practices are widely seen in all walks of life (see Luo *et al.*, 2012; Steidlmeier, 1999). Compared to the potentially high cost of offline safe intimacies, the gifting expenses for live-streamed intimacies can be quite low. Hence, emerging livestreaming platforms provide males more chances to communicate with and befriend those desirable hostesses, who could be less accessible to most men in their offline lives. For someone like *Wuxue, the reference to traditional forms of gift-giving enables her to be (sometimes explicitly) erotically appealing to the men, while avoiding the social stigma (and legal sanctions) attached to prostitution. In addition, it enables her to earn an income many times larger than what 'regular' offline jobs would offer her.

All of this is made possible by the livestreaming technology with its semiotic and interactional affordances. In livestreaming some viewers are willing to pay very substantial sums to buy virtual gifts to please the hostesses they prefer (see Li & Wei, 2017). In return, hostesses conspicuously display their gratitude for the viewers' gifting and perform that gratitude out to an extent that a big audience can well recognize and glorify the gift sender. All of this, however, stays in the online environment and does not migrate offline: the courtesy of the gift is responded to by means of a dramaturgy of online flirtation. The livestreaming hostesses usually respond more actively, elaborately and intimately to those big spenders, in words, facial expressions, body postures and gestures. In other words, with a certain amount of payment in the form of gifting, a viewer can get involved in specific public but intimate genres of interaction, ranging from being mentioned by name to being air-kissed and offered a love confession. Interactional events such as these can only happen in the tightly circumscribed online timespace configurations provided by internet applications; and when they happen, they happen according to the normative formats befitting this specific chronotope.

Conclusion: Ludic Selfie Chronotopes

In his classic *Homo Ludens*, Johan Huizinga (1950/2014) emphasized the playful character of many social, cultural and political practices. In our tendency to organize societies along rational management patterns, Huizinga insisted, we risked losing sight of the fact that much of what people do is governed by an *ir*rational logic, a ludic pattern of action. Even more, much of what we see as the rational organization of societies is grounded, in fact, in play. Huizinga (1950/2014) listed several features of 'play'. Play is *significant*, for instance: it is a site of meaning-making in which 'something is at play'; it is at the same time relatively *unregulated* and unconstrained by established rules and forms of control; it is also an *authentic* activity in which we observe the unconstrained 'playing out' of the self; it is an *enclosed* activity in the sense that it often requires a particular spatiotemporal organization different from that of other activities (a 'playground'); and finally, it is also a *serious* activity demanding focus, intensity and skill (see Blommaert, 2018 for a discussion).

We have examined 'playgrounds' here – technologically mediated and configured enclosed timespace in which ludic activities revolving around authenticity can be played out. With respect to this authenticity, it must be underscored that it is perfectly normal to *play someone else while expressing some essential 'self'*. In fact, forms of play in which roles are assumed by players, masks or other garments are worn or names are being changed for the duration of the event are found everywhere. In the online world, it suffices to think of highly developed communities such as those of cosplay and gaming to see the point; but think also of the widespread use of aliases or nicknames on social media platforms. Just as we can distinguish a Foucauldian 'care of the self' in various forms of play, we see a 'care of the selfie' in online play as well. This selfie, we hope to have illustrated, demands forms of knowledge and skill specific to the online chronotopes in which it is presented and performed. We have seen complexes of norms at play in our examples, in which older and established cultural material was blended with the particular affordances of online platforms in such a way that different forms of identity work and male-female relationships could be constructed and enacted in playful ways – by elaborate forms of graphic doctoring of images, delicate forms of interaction and joint choreographies of the body and the features of the online apps. These playful practices are, however, significant and serious, and certainly in our discussion of *Wuxue's work, something 'was at play' – there was a real, 'hard' economic transaction buried within the ludic, frivolous and artful interactional work she performed for her audience, and this transaction takes place in a neoliberal competitive market arena. There is nothing 'virtual' to the income she generates through her talk shows, even if the stuff she offers in the transaction is just a 'selfie', a semiotic, immaterial artifact that needs to be meticulously and carefully constructed and checked, just as *Fang showed us, in order to be ready for economic transaction.

Online identity work and processes of community formation remain poorly understood social facts, often suffering from reductionist interpretations grounded in a pre-internet sociological imagination. We believe it is helpful to approach the complexities of such new social facts with the help of alternative frameworks as we have attempted to illustrate here. In the cases we have discussed, we detect traces of significant socioeconomic change. The women engaging with the ludic selfie chronotopes offered by internet providers can enter a labor market and develop economic activities that are not legitimately accessible, or more strictly policed, in offline spheres of society. Of course, such new economic activities will always look insignificant when measured against the standards of the mammoth Chinese formal economy; at the same time, as we have mentioned earlier, they are not marginal and may constitute more than just symbolic opportunities for people often marginalized in the bigger socioeconomic game. This, in itself, should suffice as a reason to explore phenomena such as these as integral parts of the development of new social systems.

Notes

(1) This paper draws on cases analyzed in Kunming Li's PhD dissertation (Li, 2018). We are grateful to Sjaak Kroon and Massimiliano Spotti and Piia Varis for guidance and suggestions throughout the research project, and to Caixia Du, Mingyi Hou, Ying Lu, Jos Swanenberg and Hua Nie for critical discussions on the issues presented in this chapter.
(2) Goffman surely was not alone, and contemporary scholarship on social interaction emphasizes the intrinsic fusion of visual, tactile and verbal aspects in communication. See e.g. Goodwin (2007) and Bezemer and Kress (2014).
(3) For alternative surveys of practices for online self-presentation, see e.g. Adrian (2008) and boyd (2014).
(4) For 白, 富 and 美, see http://dict.youdao.com.
(5) Kress's notion of 'design' refers to the strategic semiotic work performed by subjects in interaction with others, with particular goals in mind (Kress 2010: 26–27, italics in original): '*Design* meets the interest of the *rhetor* (…) in full awareness of the communicational potentials of the resources which are available in the environment and needed for the implementation of the rhetor's interest'.

(6) The Chinese character *fang* (芳), which etymologically refers to a specific kind of fragrant grasses in ancient China and metaphorically refers to a girl's desirable appearance, is often used as a girl's call name in China. In this sense, the screen name is part of the selfie *Fang puts on stage.
(7) Data are retrieved at 23:29 on 28 September 2014 (UTC+1:00, Amsterdam).
(8) All translations from Chinese in this text are our own, unless specified otherwise. While we will consistently attempt to stay as close as possible to the Chinese originals, we opt for English stylistic equivalents.
(9) Originally, the photos are in a vertical sequence.
(10) Étage or 'floor' is often used in Tieba as a simulator to a construction in the offline world. The first post of a thread is called the First Étage and the rest in the same way in a chronological order. An étage can be maintained by others' replying to it. Changing an étage in Tieba usually means an ending of the previous conversation turn and the beginning of a new one.
(11) The original Chinese term *ni xi* is a military jargon noun, which literally means 'inverse attack'. It has been widely used on Chinese social media in its figurative sense to refer to one's procurement of life-changing social upward mobility.
(12) The term *diaosi* is widely used to describe the large groups of people feeling excluded or marginalized in China's booming socioeconomic environment. For more discussion on *diaosi*, see Yang et al. (2014) and Du (2016).
(13) Data are retrieved at 14:39:16 on 11 November 2016.
(14) The line and English captions are added by the authors for further analysis.

References

Adrian, A. (2008) No one knows you are a dog: Identity and reputation in virtual worlds. *Computer Law & Security Review* 24 (4), 366–374.
Appadurai, A. (1996) *Modernity at Large: Cultural Dimensions of Globalization*. Minneapolis: University of Minnesota Press.
Bezemer, J. and Kress, G. (2014) Touch: A resource for meaning making. *Australian Journal of Language and Literacy* 37 (2), 77–85.
Blommaert, J. (2017) Ludic membership and orthopractic mobilization: On slacktivism and all that. *Tilburg Papers in Culture Studies* 193.
Blommaert, J. (2018) *Durkheim and the Internet: Sociolinguistics and the Sociological Imagination*. London: Bloomsbury.
Blommaert, J. and De Fina, A. (2017) Chronotopic identities: On the timespace organization of who we are. In A. De Fina, D. Ikizoglu and J. Wegner (eds) *Diversity and Super-Diversity. Sociocultural Linguistic Perspectives* (pp. 1–15). Washington DC: Georgetown University Press.
Blommaert, J. and Varis, P. (2011) Enough is enough: The heuristics of authenticity in superdiversity. *Working Papers in Urban Language & Literacies* 76.
Blommaert, J. and Varis, P. (2015) Enoughness, accent and light communities: Essays on contemporary identities. *Tilburg Papers in Culture Studies* 76.
boyd, d. (2014) *It's Complicated: The Social Lives of Networked Teens*. New Haven: Yale University Press.
Castells, M. (1996) *The Rise of the Network Society*. London: Blackwell.
CNNIC (2016, August 3) *zhong guo hu lian wang luo fa zhan zhuang kuang tong ji bao gao* [Statistical report on China's Internet development]. Retrieved from www.cnnic.cn/gywm/xwzx/rdxw/2016/201608/W020160803204144417902.pdf.

Du, C. (2016) The birth of social class online: The Chinese precariat on the internet. PhD thesis, Tilburg University.

Foucault, M. (1986) *The Care of the Self* (Vol. 3, The History of Sexuality) (R. Hurley, Trans.). New York: Pantheon.

Goffman, E. (1959) *The Presentation of Self in Everyday Life*. New York: Doubleday Anchor.

Goffman E. (1967) *Interaction Ritual: Essays on Face-to-Face Behavior*. Garden City, NY: Doubleday Anchor.

Goodwin, C. (2007) Participation, stance and affect in the organization of activities. *Discourse & Society* 18 (1), 53–73.

Huizinga, J. (2014) *Homo Ludens: A Study of the Play-Element in Culture*. New York: Roy Publishers (Original work published 1950).

iiMedia Research (2016) *ai mei zi xun: 2016 nian zhong guo zai xian zhi bo hang ye zhuan ti yan jiu* [iiMedia research: Research on China's online livestreaming industry in 2016]. Retrieved 12 December 2016, from www.imxdata.com/archives/6312.

Indalecia, T. (2010, 30 April) Exploring identity in the virtual world – Is that REALLY you? *Psychology Today*. Retrieved from www.psychologytoday.com/blog/curious-media/201004/exploring-identity-in-the-virtual-world-is-really-you

Kress, G. (2010) *Multimodality: A Social Semiotic Approach to Contemporary Communication*. London: Routledge.

Kress, G. and Van Leeuwen, T. (2001) *Multimodal Discourse: The Modes and Media of Contemporary Communication*. New York: Oxford University Press.

Li, C. and Wei, L. (2017) *28 sui kuai ji nuo yong gong kuan yi nian da shang zhi bo ping tai 890 wan bei bu* [A 28-year-old accountant arrested for his embezzlement of 8.9 million RMB to pay livestreaming platforms within one year]. Retrieved from http://news.cyol.com/content/2017-05/19/content_16092262.htm.

Li, K. (2018) The capitalization of feminine beauty in online China. PhD thesis, Tilburg University.

Li, K., Spotti, M. and Kroon, S. (2014) An e-ethnography of Baifumei on the Baidu Tieba: Investigating an emerging economy of identification online. *Tilburg Papers in Culture Studies* 120.

Luo, Y., Huang, Y. and Wang, S.L. (2012) Guanxi and organizational performance: A meta analysis. *Management and Organization Review* 8 (1), 139–172.

Mead, G.H. (1934) *Mind, Self and Society*. Chicago: University of Chicago Press.

Mortensen, K.K. (2017) Flirting in online dating: Giving empirical grounds to flirtatious implicitness. *Discourse Studies* 19 (5), 581–597.

Steidlmeier, P. (1999) Gift giving, bribery and corruption: Ethical management of business relationships in China. *Journal of Business Ethics* 20 (2), 121–132.

Van Dijck, J. (2013) *The Culture of Connectivity: A Critical History of Social Media*. Oxford: Oxford University Press.

Yang, P., Tang, L. and Wang, X. (2014) Diaosi as infrapolitics: scatological tropes, identity-making and cultural intimacy on China's Internet. *Media, Culture & Society* 37 (2), 197–214.

Youdao dictionary. Retrieved from http://dict.youdao.com.

5 The Mass Mediation of Chronotopic Identity in a Changing Indonesia

Zane Goebel

Introduction[1]

This chapter examines how a particular chronotopic formulation, that is inhabited by populations of deviant civil servants or bureaucrats,[2] emerged over a relatively short period of time within a particular social domain: the local Indonesian newspaper, *Suara Merdeka* ('Voice of Freedom') during the period between June 2003 and January 2004. While this period was chosen because it aligned with my fieldwork in a government office, it is also important because it was part of large scale and long-term processes of change in Indonesia. In particular, this period of intensive reportage about bureaucrats was preceded by external pressure from the IMF and the World Bank to implement development policies in return for aid in the late 1990s (Goebel, 2018), a regime change and reform agenda that imitated some of the IMF and World Bank agendas on good governance (1998–2002), ongoing local and presidential elections (2003–2004), and a loosening of media laws (1998 onwards) that allowed criticism of the bureaucracy in Indonesia for the first time in nearly two decades.

To account for this rapid case of 'iconization' (Irvine & Gal, 2000) of bureaucratic personhood, I draw on reinterpretations of Bakhtin's (1981) work as it relates to semiosis, chronotopes and scale (e.g. Agha, 2007a; Blommaert, 2016; Lempert, 2014). Here it is useful to offer some working definitions of each term. Semiosis refers to the communicative processes where signs are recognized, valued, reused and where these processes contribute to a change or solidification of the meanings of a sign or signs. Chronotopes can be thought of as a special case of semiosis in that chronotopes are a sometimes ephemeral and sometimes more enduring product of a communicative event. Scale refers to one time and place or 'timespace' that is spatiotemporally separated from another. In looking at the collected newspaper texts, I identify a semiotic phenomenon that I refer to as an 'interdiscursive hub' (IH), whereby multiple fragments from prior stories are recombined in a new story. These fragments not only point to particular characteristics of civil servants, but they also undergo a reconfiguration process that generalizes these traits to all civil servants. With reference to Agha (2007a: 38–45) and Hanks (1992), I explain this reconfiguration by observing that typically there is a co-occurrence of reported talk or speeches made by politically powerful figures with a rescaling via the use of text fragments that act like universal select deictics (e.g. every, all, any). These interdiscursive hubs and the prior stories that contributed to them all helped add semiotic density through contributing characterological emblems to the figure of the Indonesian civil servant. Ultimately, this mass mediation and the series of chronotopes that it produces, contributes to a more enduring chronotopic formulation that is inhabited by an invariable population, which I refer to as a 'mass mediated chronotopic identity'.

Mass Mediated Chronotopic Identities

The idea of chronotope was initially developed by Bakhtin (1981) and loosely defined as a constellation of actors, events, places and time that were represented in novelistic discourses. Within linguistic anthropology and sociolinguistics this concept has received sustained attention (e.g. Blommaert, 2016; Lempert & Perrino, 2007; Rutherford, 2015; Swinehart & Ribeiro, 2019). All extend the ideas of chronotope to include other communicative activities, while noting that they are constructed or 'recombined' from all sorts of signs from other chronotopes (Agha, 2007b; Blommaert, 2016). Thus, here we can define a chronotope as a product of a communicative event that is inhabited by a particular participant constellation who are engaged in a particular social practice (encompassing demeanors and embodied language in a particular timespace). Note that while most chronotopic formulations are emergent and ephemeral, some seem to be more enduring. The perception of enduring-ness emerges via mass mediated chains of chronotopes that are linked via imitations of some of the signs found in earlier chronotopes. As a specific case of what Agha (2007b: 320) refers to as a more general class of 'cultural chronotopes', the idea of mass mediated chains of connected chronotopes inhabited by an invariable population helps us distinguish from a different case of chronotopic formulation referred to as a 'chronotopic identity' (Blommaert & De Fina, 2017). The latter is fruitfully distinguished by simply noting that it is one inhabited by a couple of different actors.

Mass mediated chronotopic identity formation is part of larger processes of enregisterment and semiotic register formation (e.g. Agha, 2007a; Goebel, 2015; Inoue, 2006), that are reliant upon the existence of one-to-many participation frameworks (e.g. school classrooms where the teacher is the 'one' and the pupils the 'many', or the television broadcast which is the 'one' and the audience the 'many'). These participation frameworks are infrastructures that engender the imitation of semiotic forms. Different instances of these infrastructures (e.g. a wealthy private school and an underfunded public school) can produce quite different chronotopic formulations in the same timeframe though not the same space, such as 'white collar worker', 'blue collar worker', 'jocks', 'burnouts', 'nerds' (Bourdieu, 1984; Bucholtz, 1999; Eckert, 2000; Heller *et al.*, 2015). These registers and associated chronotopes provide the non-normative models that are compared with normative models via evaluative commentaries that emerge within these very same infrastructures. Such commentaries, often made by authoritative figures, typically make imprecise copies or imitations of semiotic fragments and recontextualize them in another time and space. This imitation helps to keep fragments of these registers and chronotopes circulating, while making semiotic material available to be recombined to form new chronotopes (e.g. Agha, 2007a, 2007b; Bauman & Briggs, 1990; Lempert, 2014). While the semiotic make-up of these chronotopic formulations constantly changes across communicative events, as Blommaert (2016) points out, major changes to some chronotopes can occur over long timeframes, while others are much more rapid.

In cases of rapid change *in* or emergence *of* a particular chronotopic formulation inhabited by an invariable population, enregisterment processes need to be turbo-charged. Sociologists have pointed to some of the factors that contribute to this turbo-charging (e.g. Collins *et al.*, 2000). These include economic downturn and high unemployment, an ongoing election campaign – often one that focuses on youth crime (typically the victims of the economic downturn) – and a media frenzy where imitation of political messages increases in frequency within the same media outlet as well as across media outlets. Linguistic anthropologists also point out that in addition to an upscaling of instances of imitation, 'iconization' needs to occur (Irvine & Gal, 2000: 37).

Irvine and Gal (2000: 37) argue that iconization is the process whereby signs that have situation, person and activity specific indexical inter-relationships are transformed to be understood as an essential and enduring feature of groups, rather than of an individual involved in a specific interaction. In a sense, iconization rescales small-scale phenomena into large-scale ones or it reformulates one person's practices as an enduring characteristic of a whole invariable population. Attention to the work of Hanks (1992) and Agha (2007a: 38–45) on the reflexive nature of deictics (that is, how the construal of deictics is reliant upon other co-occurring linguistic and non-linguistic signs) is useful for fleshing out one aspect of iconization.

The meaning of deictic forms emerges as it co-occurs with other forms in ongoing discourse (Agha, 2007a: 38; Hanks, 1992). Basically, this means that deictics, such as 'yesterday' and 'tomorrow', 'here' and 'there', and pronouns ('I' and 'you') can only find a referent via reference to the other sign and text fragments within the ongoing interaction. For example, where the interaction is happening, who is speaking and when. While the situational meanings of deictics basically evaporate as an interaction progresses (Agha, 2007a: 38; Hanks, 1992), the presence or absence of particular deictics can also temporally formulate activities, personhood and so on, as more or less enduring general phenomena. This is achieved through the use of particular types of nouns which act as 'selective deictics' (Agha, 2007a: 42–43). In English, these include 'universal selective deictics', such as 'any', 'every' and 'all', and 'particular selective deictics', such as 'some' and 'somebody'. When co-occurring with particular verb configurations, we get to see how they construe an utterance as being decreasingly anchored to a specific time, place and participant constellation.

Consider, for example, the following five sentences that can be found and are explained in Agha (2007a: 42–43): '(a) Did the birds sing?, (b) The bird sang, (c) A bird sang, (d) A bird sings and (e) Birds sing'. Text (a) has a specific referent indicated by the determiner 'the'. Text (a) is also deictically anchored to a specific time, through tense ('sing') and its co-occurrence with an interrogative ('did') which presupposes situated interaction and thus a specific time and place of an unfolding conversation about a particular group of birds. As we move through the examples, some of the deictic anchoring starts to fall away. In text (b) we get a statement, which is still about a specific referent. Text (b) still potentially presupposes a situated conversation, although there is no longer an interrogative that erases any connotation of immediacy. In text (c) there is no longer a specific referent, it could have been any bird and those involved in the conversation would not be able to see this referent at the time of this specific interaction. The disappearance of deictic anchoring or 'indexical ground' (Hanks, 1992) is complete in text (e) where the use of a plural form and tense co-occur to make this a statement about birds in general that does not provide any information about when and where the statement is made.

This example of the iconization of all birds as being able to sing, illustrates a more general phenomenon that is one part of processes of enregisterment and chronotopic configuration as it relates to mass mediated chronotopic identities. In the rest of this chapter, I will draw on all of this theoretical machinery as I attempt to understand how the chronotopic formulation of civil servanthood emerged in newspaper reports published between June 2003 and January 2004. These reports emerged at a particular historical juncture where censorship of negative reportage about those involved in governance declined and where the economic meltdown of the late 1990s attracted sustained help under the guise of good governance from the IMF and the World Bank. The next section sketches this historical, economic and political backdrop, while the following one focuses upon the local news stories that emerged as a result of these complex events.

Fifteen Years of Rapid Change

Major changes beset civil servants' life worlds in Indonesia from 1998 onwards. Prior to 1998, work as a civil servant (*pegawai negeri*) was highly desired, despite historically low wages. In addition to the social status attached to such positions, there was also the possibility of receiving tips or payment for services (*suap*) as a means of supplementing income. During the Soeharto period (1965–1998), this practice was commonly censored from public discussion because of civil servants' political value as members of the government party, GOLKAR. However, since 1998 media censorship has been lifted (Kitley, 2000) as part of a rapid democratization process and a radical move to politically and fiscally decentralize governance (e.g. Aspinall & Fealy, 2003). This co-occurred and in part was driven by increasing calls for good governance from global actors, such as the IMF and World Bank (e.g. Camdessus, 1998; Lindsey & Dick, 2002; World Bank private sector development unit East Asia and Pacific region, 2001).

Since the political and fiscal decentralization that started in 2001, there was increasing pressure on civil servants to be more responsive, efficient and corruption-free as a succession of new Indonesian governments attempted to embrace ideas of democracy and good governance (e.g. Assegaf, 2002; Brietzke, 2002; Rohdewohld, 2003). For example, three policy documents from the period 2002–2004 from the State Ministry of Administrative Capacity listed corruption, inefficient and ineffective mechanisms, and lack of structured supervision and accountability procedures as serious shortcomings (Kementerian Pendayagunaan Aparatur

Negara, 2002, 2003, 2004). Thinking about these issues was underpinned not just by outside pressures from aid agencies and the World Bank, but also by some of the new emerging political parties who made bureaucratic accountability and corruption an election issue (Tomsa, 2012).

During the election campaign for local parliamentary seats that started in 2003, these issues also became very prominent in the local and national newspaper media. To get some sense of just how often these ideas were imitated in the local public sphere during the period I focus on here, we can look at the online front-page stories of the Semarang based newspaper *Suara Merdeka* ('Voice of Freedom'). With the help of a research assistant, we browsed the front pages, found over a thousand online stories from *Suara Merdeka* in 2013, and downloaded those that negatively reported about the bureaucracy between July 2003 and February 2004. From July, reportage gradually increased as a percentage of the overall number of published stories, peaking in January 2004 with around 19% of stories negatively reporting about civil servants. Many of these stories repeated the themes about bureaucratic personhood found in the 2002 reports submitted by the Ministry of Administrative Reform and more generally those found in IMF and World Bank reports on good governance in Indonesia. For example, there were regular headlines and stories about corruption and lack of accountability procedures. There were also many stories about inefficient and ineffective processes. In the following section, I will take a closer look at some of these stories.

Mass Mediated Chronotopes of Civil Servanthood

The data that I present below was gathered as part of a larger project on language practices in the Indonesian civil service that began with five months of fieldwork in a government office in Semarang, the provincial capital of Central Java, between August 2003 and January 2004 (Goebel, 2007, 2014). The data presented here was thus gathered some 10 years after I had left the field and was initially gathered to help contextualize my study as I worked on my interview material (Goebel, 2016, 2019). As I narrowed my focus to reports about the civil service, I recruited a number of Indonesian research assistants who helped me go through these stories again to come up with some keywords and combinations of keywords.

These key words included those associated with leadership (*pimpin, pemimpin, pimpinan* and *kepemimpinan*), guidance (*pandu* and *pemanduan*), training/socialization (*kader, kaderisasi, bina, binaan, pembinaan, bimbing, bimbingan* and *pembimbingan*), management (*manajemen, sistem manajemen pemerintahan* and *sistem manajemen*), human resources (*SDM*) and combinations of these words with bureaucracy (*birokrasi, birokrat, pegawai negeri sipil, PNS, aparat* and *aparatur*), and efficiency (*kinerja*). Using these keywords, we then revisited the online news database discussed above and looked at the other sections within this newspaper. This narrowed down our database to a hundred or so stories.

In looking at the stories, I started to notice regular instances of imitation and iconization. I define the co-occurrence of these two features with instances of quotations and instances of authorization by powerful figures as 'interdiscursive hubs' (IH). Out of these stories, I then focused upon the themes of serving the public, transparency, efficiency and effectiveness. Because of the volume of stories, in the rest of this section I have just chosen five stories to illustrate the process of chronotopic configuration that occurred in the period from mid-June until mid-August 2003. I start with an excerpt of a story that was published on 16 June, 2003 because it has semiotic features that demonstrate what I mean by an IH.

The number of bureaucrats (13,000) on line 1 helps to generalize the claims that follow about the characteristics of civil servants (*pegawai negeri sipil* or *PNS* for short). Although the story is deictly anchored to a place, Karanganyar, continued use of *PNS,* and the use of *para* (a classifier for human groups) and *staf* (staff) without the use of particular selective deictics helps to imply 'all' civil servants, rather than just some living in the Karanganyar regency. In a sense, *para* and *staf* function as a type of universal selective deictic. The story is also characterized by quotations (lines 4–9, 9–18 and 20–24) made by a relatively powerful figure, the area head of human resources. The citation of a powerful figure, was common in many of the stories and more generally seems to add authority to the text.

Excerpt 1 Civil servants, efficiency, absenteeism, motivation and political affiliation (G8–78, 2003)[3]

Original	*Translation*
1 *Lebih dari 13.000 pegawai negeri*	More than thirteen thousand
2 *sipil (PNS) di lingkungan Pemerintah*	civil servants (PNS) from
3 *Kabupaten (Pemkab) Karanganyar akan*	within the regional government
4 *ditertibkan ... 'Kalau tidak orang daerah*	(Pemkab) of Karanganyar will
5 *asli atau kerabat dekatnya, PNS tidak*	be tidied up ... 'If you are not
6 *bisa naik jabatan pada jenjang yang*	a local or a friend, [then] a civil
7 *lebih tinggi, sehingga terjadi pengkotak-*	servant can never be promoted
8 *kotakan. Oleh karenanya, hal itu perlu*	causing [them] to be boxed in.
9 *Dibenahi', tandasnya ... 'Para pejabat*	Because of this, this is a matter
10 *untuk benar-benar memahami peran dan*	that needs to be tidied up', he
11 *fungsinya masing-masing sehingga beban*	said firmly. By having a deep

12 *tugas yang menjadi tanggung jawabnya*
13 *akan berhasil dengan baik...*

14 *Pengembangan sistem dengan*
15 *memberikan penghargaan dan*
16 *hukuman bagi staf yang berprestasi dan*
17 *bermasalah atau mangkir juga perlu*
18 *untuk meningkatkan motifasi kerja',*
19 *tandasnya.*

20 *'Kami akan membuat evaluasi terhadap*
21 *kinerja para pejabat dan staf masing*
22 *unit kerja guna mengetahui seberapa*
23 *jauh tanggung jawab mereka dalam*
24 *melaksanakan tugasnya', tandas dia...*

25 *Pada bagian lain ia mengatakan, PNS*
26 *dilarang menjadi anggota salah satu*
27 *partai politik...*

understanding of their respective roles and functions, senior civil servants work responsibilities can be successfully carried out'.
'The development of a system of rewards and punishments for staff who do well and perform poorly or are regularly absent without leave also need to increase their motivation to work', he said firmly.
'We are going to evaluate the efficiency of senior civil servants and their staff in their respective departments so that we understand how responsible they are in undertaking their duties', he firmly said.
In another part he said that civil servants are forbidden from becoming members of political parties.

The commentaries about the characteristics of this group of civil servants is of special interest. We find out on lines 4–8 that for this group it seems difficult to get promoted without some sort of nepotism (either being a local or a friend of the person doing the promoting). Of interest here too is the emerging definition of *kinerja* 'efficiency' (line 21), which is linked to the need for civil servants and senior civil servants to understand their responsibilities (lines 9–13), presupposing that they currently do not. This characteristic of not understanding their role is further developed on lines 14–24 as the author represents civil servants as being good at their job (*berprestasi*), problematic (*bermasalah*), a group who is regularly absent without leave (*mangkir*), a group who are required to increase their motivation to work (line 18), a group whose efficiency (*kinerja*) needs to be evaluated via the extent that they take on their responsibilities (lines 20–24), and finally a group who needs to be reminded to stay politically neutral (lines 25–27). In linking this analysis with ideas around chronotopes, we can say that this discursive work associates civil servants to deviant practices in a space, Karanganyar, and time, the period being reported. The process of iconization helps create a sense of an enduring and invariable population who inhabit this chronotopic formulation.

Of note too, is that here and in the other stories the voice of the quoted civil servant is typically Indonesian, although the use of *kemlinthi* on line 5 of Excerpt 2 below is an exception that also attracts an immediate translation to Indonesian by the author of the story. The quoting of someone else (represented) as using Indonesian, helps to re-link the national language, Indonesian, to the context of government and civil servants, while reproducing one exemplary model of Indonesian speakership that has a long history in language development policy in Indonesia (Moeliono, 1986). Each of the above-mentioned characteristics are imitated (i.e. not replication-as-precise-copy) in subsequent stories, some of which we will focus on in the next few excerpts. Before doing so, however, we will focus on another interdiscursive hub. The next one, Excerpt 2 is from a story published on 8 July 2003.

Excerpt 2 Civil servants should be modest and not arrogant and remember the people (P27–81S, 2003)

Original	Translation
1 *Sekretaris Daerah Wonogiri Drs H*	The Wonogiri area secretary,
2 *Triwibowo MM mengatakan, figure*	Drs H Triwibowo MM[4], said
3 *pejabat sebagai aparatur pemerintah*	it is hoped that the figure of a
4 *dan pemimpin masyarakat, hendaknya*	senior civil servant, as part of
5 *jangan sampai bersikap kemlinthi*	the government and a leader
6 *(banyak tingkah)....Menurut*	of the people is someone who
7 *penuturan Sekda, generasi sekarang*	shouldn't have an attitude
8 *harus memiliki kesadaran sejarah*	of indifference. According
9 *kemerdekaan yang tewujud berkat*	to the area secretary, the
10 *perjuangan para pejuang yang tak*	current generation needs
11 *ternilai besarnya.*	to understand [our] history
	of independence which has
	been shaped by the goodwill
	of freedom fighters, whose
	contribution cannot be
	quantified.
12 *"Dengan memiliki kesadaran itu, kita*	'By having this understanding,
13 *akan merasa kecil dan akan terjauhkan*	we will feel small and will
14 *dari sikap keangkuhan, kecongkakan,*	distance ourselves from
15 *dan kesombongan,' katanya. Sekda*	conceitedness, pride and
16 *mengingatkan, para pejabat dan*	arrogance', he said. The area
17 *pemimpin rakyat hendaknya tidak*	secretary also reminded senior
18 *mudah lupa kepada nasib bangsa.*	civil servants and leaders that
	it is hoped that they don't
	easily forget the people.

As with Excerpt 1, this story reports on another relatively powerful figure's comments about civil servants. In this case, it is the area secretary for the regency of Wonogiri (his boss being the Regent, or *Bupati*). The text also uses a classifier, *figur*, that acts as a type of universal selective deictic. This helps generalize the traits mentioned in the rest of the story. In particular, the area secretary is quoted as asking and reminding civil servants to act appropriately when dealing with the public. Not doing this is described on lines 5–6 as acting inappropriately (in Javanese *kemlinthi* and translated into Indonesian as *banyak tingkah*). This is later, on lines 14–15, described as conceitedness (*keangkuhan*), pride (*kencongkakan*) and arrogance (*kesombongan*). These negative traits are then linked with the need not to forget about or ignore the fate of their public (lines 15–18). As an IH, this story provides imitable texts in the area of the three inappropriate characteristics as well as an emerging one about needing to pay attention to the needs or fate of the public, which is a focus of Excerpt 3. Before turning to Excerpt 3, we can also link all of the above to processes of chronotopic formulation. As with Excerpt 1, we can say that this discursive work links a particular subset of civil servants, those who lead, to other deviant practices in a space, Wonogiri, and time, the period being reported. Note too that the process of iconization helps create a sense of an enduring and invariable population of leaders who inhabit this chronotopic formulation.

While most stories were negative, there were some that were positive, as in Excerpt 3. This article, published on 14 July 2003, discusses the decision of the provincial governor to keep one of his regents because he has been evaluated as engendering efficiency in the civil service, which in turn has contributed to efficient service to the public.

Excerpt 3 Efficiency and serving the public well (G8–58J, 2003)

Original	Translation
1 Setelah mengevaluasi kinerja	After evaluating [his] efficiency
2 dalam enam bulan sejak menjalani	in carrying out his task as
3 jabatannya sebagai penjabat [b]	a regent, starting on 17th of
4 upati, terhitung mulai 17 Desember	December 2002 until the 16th
5 2002 hingga 16 Juli 2003, melalui	of July 2003, via a letter, the
6 surat Gubernur kembali menugasi	Governor again gave Tjipto
7 Tjipto Hartono untuk tetap berada di	Hartono the task of staying
8 pos jabatannya hingga penyelesaian	on in his senior post until the
9 pemilihan bupati (pilbup) tuntas...	end of the general elections for regents (pilbup)...
10 Gubernur Mardiyanto, dalam suratnya	In his letter Governor
11 menilai, kinerja Tjipto cukup baik,	Mardiyanto positively

12 *sehingga belum perlu diganti. Terutama*	evaluated Tjipto's work leading
13 *dalam memimpin roda pemerintahan*	to [his position] that [Tjipto]
14 *untuk <u>memberikan pelayanan pada</u>*	did not yet need to be replaced.
15 *<u>masyarakat.</u>*	In particular, [his] leadership of
	the government in their efforts
	<u>to serve the public.</u>

The import of this text is how the idea of *kinerja* (efficiency) on lines 1 and 11 is recontextualized and more explicitly linked with giving good service to the public (lines 12–15). In terms of semiotic features, this example is distinguishable from an IH because of the presence of deictic anchoring. While it still has elements of authority, such as the reference to the letter from the Governor (*gubernor*) to the Regent (*bupati*) about his efficiency (lines 5–6), this story focuses on a specific referent and his practices, in this case the Regent and his efficiency. The presence of this form of deictic anchoring, i.e. a specific Regent rather than all Regents, is the most common feature that distinguishes these texts from IHs.

The imitation of characteristics found in one IH in other stories was a common feature in many of the stories during the 2003 period. In Excerpt 4, we see imitation of a part of a sentence from Excerpt 3 (underlined in Excerpt 3 on lines 14–15), together with some new generalizations relating to two other emerging characteristics; engaging in collusive practices and becoming more effective in raising government revenue. Unlike the previous hubs, the authoritative figure here is a member of a non-governmental organization who is offering commentary as part of an interview with a reporter from *Suara Merdeka*. The interview was published on 23 July 2003.

Excerpt 4 Raising revenue and serving the public well (Anindito, 2003)

Original	*Translation*
1 *Selama ini terjadi kesalahan*	Until now, there has been an
2 *persepsi dalam menjabarkan*	incorrect perception when
3 *maksud mewirausahakan birokrasi*	discussing the meaning of
4 *di era otonomi daerah. Ada yang*	encouraging entrepreneurship
5 *beranggapan mewirausahkan birokrasi*	in the bureau-cracy in the
6 *itu agar para PNS di kantor dinas/*	regional autonomy era. There
7 *instansi Pemkab dituntut bertindak*	are those who consider [the
8 *menjadi seperti seorang wirausaha atau*	meaning] of entre-preneurship
9 *pengusaha.*	in the bureaucracy as requiring
	civil servants to act like
	entrepreneurs or businesspeople
	in their offices/departments.

10 *Kantor dinas dituntut 'berbisnis' agar*
11 *memberi nilai tambah untuk PADS.*
12 *Padahal yang dimaksud yakni*
13 *memberdayakan institusional, bukan*
14 *menciptakan 'pengusaha' dalam*
15 *lingkungan birokrasi. ...*

16 *Para birokrat atau aparatur*
17 *pemerintah, kalau ingin sukses perlu*
18 *bertindak dan berperilaku sebagai*
19 *seorang wirausaha terutama dalam*
20 *menyediakan dan* <u>*memberi pelayanan*</u>
21 <u>*kepada masyarakat...*</u>

22 *Birokrat harus berhati-hati. Sebab*
23 *institusi pemerintah (birokrat) dan*
24 *pengusaha, mempunyai tujuan berbeda.*
25 *Sebelum era reformasi muncul pameo,*
26 *'Penguasa merangkap pengusaha dan*
27 *pengusaha merangkap penguasa'.*
28 *Kalau sekarang pameo itu harus*
29 *dihilangkan.*

30 *Pemerintah harus* <u>*melakukan*</u>
31 <u>*pelayanan sebaik-baiknya kepada*</u>
32 <u>*masyarakat*</u> *agar pada waktunya nanti*
33 *jika dipilih lagi oleh para konstituen*
34 *akan tetap konsisten dengan sikapnya*
35 *sebagai abdi masyarakat.*

Government departments have been required to 'be business-like' so that they can increase regional revenue. But in fact, what was meant was to invigorate departments, rather than create 'entrepreneurs' within the civil service.

If bureaucrats or civil servants want to be successful, [then they] need to act like and have the characteristics of someone in business, especially in the preparation and <u>delivery of service to the public...</u>

Bureaucrats have to be careful. Because government institutions (bureaucrats) and entrepreneurs have different tasks. Before the reform era there was the slogan 'he politically powerful double as entrepreneurs and entrepreneurs double as the political powerful'. But now, that slogan has to be erased.

The government must provide the <u>best service possible to the people</u> so that in the future, when the time comes to be elected again by their constituents, they will have [demonstrated] a commitment to be a servant of the people.

As with Excerpts 1 and 2, this particular representation does not use any form of particular selective deictics when discussing PNS (civil servants). Instead, we find the use of *para* (line 6), which as noted earlier functions as a universal selective deictic. This usage helps to generalize the characteristics discussed in the story to all PNS. The first are PNS who are confused about the meaning of being business-like (lines 1–9). It is later revealed that being business-like was initially confused with increasing the revenue base of a government department (lines 10–15), and that what this actually meant was giving service to the people (lines 19–21 and 30–32), and being a servant of the people (line 35). Note that these latter two examples (underlined) represent imitations of text from Excerpt 3. In contrast, being 'business-like' is not to be confused with either running your own business while in the employ of the government (lines 12–15), or past practices where the government works in a close, collusive way with the business world (lines 25–29). Note too that the imitation of texts from Excerpt 3 represents the semiotic material that links these chronotopic formulations to produce a chain, while also helping to increase the sense of enduring-ness of a chronotope inhabited by an invariant population of deviant civil servants.

Before looking at excerpts from the last story, I will briefly summarize the stories that were published before it, but after the fragment of the story represented in Excerpt 4 above. Each of these stories added to (i.e. increased semiotic density) or reinforced already circulating characteristics that were increasingly becoming emblems of bureaucratic identity and part of a solidifying chronotopic formulation inhabited by an invariable population of civil servants. On 26 July a story was published about tertiary students from the Brebes regency protesting plans for 297 village heads and other civil servants to go on a tour to Bali to study successful agriculture and irrigation techniques (WH-20, 2003). The story highlighted that 20 village heads from Brebes had declined to participate in the 'picnic' to Bali, noting the need to better spend government money on needed communication infrastructure. In addition to adding the characteristic of being involved in junkets that waste the peoples' money, these protestors also tied the study tour to political motives, noting that it was merely a junket to politicize this group of civil servants. Five days later, an abridged version of this story reappeared. The focus of this article continued to be on the inappropriateness of junkets, but this time within a frame of 'good governance' (explicitly spelt using English) and the offering of a better alternative by the 20 dissenters; namely remaining in their office so that they could be close to their respective publics (D12-80E, 2003).

On 11 August another story linked the need for efficiency within the civil service with generalized statements around the relationship of efficiency to development, public prosperity, and serving the public (Bachri, 2003). This story resembled an IH because it contained quotes made by an authorative figure and used universal selective deictics, while introducing two new potentially imitable characteristics; development and public prosperity. Another story that added semiotic density to ideas around inappropriate links between money and civil servants (e.g. collusion and junkets) was published three days later with the outgoing Regent of Magelang giving a speech in a public forum about what characterized an ideal regent (PR-42S, 2003). Of special note here, is the need for them to seek office because they want to be a servant of the people, rather than seeking office for financial gain.

In the last story that I will look at (Excerpt 5), a number of the characteristics examined thus far are imitated, while a new characteristic is introduced. This story, published on 20 August 2003, is an opinion piece written by an academic from the Faculty of Social and Political Science at the prestigious government funded institution, Diponegoro University.

Excerpt 5 An academic's view of the bureaucracy (Amirudin, 2003)

Original	Translation
1 Saya melihat, dilema yang paling	I see the most basic dilemma is
2 mendasar adalah perilaku disiplin dari	the discipline of bureaucrats,
3 aparat birokrasi, terutama disiplin	especially in regards to time,
4 terhadap waktu, anggaran, dan komitmen.	money, and commitment.
5 Perilaku disiplin ini memang sulit	Discipline is indeed hard
6 ditegakkan ... Pengertian masyarakat	to maintain ... [Because]
7 dalam konteks tertentu, termasuk	the people's understanding
8 juga unsur birokrasinya. Artinya,	of discipline in certain
9 kebutuhannya untuk berprestasi	contexts, including within
10 sangatlah rendah sehingga mereka	the bureaucracy [is unclear].
11 lebih suka berprinsip 'gengsi lebih	What is understood is that the
12 penting daripada prestasi' atau	need for achievement is very
13 'uang lebih berharga daripada kerja'.	low while in contrast they
14 Dengan dorongan prestasi yang rendah	have the principle 'putting
15 didukung pengendalian diri yang	on airs and graces is more
16 lemah, lahirlah perilaku birokrasi yang	important than Achievement'
17 tidak berdisiplin.	or 'money is more important
	than work'. A low push for
	achievement supports weak
	self-monitoring, giving birth
	to undisciplined bureaucrats.

Like Excerpts 1, 2 and 4, this text resembles an IH because of its imitation of multiple characteristics from past stories, including inappropriate use of time and money, and a new one, commitment to work (lines 3–5). What 'commitment to work' means is only slightly elaborated through the contrasting of the prioritization of money and appearance (*gengsi*) over working to do a good job (lines 10–13). As with the other IH, this report is also one associated with an authorative figure, in this case an academic. Through the use of lexicon that acts in similar ways to universal selective deictics, the story also helps to generalize the characteristics to all bureaucrats. This is most notable through the use of *aparat* 'those involved' on line 3 and *unsur* 'general' on line 8. While *unsur* can have the meaning of a 'part of' the earlier occurrence of *aparat* and the author's later use of *perilaku* 'behavior' on line 16 suggest a reading of 'general' here. As with Excerpt 4, this excerpt can be seen as one further chronotopic formulation that is linked, via imitation, to prior ones, helping to give a sense of enduring-ness that applies to a whole population.

Conclusion

Prior to 1998, Indonesian civil servants were relatively well-respected and had become legitimate participants in a large political machine. This all changed with the collapse of Soeharto's authoritarian regime in May 1998. In keeping with the thematic focus of this volume, it is important to highlight that the chronotopic formulation that had been constructed through imitation and iconization, and which was inhabited by an invariable population of deviant Indonesian civil servants, was emerging at this scale for specific reasons. These included a confluence of a severe economic downturn that occurred after the Asian financial crisis of 1997 onwards, sustained pressure from the IMF and World Bank since the mid-1990s to reform the bureaucracy, uptake of elements of these reforms within the government, regime change, deregulation of the media, relaxation of previously heavy-handed censorship laws that stopped any form of criticism of the government and its bureaucracy, and big bang democratization and political and fiscal decentralization.

In this chapter, I have focused on a tiny slice of timespace from this period – newspaper reports published in the online version of *Suara Merdeka* ('Voice of Freedom') between June 2003 and January 2004 and referred to the discursive outcomes of each of these stories as 'mass mediated chronotopic identities'. This focus adds to work being done on chronotopic identities more generally (Blommaert & De Fina, 2017) by focusing squarely on a different participation framework; the one-to-many framework of mass mediation. In focusing on just a few of the hundreds of stories about bureaucrats that could be found in this newspaper, I drew on work on enregisterment and chronotopic configuration (Agha, 2007a, 2007b; Blommaert, 2016; Blommaert & De Fina, 2017) to show how particular characteristics were being represented and recombined to formulate chronotopes inhabited by invariant populations. By focusing on the co-occurrence of several discursive practices, that I referred to as interdiscursive hubs, I demonstrated how mass mediated chronotopic identities were constructed as invariable populations, which contrasts with Blommaert and De Fina's (2017) conceptualization of identities that seems to imply small variable populations.

In proposing the idea of interdiscursive hubs – i.e. the co-occurrence of the imitation of prior semiotic material, the adding of new characteristics, the quotation or reporting of speech by authorative figures, and the more general creation of nomic truths through the use of lexicon that acted like universal selective deictics – and exploring their connections – we get a sense of how mass mediated semiotic fragments get recombined to form recognizable chronotopic identities. The last element of these hubs, the creation of nomic truths, deserves special consideration. As a form of what Irvine and Gal (2000) refer to as 'iconization', the construction of nomic truths rescales small-scale phenomena into a large-scale one and thus also provides an impression that a particular phenomenon, identity, or process is more common and enduring than it may actually be. This points to some of the limitations of my claims.

In this case, I am only claiming that the mass mediated chronotopic identity of the primarily deviant civil servant is one that is recognizable to the actors involved in constructing the stories. For reasons of space, I have ignored discursive connections between these stories and stories in other newspapers, between these stories and government policy, between all of this and the communicative life worlds of civil servants. Elsewhere, I have started this work (Goebel, 2019; Goebel & Manns, 2018). Briefly, and as we might expect, in one office setting Indonesian civil servants strategically imitated some semiotic features of these mass mediated chronotopic identities, while also contrasting themselves with these chronotopic identities.

Notes

(1) This chapter draws much from my recent article in *Language and Communication* (Goebel, 2017). It is printed here with the permission of the journal's publisher. The feedback given by especially Robert Moore, Rachel Reynolds, Brent Luvaas and Anna De Fina is highly acknowledged, although all errors, omissions and misinterpretations are mine. I would also like to thank a number of research assistants who have helped me gather and code the newspapers, including Hery Santosa and Eni Goebel. The research was partly funded by the Australian Research Council (DP130102121).
(2) To avoid any assumption that being labelled a bureaucratic is a-priori negative, I use 'civil servant' wherever possible and only use bureaucrat where the stories have used an approximation of the English bureaucrat or bureaucracy or where it is stylistically more appropriate, as in 'bureaucratic personhood'.
(3) Reporters names are often coded, as is this one here. I use these codes as in-text citations unless a full name is given in the newspaper story. The full citation can be found under the list of newspapers cited found at the end of this chapter.
(4) It is common to have titles as part of names; the more titles the more prestige. In this instance 'Drs' points to a bachelor degree, 'H' to Haji, and 'MM' to masters level study.

References

Agha, A. (2007a) *Language and Social Relations*. Cambridge: Cambridge University Press.
Agha, A. (2007b) Recombinant selves in mass mediated spacetime. *Language & Communication* 27 (3), 320–335.
Aspinall, E. and Fealy, G. (eds) (2003) *Local Power and Politics in Indonesia: Decentralisation and Democratisation*. Singapore: Institute of Southeast Asian Studies.
Assegaf, I. (2002) Legends of the fall: An institutional analysis of Indonesian law enforcement agencies combating corruption. In T. Lindsey and H. Dick (eds) *Corruption in Asia: Rethinking the Good Governance Paradigm* (pp. 127–146). Annandale, N.S.W.: Federation Press.
Bakhtin, M. (1981) *The Dialogic Imagination. Four Essays* (edited by M. Holquist; translated by C. Emerson and M. Holquist). Austin: University of Texas Press.
Bauman, R. and Briggs, C. (1990) Poetics and performance as critical perspectives on language and social life. *Annual Review of Anthropology* 19, 59–88.
Blommaert, J. (2016) Chronotopes, scales and complexity in the study of language in society. In K. Arnaut, M.S. Karrebæk, M. Spotti and J. Blommaert (eds) *Engaging Superdiversity: Recombining Spaces, Times and Language Practices* (pp. 47–62). Bristol: Multilingual Matters.
Blommaert, J. and De Fina, A. (2017) Chronotopic identities: On the timespace organization of who we are. In A. De Fina, D. Ikiszoglu and J. Wegner (eds) *Diversity and Superdiversity: Sociocultural Linguistic Perspectives* (pp. 1–15). Washington: Georgetown University Press.
Bourdieu, P. (1984) *Distinction: A Social Critique of the Judgement of Taste*. Cambridge, Massachusetts: Harvard University Press.
Brietzke, P. (2002) Administrative reforms in Indonesia? In T. Lindsey and H. Dick (eds) *Corruption in Asia: Rethinking the Good Governance Paradigm* (pp. 109–126). Annandale, N.S.W.: Federation Press.
Bucholtz, M. (1999) 'Why be normal?': Language and identity practices in a community of nerd girls. *Language in Society* 28 (2), 203–223.
Camdessus, M. (1998) The IMF and good governance. *Address to Transparency International Paris*, France, 21 January. Accessed at www.imf.org/external/np/speeches/1998/012198.htm on 12 August 2015: IMF.
Collins, J., Noble, G., Poynting, S. and Tabar, P. (2000) *Kebabs, Kids, Cops and Crime: Youth, Ethnicity and Crime*. Sydney: Pluto Press.
Eckert, P. (2000) *Linguistic Variation as Social Practice: The Linguistic Construction of Identity in Belten High*. Oxford: Blackwell.
Goebel, Z. (2007) Enregisterment and appropriation in Javanese-Indonesian bilingual talk. *Language in Society* 36 (4), 511–531.
Goebel, Z. (2014) Doing leadership through signswitching in the Indonesian bureaucracy. *Journal of Linguistic Anthropology* 24 (2), 193–215.
Goebel, Z. (2015) *Language and Superdiversity: Indonesians Knowledging at Home and Abroad*. New York: Oxford University Press.
Goebel, Z. (2016) Represented speech: Private lives in public talk in the Indonesian Bureaucracy. *Pragmatics* 26 (1), 51–67.
Goebel, Z. (2017) Imitation, interdiscursive hubs, and chronotopic configuration. *Language & Communication* 53, 1–10.
Goebel, Z. (2018) Reconfiguring the nation: Re-territorialisation and the changing social value of ethnic languages in Indonesia. In S. Kroon and J. Swanenberg (eds)

Language and Culture on the Margins: Global/Local Interactions (pp. 27–52). New York: Routledge.
Goebel, Z. (2019) Understanding rapport through scalar reflexivity. In Z. Goebel (ed.) *Rapport and the Discursive Co-construction of Social Relations in Fieldwork Settings* (pp. 53–72). Berlin: Mouton de Gruyter.
Goebel, Z. and Manns, H. (2018) Chronotopic relations and scalar shifters. *Tilburg Papers in Cultural Studies* 204.
Hanks, W. (1992) The indexical ground of deictic reference. In A. Duranti and C. Goodwin (eds) *Rethinking Context: Language as an Interactive Phenomenon* (pp. 43–76). Cambridge: Cambridge University Press.
Heller, M., Bell, L., Daveluy, M., McLaughlin, M. and Noel, H. (2015) *Sustaining the Nation: The Making and Moving of Language and Nation*. New York: Oxford University Press.
Inoue, M. (2006) *Vicarious Language: Gender and Linguistic Modernity in Japan*. Berkeley: University of California Press.
Irvine, J. and Gal, S. (2000) Language ideology and linguistic differentiation. In P.V. Kroskrity (ed.) *Regimes of Language: Ideologies, Polities and Identities* (pp. 35–84). Santa Fe: School of American Research Press.
Kementerian Pendayagunaan Aparatur Negara (2002) *Keputusan Menteri Pendayagunaan Aparatur Negara [Decree of the Ministry of National Administrative Capacity]: tentang pedoman pengembangan budaya kerja aparatur negara [Policy Guidance about the Development of Work Culture within the National Administration]*, 25/KEP/M.PAN/4/2002. Jakarta: Kementerian Pendayagunaan Aparatur Negara [Ministry for National Adminstrative Capacity].
Kementerian Pendayagunaan Aparatur Negara (2003) *Keputusan Menteri Pendayagunaan Aparatur Negara [Decree of the Ministry of National Administrative Capacity]: tentang pedoman penyelenggaraan pelayanan publik [Policy Guidance about the Carrying Out of Public Services]*, 63/KEP/M.PAN/7/2003. Jakarta: Kementerian Pendayagunaan Aparatur Negara [Ministry for National Adminstrative Capacity].
Kementerian Pendayagunaan Aparatur Negara (2004) *Keputusan Menteri Pendayagunaan Aparatur Negara [Decree of the Ministry of National Administrative Capacity]: tentang pedoman penyusunan indeks kepuasan masyarakat unit pelayanan instansi pemerintah [Policy Guidance about the Creation of a Publick Satisfaction Indexs in Relation to Carrying Out of Public Services by Specific Government Departments]*, KEP/25/M.PAN/7/2003. Jakarta: Kementerian Pendayagunaan Aparatur Negara [Ministry for National Adminstrative Capacity].
Kitley, P. (2000) *Television, Nation, and Culture in Indonesia*. Athens: Ohio University Press.
Lempert, M. (2014) Imitation. *Annual Review of Anthropology* 43 (1), 379–395.
Lempert, M. and Perrino, S. (2007) Entextualization and the ends of temporality. *Language & Communication* 27 (3), 205–211.
Lindsey, T. and Dick, H. (eds) (2002) *Corruption in Asia: Rethinking the Good Governance Paradigm*. Annandale, N.S.W.: Federation Press.
Moeliono, A.M. (1986) *Language Development and Cultivation: Alternative Approaches in Language Planning*. Canberra: Pacific Linguistics.
Rohdewohld, R. (2003) Decentralization and the Indonesian bureacracy: Major changes, minor impact? In E. Aspinall and G. Fealy (eds) *Local Power and Politics in Indonesia: Decentralisation and Democratisation* (pp. 259–274). Singapore: Institute of Southeast Asian Studies.

Rutherford, D. (2015). Introduction: about time (Special Collection: Kinship Chronotopes). *Anthropological Quarterly* 88 (2), 241–249.

Swinehart, K. and Ribeiro, A. (2019) When time matters. *Signs and Society* 7 (1), 1–5.

Tomsa, D. (2012) Moderating Islamism in Indonesia: Tracing patterns of party change in the prosperous justice party. *Political Research Quarterly* 65 (3), 486–498.

World Bank private sector development unit East Asia and Pacific region (2001) *Indonesia: World Bank Group Private Sector Development Strategy (Report No. 21581-IND)*. Retrieved from http://documents.worldbank.org/curated/en/656131468756282891/pdf/multi-page.pdf.

Wortham, S. (2006) *Learning Identity: The Joint Emergence of Social Identification and Academic Learning*. Cambridge: Cambridge University Press.

Newspaper articles cited

Amirudin (2003, 20 August) Disiplin birokrat kendala Gubernur. *Suara Merdeka*. Retrieved from http://suaramerdeka.com/harian/0308/20/kha1.htm on 09 September 2013.

Anindito (2003, 23 July) Keliru, persepsi birokrat boleh bisnis. *Suara Merdeka*. Retrieved from http://suaramerdeka.com/harian/0307/23/slo28.htm on 17 September 2013.

Bachri, S. (2003, 11 August) Kebijakan pembangunan Pemkab diminta tak diskriminatif. *Suara Merdeka*. Retrieved from http://suaramerdeka.com/harian/0308/11/dar2.htm on 09 September 2013.

D12-80E (2003, 31 July) Kades Kecamatan Wanasari tolak 'Piknik' ke Bali. *Suara Merdeka*. Retrieved from http://suaramerdeka.com/harian/0307/31/dar2.htm on 17 September 2013.

G8-58J (2003, 14 July) Gubernur pertahankan Tjipto Hartono. *Suara Merdeka*. Retrieved from http://suaramerdeka.com/harian/0307/14/slo25.htm on 16 September 2013.

G8-78 (2003, 16 June) Tiga belas ribu lebih PNS di Karanganyar ditertibkan. *Suara Merdeka*. Retrieved from http://suaramerdeka.com/harian/0306/16/slo17.htm on 24 September 2013.

P27-81S (2003, 08 July) Sekda Wonogiri: Pejabat jangan banyak tingkah. *Suara Merdeka*. Retrieved from http://suaramerdeka.com/harian/0307/08/slo27.htm on 11 September 2013.

PR-42S (2003, 14 August) Jabatan Bupati bukan tempat nyaman untuk mencari uang. *Suara Merdeka*. Retrieved from http://suaramerdeka.com/harian/0308/14/dar20.htm on 09 September 2013.

WH-20 (2003, 26 July) Disorot, studi banding Kades. *Suara Merdeka*. Retrieved from http://suaramerdeka.com/harian/0307/26/dar4.htm on 17 September 2013.

6 Chronotopic Identities and Social Change in Yangshuo, China

Shuang Gao

Introduction

It was a nice summer afternoon in Yangshuo, a tourism site in southern China. I was sitting in a quiet coffee shop, having a chat with Steve. Steve was from Ireland. He is one of the many travelers who had stayed here for months, taking the time to relax among the Karst scenery. Like many other backpackers here, he was on a low budget and supported his traveling expenses by teaching English part-time at local language schools, as well as doing some flexible-hour IT work online, a job he's been doing for years. As we started talking, he explained to me what this downtown area is like: 'Most of the tourism things seem to be concentrated on West Street, which is good I guess, because we can sit here [on Guihua Road] now, and it's not extremely busy'. Such an observation not only presents a rough geographical layout of the area in terms of its tourism activities, but also indicates his stance towards the contrasting differences between West Street and other streets nearby. He goes on to elaborate what he means:

> Steve: When you first go to a city, you go to where the guidebook tells you to go, or where it's popular, so you go to West Street. And then you'll discover, okay, this is like everywhere, this is like Khaosan road in Bangkok, or Temple Bar in Dublin. It's where the expensive, noisy bars are all there, souvenir shops are, well, you know. I don't know, it's, it's terrible … People just go because it's convenient. And they don't know any better. If you are willing to look around, there are so much, so much better place at Yangshuo. I most prefer here. And I prefer the older parts of Yangshuo, with traditional bars. I would most like to have a drink there … There's a term we would

	use to describe it, tourist trap, yeah tourist trap. In many parts of the world, they have beautiful places, but they use it too much, with many bars, restaurants, McDonald's, KFC's. I can understand they're trying to make money, but you may end up destroying what makes it unique in the first place … The first thing I thought on West Street is how out of place McDonald's was.
Shuang:	Out of place?
Steve:	Yeah,
Shuang:	What do you mean?
Steve:	Out of place means it should not be here.
Shuang:	Why, why it should not be here?
Steve:	Because you have so many beautiful mountains here, things you have never seen. And you have things in the way of the beautiful view. Its giant yellow M, with … It's pretty disgraceful. I don't know why they were allowed to do this, because the thing about Yangshuo is no matter where you are, you are got to see a beautiful view. So you shouldn't put terrible things, like a giant yellow M from McDonald's to block these views.

Here, Steve elaborates on the differences between West Street and surrounding areas, highlighting the disjuncture in terms of the old and the new, and the past and the present ('I most prefer here [Guihua road]. And I prefer the older parts of Yangshuo, with traditional bars'), with McDonald's being singled out as one of the telling features of the new semiotic landscape. He also makes clear his stance towards the new development ('disgraceful', 'out of place', 'terrible'), and explains how he organizes his everyday social life accordingly. Such discourses on social change constantly emerge during my fieldwork, with people explaining to me how the place has been changing, and how they position themselves in relation to these changes. In talking about social change, people invoke histories of the place and make moral and aesthetic evaluations while aligning with different timespace organizations, or chronotopes (Bakhtin, 1981).

This chapter examines the social change of West Street, Yangshuo during the past few decades with a view to understand how people caught up in social change negotiate and adapt their social position and identity. Data were collected during ethnographic fieldwork in 2011, including policy documents, public signage, observations, and interviews with local people. Documents and public signage show the material, historical, and semiotic aspects of social change, whereas interviews and observations help us understand how people make sense of such social change through their own narrative and action. It is shown that as people talk about social change, they inevitably produce discourses of comparison, contrasting the past and the present in terms of its material and semiotic timespace organizations. But such narratives revolve around not just describing social change, but also justifying their own social behavior and action in relation to different timespace configurations. In other words, the material, semiotic, and experiential aspects of social change are interconnected. I found it useful therefore to draw upon the notion of chronotope, or timespace (Bakhtin, 1981) in the analysis of my ethnographic corpus. Starting from the concept of chronotope avoids 'an analytical separation of behavior and context' (Blommaert, 2015a: 4) and emphasizes instead the agency of timespace organization in shaping people's experience and social behavior (Blommaert, 2015a, 2015b; Blommaert & De Fina, 2016).

In the following sections, I first discuss how the notion of chronotope informs our understanding of social change, paying special attention to chronotopic contrasts (Agha, 2007), chronotopic identity (Blommaert, 2015), and power geometry of space (Massey, 1994). I then introduce the research site of West Street, Yangshuo and present a short history of the place in terms of its spatial, demographic, and semiotic change. I then show how people negotiate their own social positions and identity amid social change by looking at their narratives, focusing on how social identity and persona is chronotopically organized (Agha, 2007; Blommaert & De Fina, 2016), that is, how in this process of social change, people have to re-negotiate their social positioning and identity and re-organize their social life. I identify two chronotopes through which people negotiate their social identity, the chronotope of tourism economy and the chronotope of countryside living. The chapter concludes with a discussion of how chronotopes can contribute to our understanding of social change and help critique social differentiation and inequality under globalization.

Chronotopes, Social Change and Identity

Globalization has prompted sociolinguistic scholars to adopt more accurate analytical tools and concepts which do justice to, as opposed to reducing, the increasingly complex empirical phenomena in society (Blommaert, 2010, 2015b). One aspect is how concepts like context, community, place and space are no longer understood simply as objective and given entities, but as social and discursive constructs (Blommaert, 2012; Gao, 2012a; Johnstone, 2010; Rampton, 2000). Recently, the notion of chronotope has been re-introduced to achieve an even more in-depth understanding of the intrinsic connectivity between context and social behavior. Blommaert (2015a) and Blommaert and De Fina (2016) suggest that the concept of chronotope is particularly useful in understanding complexity under globalization, as it avoids analytical pitfalls that separate human experience and behavior from social context (Blommaert, 2015a, 2015b). First proposed by Bakhtin (1981), chronotope highlights the inseparability of timespace in enabling plot development and character performance in literary works. Timespace, in other words, is not simply an objective and passive entity, as usually implied by the use of terms like contexts, backgrounds or settings, but has agency in shaping character and plot development (Bakhtin, 1981). Agha (2007) proposed the notion of 'cultural chronotope' to refer to 'a semiotic representation of time and place peopled by certain social types' (Agha, 2007: 321), highlighting the interconnectivity of 'depictions of place-time-and-personhood' (Agha, 2007: 320; see also Blommaert & De Fina, 2016).

The notion of chronotope has been usefully deployed to analyze a variety of social and cultural phenomena (e.g. Dick, 2010; Karimzad & Catedral, 2017; Park, 2017). In an early study, Woolard (2013) uses the concept of chronotope to analyze how 'individuals make sense of the changes that have taken place across time in their relationships with the Catalan language' (Woolard, 2013: 211). She suggests that there are three chronotopic frames through which people construct their ethnolinguistic identities based on different language ideologies and political stance: the biological chronotope, the sociohistorical chronotope, and the chronotope of adventure time in everyday life. Following this line of research, in this chapter, I use the notion of chronotope to analyze how residents make sense of social change in West Street, Yangshuo. First, in talking about their life in Yangshuo, a place that has changed a lot during the past few decades, my participants inevitably invoke the history of the place wherein the present and the past have become a reoccurring point of reference in their narratives. However, such narratives are not just descriptive discourses; people sharing the same physical space may not necessarily share the same experience, as 'social contexts are ... constructed though interpretative processes' (Woolard, 2013: 211; see also Blommaert, 2015). The variety of interpretative frames people draw upon points to the multiplicity of chronotope, and potential tensions between contrasted chronotopes for people inhabiting the same place. In other words, we need to pay attention to what Agha (2007: 230) calls 'chronotopic contrasts' wherein social norms, values and personhood can be foregrounded, negotiated and contested. Second, narratives of social change are also evaluative and metapragmatic discourses through which people articulate their stance (Du Bois, 2007) and construct their social identity as they navigate between multiple chronotopes. In their narratives of social change, people are not just trying to make sense of their place of living, but also justifying their social position and identity in relation to social change, especially through making moral judgements and negotiating the legitimacy of their desired social activity and personhood. In this sense, stance and social identity are integral to chronotope; social identities are 'chronotopically organized' (Blommaert & De Fina, 2016). Making sense of social change involves making sense of who I am, why I do what I do, and how I fit in here. As Blommaert (2015a) suggests,

> change in timespace arrangements triggers a complex and massive change in roles, discourses, modes of interaction, dress, codes of conduct and criteria for judgment of appropriate versus inappropriate behavior, and so forth ... timespace reordering involves a complete reordering of the normative codes of conduct and redefines the space of what is possible and allowable in performing identity work. (Blommaert, 2015a: 4)

Third, due to the moral and ideological dimensions of chronotope mentioned above, it is important to examine the underlying ideologies informing people's varied chronotopic identities as they adapt to social changes. One key to understanding social change is how social order can be reorganized based on new regimes of value (Appadurai, 1986: 4), such that social behavior and activity associated with the new regimes of value are expected, desired or even normalized (Blommaert, 2016), whereas behaviors and activities incompatible with the new regimes of value can be rendered illegitimate, obsolete, or transgressive (Blommaert, 2015a: 3). Uncovering the ideological nature of chronotope can shed light on identity politics, or the power geometry of space (Massey, 1994) under globalization, that is how people are differentially positioned in relation to flows and movements. As Massey (1994) notes:

> this point concerns not merely the issue of who moves and who doesn't [...] it is also about power in relation to the flows and the movement. Different social groups have distinct relationships to this anyway differentiated mobility: some people are more in charge of it than others; some initiate flows and movement, others don't; some are more on the receiving end of it than others; some are effectively imprisoned by it. (Massey, 1994: 149)

This observation of 'differentiated mobility' wherein some people might be 'imprisoned' (Massey, 1993: 61) echoes what Blommaert (2010: 154) calls 'soft marginalization', i.e. 'the marginalization of particular cultural features, identities, practices and resources such as language'. Narratives of social change in this sense constitute important discursive sites for uncovering and critiquing social differentiation and inequality under globalization.

In the following sections, I provide a brief introduction to West Street, Yangshuo in terms of its geographic, demographic and semiotic changes over the past few decades before moving on to discuss how tensions emerge in this process and how people adapt their social identities and try to find a sense of belonging amidst contrasted chronotopes.

The Transformation of West Street: From Neighborhood to 'Global Village'

West Street used to be a neighborhood street in Yangshuo County, Guangxi Zhuang Autonomous Region in southern China. The County has always been well known for its natural scenery and was once a natural resort for imperial officials during the Song Dynasty (1100s) due to its special Karst geography (Wang, 2006). For the most part of its history, the local people have been making a living mainly on agriculture and fishery. In the year 1978, with the implementation of the opening-up and reform policy of China, Yangshuo was designated by the national central government as one of the first places to receive international travelers due to its beautiful natural scenery. People would arrive at this little town from the nearby city on ships via the famous Li River, and West Street, a neighborhood street on the west bank of the river, also became the first place travelers stop by after their journey on the river.

During this early period of tourism development, however, Yangshuo was still under the planned economy, and tourism-related businesses were state-owned and managed. This is because travelling to China was considered as foreign affairs and tourism was more of a matter of political responsibility (Zhang, 2003: 25–26). Therefore, despite this emerging international tourism, Yangshuo people were not much involved in its development. As one of my interviewees, Liu, a local artist who came to West Street in the early 1990s from a nearby village to sell his paintings, told me, 'the local government did not care much about our business. Yangshuo did not have much publicity in the nineties. The government did not try to get enough publicity, nor had clear plans to develop any tourism sites.'

The early development of West Street was thus largely based on individuals' initiatives. Tian, a coffee shop owner in Yangshuo since the year 2000, recalled,

> most people, they just searched their backyards for old wooden boards or 'ancient' stones, and sold them. That's it. Those kinds of old stuff, which

looked like ancient treasures. Hahaha. They were just not sure about what they should sell except that the foreigners might be interested in this kind of stuff.

First wave of development

While these early family businesses helped the local tourism development to some extent, its significance as an important part of the local tourism industry was only recognized in the late 1990s. Around the turn of the century, the local government started to turn to tourism as a new and important growth point for the local economy. This transformation towards a tourism-based economy is justified back then by a local government official as below:

> We must recognize that tourism is an economic industry and has a large demanding market. And more importantly, it requires relatively fewer investment capitals and yet brings quick economic returns. This is a great advantage compared with other industries ... It could not only provide a large market for agricultural, industrial and other business products, but also help stimulate the development of transportation, communication, food industries, and entertainment. (Zhao, 1999: 45–46)

This economic transformation prompted the local government to adopt more pragmatic and flexible practices in order to provide the necessary institutional support and infrastructures for a tourism-based economy. This mainly includes unleashing the private entrepreneurship by prioritizing and depending on private capitals on the one hand, and strategically exploiting and mobilizing varied resources to facilitate the overall development of the tourism industry on the other. As Tan Zibao, Vice Secretary of the Communist Party of China Yangshuo County Committee states, such change 'requires a departure from the old production-based development ideology to one focusing on circulation, flows and service' (Tan, 1999: 31–32). A series of development plans were then initiated to mobilize and manage various tourism resources.

West Street since then has undergone great geographical and demographic changes, no longer being a residential neighborhood with small family businesses. With the establishment of the local tourism development promotion committee in 1999, the 'West Street Protection and Development Project' was initiated to revitalize the residential neighborhood. This project involves the renovation of the old residential houses on West Street, with the major requirement concerning the general outlook of the neighborhood so that all houses should now be renovated according to the traditional style of white walls, and cyan-blue roofs. This revitalization aims at re-authenticating this traditional Chinese neighborhood according to Ming-Qing style, which has already been a great attraction for tourists. In the meantime, as one of the first tourist destinations open to foreigner travelers, Yangshuo has a relatively large number of foreign residents. Such cultural and linguistic diversity were capitalized and promoted by the local government as West Street was advertised widely as a 'global village', in particular as it tries to attract more domestic Chinese travelers to experience a western style of living (Gao, 2012a).

During this time, under favorable investment policies, businesses on West Street became more diversified, including more private businesses investments not only by local residents, but also residents from neighboring villages and travelers from China and abroad. As my interviewee Tian, who came to West Street, Yangshuo from a town nearby and opened a coffee shop with his family in 2000, said:

> The majority of businesspersons were actually local residents and it was all family business. There were also people from other large cities, like Beijing or Shanghai, and foreigners as well. They were quite tired of the busy city life and had come here to just live the simple life in this quiet countryside, instead of thinking about making money here. The houses were actually quite primitive and old, maybe used as storage rooms before. And the walls inside were dark. I think that's because they had been using woods for fire, and the smoke darkened the walls. But we only made very simple renovations when we came in. For us [Tian, his sister, and his brother-in-law], we just painted the walls and nothing else.

Around the same time, the local government also decided that tourism forms needed to be diversified, i.e. 'from only scenery tourism to be expanded to include culture, agriculture, exploration, entertainment, and learning' (Tan, 1999: 33). One of these is the so-called English Educational Tourism. Due to its relatively high density of foreigners, coming to Yangshuo to speak English with foreigners represents a rare opportunity for Chinese people and soon became another attraction of the local tourism industry (Gao, 2012b).

In the early phase of tourism development till the mid-2000s then, the former residential neighborhood was gradually changed both demographically and economically. West Street was developing into a street of business shops for travelers, and meanwhile Chinese learners of English also arrived to practice their spoken English, which thus to some extent redefined the functionality of the neighborhood.

Second wave of development

A more profound change came around the mid-2000s after the severe SARS outbreak in the early 2000s. Yangshuo started a more comprehensive tourism development plan through economic-geographical expansion in an effort to revitalize its tourism economy. In 2003, several connected streets nearby, including Xianqian Road, Binjiang Road, Guanlian Road, Chengzhong Road, Fuqian Lane, Guihua Road, started to invite bids for real estate development and existing old houses were renovated in accordance with the style of West Street so as to establish a 'big West Street', a concept proposed by the local state to expand the scope of the so-called 'global village' (Huang, 2009: 21–22) (see Figure 6.1).

Under the new institutional framework which prioritizes entrepreneurship and private capital investment, different geographical locations of Yangshuo acquired different economic values and attracted different business forms. The old West Street now represents the center of the 'global village', and space on West Street became more desirable and expensive for business investors. As Liu recalls:

> They [businesspersons] came and bid for the rental prices because they were trying to secure a place for their business. They used to pay rents like

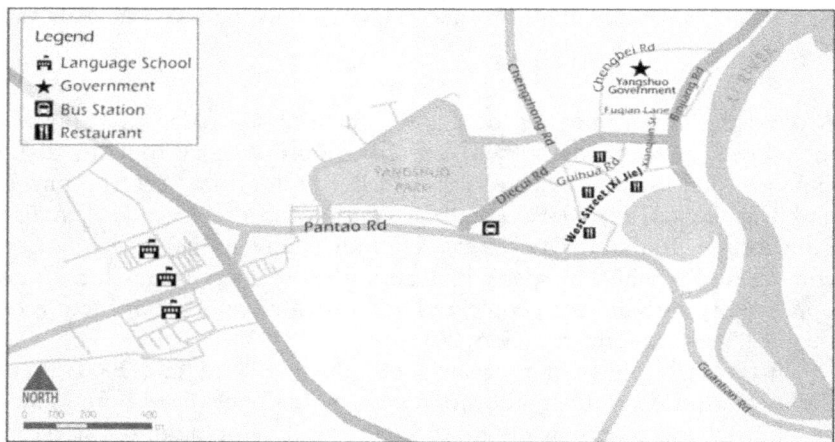

Figure 6.1 Impressionist map of Yangshuo (courtesy of Leonardo Zurita-Arthos)

700,000 yuan a year in big cities like Shanghai, so here they very willingly offered to pay us 200,000. They offered such good price themselves. But we'd never seen so much money before. So that's how now almost all the businesses are opened by non-locals.

Thus, as the businesspersons came and brought the rental price up, from tens of thousands to a sudden increase by tenfold to hundreds of thousands per year, more house-owners on West Street also started to rent their houses out, becoming the new-rich of the County. These newly-opened or renovated businesses on West Street since the mid-2000s changed the types of businesses on West Street by running more fancy-looking establishments, in particular night clubs. As Liu explained to me:

Now if you still operate the business like before, putting out tables and let customers drink over beer and chat for hours, it definitely won't work, you get nothing! ... If you don't do clubs, it's very likely you lose your money, because only selling expensive drinks bring profit.

Apart from selling more expensive drinks, these new clubs also tend to have more fancy outlooks, louder and faster dance music, and sometimes also pole-dancers (see Figure 6.2).

Figure 6.2 House Lizard Bar near West Street (photo by author, 2011)

These night clubs not only provide entertainment, but also establish a night club culture.

For our purpose here, this quick growth and spreading of night clubs on West Street increases the chances of containing and channeling the use of space (Blommaert *et al.*, 2005: 221), thereby making night clubs an increasingly hegemonic culture of the 'global village' at the expense of other types of businesses.

Since the mid-2000s, with the increasing number of fancy businesses and soaring rental fees, some former business owners had chosen to relocate to streets nearby. For one thing the rental price there is cheaper; for another, it has the quietness and casualness for which they had decided to stay here in the first place. As Tian told me:

> It has become too difficult to do business there on West Street, because the rental fee has increased so much. It makes little sense to be there, too much pressure. Like many other people, we arrived here for a simple life, and opened these businesses just to make a living. But with the rental fees so high, we would have to work under great pressure. We could make money there, but that's not the life we want.

Since these businesses tend to locate in the relatively newly developed surrounding streets, they tend to be popular among international travelers who have stayed in Yangshuo for quite a while and know the place better, like Steve mentioned in the beginning. They would come here at night to enjoy the music and have a chat with friends over beer. However, the promotion of West Street as a place for practicing spoken English, as mentioned earlier, also means that these places tend to be frequented by English conversation seekers, which, as I will show below, causes tensions.

In this section, I have shown the social change of West Street over the past few decades from a residential neighborhood to the business center of the so-called global village. The next section presents three cases of people living in the 'global village', focusing on how they negotiate their social positions and identity in relation to social change.

Contrasted Chronotopes in Narratives of Social Change

'This is too much'

Most foreign residents in Yangshuo, like Steve mentioned in the beginning of the chapter, are low budget international travelers who have stayed to enjoy its natural scenery while supporting themselves financially through taking up English language teaching jobs at local language schools. One of my interviewees, Jason, is a backpacker in his late twenties from South Africa. He said he decided to come to Yangshuo after seeing some photos of its natural scenery by chance:

> I really like the mountains and the beautiful surroundings. So I thought I would rather sacrifice some money and big city life, and go somewhere small for a year or maybe longer, and have a nice lifestyle.

Here, Jason highlighted the chronotopic organization of social identity: here in the beautiful natural scenery of Yangshuo he can have 'a nice lifestyle' as a backpacker which is not possible back home where people are concerned with 'money' in 'big city life'. In other words, he constructed his life here now within a chronotope of countryside living. As a long-term resident here, Jason also has a network of friends. His job as an English language teacher helped provide his living expenses here, but also provided an opportunity to know fellow teachers/backpackers as friends. During his free time, as a trained musician, he also played guitar at a western bar on Guihua Road. The bar was opened together by a Belgian and a Chinese musician around 2005, and is now taken care of by the Chinese owner alone. It is popular among international travelers. Jason played live music there sometimes in the evenings with his band members, who are also travelers from different parts of the world:

> Even I've been here like nine months now, it's still like every day is getting better and better. I enjoy life more and more ... and I have friends maybe from every country in the world ... And then local, lots of local Chinese friends as well in town. So it's a very nice community of people.

For Jason, playing guitar in the bar in the evenings (timespace) therefore constitutes a fractal part of the chronotope, or micro-chronotope (Blommaert, 2016: 97), of countryside living in Yangshuo wherein he could enjoy a nice lifestyle as a traveler and guitarist. However, bars are among the most frequented places by English language learners in Yangshuo due to its popularity with international travelers. As mentioned earlier, one aspect of social change in Yangshuo involves the development of an English language learning industry wherein the opportunity to speak to English speakers in a natural environment, as opposed to classroom learning, is promoted (Gao, 2016). The multiplicity of space (Blommaert *et al.*, 2005) opens up the potential for multiple social activities and therefore tensions over what kind of social activities and identities are considered legitimate. Jason recalled once someone even came to him with a dictionary after his performance. He loves interacting with different people, he said, but 'this is too much'. Jason thus had learnt to retreat to upstairs whenever he finished his performance to minimize this kind of encounters.

In this case, we see that Jason has to negotiate his social identity along two contrasted chronotopes. An evening at the bar presents leisure time ('have a nice lifestyle', 'enjoy life', 'nice community of people') within a chronotope of relaxing countryside living wherein he can relax among friends and enjoy being a guitarist. However, since the bar is popular among international travelers, domestic Chinese people would also go there to practice spoken English (Gao, 2016). In other words, bars are not just a space of socialization and entertainment, but also a potential space for English language learning. People like Jason can be chosen as an interlocutor simply for the fact that he is an English speaker. Therefore, Jason is caught up in two different social identities within two contrasted chronotopes: one chronotope of countryside living wherein he can take the time to relax and have fun as a guitar player, and the other a chronotope of tourism economy wherein he can be approached or interrupted as a(n) teacher/interlocutor of English for Chinese students. To avoid being approached as an English language teacher in his spare time, he has come up with the strategy of going upstairs after performance, thereby re-negotiating his identity through re-organizing timespace.

To some extent, Jason represents most long-term international tourists in Yangshuo, who enjoy the various sight-seeing opportunities as well as the international communities, but at the same time have to subject themselves to constant disturbance from potential conversation-seekers who would like practice their English. Being in a tourism site which capitalizes on English language learning in a natural environment, his English is recognized as a valuable linguistic resource in Yangshuo. At the same time, the value of language nevertheless also works against him when he tries to refrain to a relaxing life as a guitar player in the local bar. Jason has to negotiate his own social identity constantly between these contrasted chronotopes. Accordingly, his daily life is constantly caught up in these different regimes of value associated with different chronotopes, presenting a dilemma of identity that he has to constantly live with.

'It's changed too much'

The social change of Yangshuo also involves the commercial development and expansion of West Street into a so-called 'global village', which, as explained above, has led to the competitive construction of more profitable businesses such as night clubs as opposed to family businesses. Notably, an increasing number of bars like the one shown in Figure 6.2 are taking over West Street, transforming it into a space of entertainment and consumption. This new development constitutes a major source of tensions for people living there.

When walking around West Street back in 2011, I saw a very eye-catching white paper poster right in front of a small family house turned into a hotel (see Figure 6.3).

The hotel was protesting against the construction of a night club right next door. It read:

> As a private business, our hotel has always dedicated itself to local charity work, donating about 650,000 Chinese yuan for the past ten years. However, we now have to close our hotel because the Housing Construction Bureau has done nothing but destroying our peaceful life here. We thus had to close since 13 May. We welcome anyone interested to come in and have a look.

Henry, the hotel owner, told me, he already had enough of the booming noise because of a night club operating on the other side of his hotel. Now, if the second night club next door is completed, his hotel could not do business anymore – there would be noise from both sides. When he came to Yangshuo in 1998 from the US and opened his hotel in 2002, it was because he liked the beautiful scenery and the nice little

Figure 6.3 Protest paper by Henry's hotel (photo by author, 2011)

neighborhood. But now everything has changed, worse than he could ever think of:

> It's changed too much. It's too bad. This is very disappointing ... because it used to be a very special street, and a very unique atmosphere draws people here. But now it's just a noisy place, you know, with bars and discos. It's lost its charm ... The discos make a lot of money every year. That's the best business on West Street. But if people like to drink, get drunk, and hear loud music, watch naked girls pole-dancing, that's what they are doing.

In talking about his situation, Henry invokes 'chronotopic contrasts' (Agha, 2007) between the past and the present. West Street in the early 2000s was framed within a chronotope of countryside living ('a very special street' with 'a very unique atmosphere'), whereas West Street now has become 'just a noisy place' within a chronotope of tourism economy. In the chronotope of countryside living, Henry runs the hotel as a charitable resident and businessman, contributing through his business to the local community. With the new development which values commercialization and profit-making, his business has become incompatible and he was struggling to fight for its existence. Within the chronotope of tourism development, night clubs are re-organizing and refining the space, and introducing new social activity like drinking and dancing ('people like to drink, get drunk, and hear loud music, watch naked girls pole-dancing'). Caught up in the overwhelming tourism development, Henry and his hotel are losing out and in crisis: there is no way back to the old special West Street years ago, and there seems to be no way forward either.

Asked what is his plan now, he said: 'I don't know, try to resolve the problem first. But I'm pretty sure I have to close the hotel. Right now I'm closed, because of the noise, because there's construction, it's unsafe.' Actually, he had tried to visit different bureaus, and tried to negotiate with the next door neighbor, but in vain. Thus, as West Street gets expanded and constructed into a 'global village', Henry and his hotel have been made 'out of place' (Blommaert, 2015a). For Henry, this eye-catching poster therefore represented perhaps a last symbolic attempt through which he tries to retain at least some control over a business he once had and an identity he was proud of ('our hotel has always dedicated itself to local charity work, donating about 650,000 Chinese yuan for the past ten years'). His social identity as a charitable businessman has been marginalized or rendered obsolete within a chronotope of tourism development which favors business competition ('The discos make a lot of money every year. That's the best business on West Street.') as opposed to community development. We see here a crisis of social identity associated with social change driven by neoliberal globalization.

'Everything is about money now'

Sun is a local Chinese in his fifties. He is well known as a local personality. He is one of the few residents who has spent most of his life in Yangshuo and was one of the early businessmen on West Street. He used to be a farmer in another village in Yangshuo, and moved to West Street to do some seal carving in 1985, and opened his café there in 1992 and ran it until 2003. He is also widely recognized for his strong interests in traditional Chinese culture: he wears traditional loose Chinese shirts and pants, keeps a Taoist hair knot, and is famous for his artistic practices in painting, calligraphy, and Chinese seal carving. He likes what West Street used to be in the 1990s. When West Street was a cozy place with family businesses for travelers, he was able to make friends with many international tourists – he learnt English by himself – who still visit him in his new place these days when they come back again. But he dislikes the present West Street. When asked what he thinks of the 'global village' as it is now, he alluded to Wenzhou, a place in southern China famous for its savvy businessmen, and said it's now a 'Wenzhou village', which means everything is about money now.

Different from Henry who was helplessly making this last attempt on West Street, Sun has left his former little café on West Street, which is now run by his former business partner. Instead, he has opened a new one in a relatively quieter street nearby where the rents are much lower. Perhaps more important to him, the new place he was renting was just next door the former residence of Xu Beihong (1895–1953), a famous painter in China. Few tourists would find their way to this relatively quiet place and on several visits I saw his restaurant was closed. He said he would rather sacrifice money for the sake of a way of living he prefers: 'Here, I have my quietness. As to whether I can have customers, I don't care.'

Here, Sun contrasts the past and present of West Street: a place where he used to run his business and hang out with friends, and now a place he condemned and characterized as simply a competitive place for money-making ('That's a gold mine there. But I don't want to go'). Relocation is a strategy of identity maintenance through re-constructing a chronotope wherein he can continue his preferred cultural activity, social life and also retain his desired identity as an artist.

However, while he had moved out from his former café, he still actually has some business there. Like before, he still provides roasted chicken, the most famous in town over the years, to the café, but only for a limited number every day. In this sense, he still retains part of his old life on West Street, though no longer physically belongs there. Moving to another street while retaining some ties with his former life therefore constitutes a middle ground between two chronotopes: living as an artist within the chronotope of countryside living at his new location and also remaining part of the tourism economy by roasting chicken for his former café. This middle ground is a result of constant tension and negotiation between desired lifestyle and reality, between past and present. When telling me that West Street is now a Wenzhou village, he also shared with me his dream image of West Street. He said it should be like *Along the River during the Qingming Festival*, a renowned Song Dynasty painting of civic life in those days. His reservation and criticism towards West Street therefore is not simply a regressive return to the good old days; rather it is about coming to terms with the social change via adapting his social identity as a chronotopic item.

Conclusion

This chapter has used the notion of chronotope to understand how people make sense of and adjust to social change in Yangshuo during the past few decades. I have shown that social change has both temporal and spatial dimensions and in their narratives of social change, people invoke the history of the place, and construct their social identity with reference to contrasted timespace configurations or chronotopes. Through examining the material, semiotic and experiential aspects of the social change of Yangshuo, I show that travelers and business owners in the 'global village' adapt themselves in different ways to social change, whether it is related to language learning, business operation, leisure activity or everyday life. Nevertheless, their seemingly diverse experiences of social change and their self-positioning can be explained through their navigation and negotiation among two main chronotopes: the chronotope of countryside living, and the chronotope of tourism economy. It is through these contrasted chronotopes that social identities are negotiated and constructed.

Social change therefore can be seen as multilayered chronotopes which have effects on how people make sense of their lives and negotiate their social identity. Social identity and social activity are chronotopically organized (Blommaert, 2015a; Blommaert & De Fina, 2016), and adapting to social change involves negotiating and adapting one's social identity as a chronotopic item. As we have seen, such negotiation and adaption take different forms and are informed by people's stance towards social change.

This chapter thus shows how social change could disrupt old social order and value systems while producing, legitimizing, and normalizing new ones. People living amidst social change are caught up in competing and contrasted chronotopes, and forced to negotiate and adapt their social identity and activity accordingly. Paying attention to the chronotopic nature of identity and chronotopic contrasts helps us better understand the marginalization and exclusion of certain social identity and cultural practices under social change driven by neoliberal globalization.

References

Agha, A. (2007) Recombinant selves in mass mediated spacetime. *Language & Communication* 27 (3), 320–335.

Appadurai, A. (1986) Introduction: Commodities and the politics of value. In A. Appadurai (ed.) *The Social Life of Things: Commodities in Cultural Perspective* (pp. 3–63). Cambridge: Cambridge University Press.

Bakhtin, M. (1981) *The Dialogic Imagination. Four Essays* (edited by M. Holquist; translated by C. Emerson and M. Holquist). Austin: University of Texas Press.

Blommaert, J. (2010) *The Sociolinguistics of Globalization*. Cambridge: Cambridge University Press.

Blommaert, J. (2012) *Ethnography, Superdiversity and Linguistic Landscapes: Chronicles of Complexity*. Bristol: Multilingual Matters.

Blommaert, J. (2015a) Chronotopic identities. *Working Papers in Urban Language & Literacies* 170.

Blommaert, J. (2015b) Chronotopes, scales, and complexity in the study of language in society. *Annual Review of Anthropology* 44: 105–116.

Blommaert, J. and De Fina, A. (2016) Chronotopic identities: On the timespace organization of who we are. *Tilburg Papers in Culture Studies* 153.

Blommaert, J., Collins, J. and Slembrouck, S. (2005) Polycentricity and interactional regimes in 'global neighborhoods'. *Ethnography* 6 (2), 205–235.

Dick, H. (2010) Imagined lives and modernist chronotopes in Mexican nonmigrant discourse. *American Ethnologist* 37 (2), 275–290.

Du Bois, J.W. (2007) The stance triangle. In R. Englebretson (ed.) *Stancetaking in Discourse: Subjectivity, Evaluation, Interaction* (pp. 139–182). Amsterdam: John Benjamins Publishing Company.

Farrer, J. (2014) Foreigner street: Urban citizenship in multicultural Shanghai. In N. Kim (ed.) *Multicultural Challenges and Redefining Identity in East Asia* (pp. 17–44). London: Ashgate.

Gao, S. (2012a) Commodification of place, consumption of identity: The sociolinguistic construction of a 'global village' in rural China. *Journal of Sociolinguistics* 16 (3), 336–357.

Gao, S. (2012b) The biggest English Corner in China. *English Today* 28 (3), 34–39.

Gao, S. (2016) Interactional straining and the neoliberal self: Learning English in the biggest English Corner in China. *Language in Society* 45 (3), 397–421.

Huang, Q. (2009) New strategies of scientific development: Implications of the 'Yangshuo phenomenon'. In T. Tang and X. Chen (eds) *Scientific Development of Guangxi Tourism: Exploring the Yangshuo Phenomenon* (pp. 17–22). Beijing: Huaxia Publishing House.

Johnstone, B. (2010) Language and geographical space. In P. Auer and J.E. Schmidt (eds) *Language and Space: An International Handbook of Linguistic Variation* (pp. 1–17). Berlin: Walter de Gruyter.

Karimzad, F. and Catedral, L. (2017) 'No, we don't mix languages': Ideological power and the chronotopic organization of ethnolinguistic identities. *Language in Society* 47 (1), 1–25.

Massey, D. (1994) *Space, Place and Gender*. Minneapolis: University of Minnesota Press.

Park, J.S. (2017) Transnationalism as interdiscursivity: Korean managers of multinational corporations talking about mobility. *Language in Society* 46 (1), 23–38.

Rampton, B. (2000) Speech community. *Working Papers in Urban Language and Literacies* 15.

Tan, Z. (1999) Some thoughts on accelerating the tertiary economy of Yangshuo. In L.J. Xu (ed.) *A Fast-developing Tourism County: Yangshuo in the Past 20 Years of Open-up and Reform* (pp. 31–34). Yangshuo: Yangshuo County Publishing House.

Wang, Q. (2006) West Street: Historical stories (西街史话). In Q. Wang. *The Wonderland of Yangshuo* (仙境阳朔,梦幻家园) (pp. 108–151). Guilin: Lijiang Publishing House.

Woolard, K.A. (2013) Is the personal political? Chronotopes and changing stances toward Catalan language and identity. *International Journal of Bilingual Education and Bilingualism* 16(2): 210–222.

Xu, Y. (1999) Introduction. In L.J. Xu (ed.) *A Fast-developing Tourism County: Yangshuo in the Past 20 Years of Open-up and Reform* (pp. 3–17). Yangshuo: Yangshuo County Publishing House.

Zhang, G. (2003) China's tourism since 1978: Policies, experiences, and lessons learned. In A. Lew, L. Yu, J. Ap and G. Zhang (eds) *Tourism in China* (pp. 13–34). New York: Haworth Hospitality Press.

Zhao, M. (1999) Thoughts on the economic development of Yangshuo. In L.J. Xu (ed.) *A Fast-developing Tourism County: Yangshuo in the Past 20 Years of Open-up and Reform* (pp. 42–47). Yangshuo: Yangshuo County Publishing House.

7 Chronotopes and Heritage Authenticity: The Case of the Tujia in China

Xuan Wang and Sjaak Kroon

Introduction

In this chapter,[1] we draw on the Bakhtinian notion of 'chronotope' as a useful heuristic of meaning making to consider heritage authenticity in the case of the Tujia in Enshi, China. Being 'the highlanders of Central China' (Ch'en, 1992), the Tujia in Enshi is a peripheral community with its minority status and associated heritage described ethnographically as something 'manipulated' locally and 'given' by the state (Brown, 2002). We observe that the historical issue of 'inauthenticity' perceived and experienced by the Tujia in Enshi is now opened for reinterpretation, as the local communities are confronted with the challenge of heritage tourism that is engendered by China's processes of modernization and globalization and revolving around a seemingly paradoxical project of designing 'inauthentic authenticity' (Wang, 2015) for tourist consumption. Following Coupland (2010, 2014), Heller (2003, 2014) and others, we take this project of heritage authenticity as part of the chronotopic phenomena of identity making, that is, becoming authentic involves the complex shaping and interplay of multi-scaled, synchronically displayed, and historically invoked timespace frames for semiotic and discursive production of authenticity, which condition as well as offer new potentials to the meanings of authenticity.

In what follows, we will illustrate that the notion of chronotope (in combination with that of indexicality, scale and complexity) can be used as an empirical tool for analyzing the timespace configurations of semiotic and discursive behaviors undertaken by the Tujia in Enshi in their renewed pursuit of heritage authenticity. Moreover, we will show that it offers an ethnographically sensitive approach to this project of heritage authenticity, which we take as a project of sociolinguistic processes that are semiotically designed, and chronotopically reorganized and reordered by the peripheral group within a historicized context and wider scheme of authenticity largely defined by the center. We will first locate our case within the current research on heritage tourism and peripheral globalization, before discussing the concept of chronotope and its heuristic purchase in relation to authenticity as identity practices, focusing particularly on authenticity as an imperative for heritage tourism. Based on this framework, we will provide an analytical description of the chronotopic nature of a major heritage tourism event we encountered in Enshi.[2] This is furthered by a historical contextualization wherein the issue of heritage inauthenticity for the Tujia in Enshi is situated, which will shed crucial light on the processes of chronotopic reordering of authenticity by the Tujia that make it possible to incorporate the logic of authenticity as defined by the globalized heritage tourism and the state identity politics into the local way of life. In the final part, we offer a critique of chronotope, authenticity, and globalization in the periphery.

Heritage Tourism and Peripheral Globalization

19 August 2013 was no ordinary day for Enshi Tujia and Miao Autonomous Prefecture, a rural minority region located in the deep mountains of Hubei Province in Central China. It was the day that marked the 30th anniversary of the founding of Enshi, the last officially recognized ethnic minority prefecture (of the Tujia, the Miao and 26 other smaller groups) in the People's Republic of China. For the local communities, this day was a reminder of the historic moment when an entirely different and significant political-cultural identity of 'minority' was given to them by the state. It was also a formal occasion to showcase and celebrate the particular(ized) cultural heritage they have assumed since that moment, to perform and reenact that heritage in a present-day context, and to marketize aspects of authenticity in relation to their identity and heritage – whether prescribed or ascribed – in order to set their foot in the new economy of heritage tourism and become part of the globalization processes in China.[3] In the fortnight leading up to the special day, dozens of major events and activities were organized in various parts of Enshi (of which one will be analyzed in detail later), combining commemoration, showcasing, celebration, performing, reenactment and marketization, with the Tujia, the largest indigenous ethnic group of the prefecture, playing the leading role.

What is witnessed is a remarkable instance of sociolinguistic globalization in the periphery (Wang *et al.*, 2014; see also Heller, 2003; Pietikäinen

& Kelly-Holmes, 2013; Pietikäinen *et al.*, 2016). In the periphery – being a geopolitical and sociocultural minority in the case of Enshi – just as in the 'center', unprecedented economic and cultural transformations as well as renewed local awareness and identity politics are to various extents taking place. For the people of Enshi, similar to disenfranchised ethnic and small-culture groups elsewhere, heritage tourism provides niched albeit compelling access to and infrastructure of globalization through which opportunities for economic and identity repositioning become available and explored. Such dynamics are captured by Duchêne and Heller (2012) as tensions between economic 'profit' and cultural-political 'profit', creating new conditions for both language and authenticity. These dynamics are densely substantiated in key moments such as the founding anniversary of Enshi – akin to events of Corsican language revitalization through heritage tourism accounted by Jaffe (2015, 2019).

What we will observe in the case of the Tujia in Enshi, also as the central argument we would like to bring from this study, is that it is through multiple chronotopic organizations of semiotic and discursive maneuvering that peripheral groups arrive at a sense of authenticity that fulfils heritage tourism as both an economic and identity project instated by globalization.

The case of Enshi focuses our gaze on specific aspects of peripherality, notably *heritage*, a notion intrinsic to ethnic and cultural identity and at the core of the local globalization processes, lodged in the new economy of heritage (thus identity) tourism. As suggested by Pujolar (2013: 56), 'heritage is indexical of peripherality within the framework of modernity'. It is through the reproduction of the modernist ideology and discourse of antiquarianism and linguistic nationalism (as described in Bauman & Briggs, 2003) that particular forms of the past and ways of life – i.e. history and tradition – are evoked, 'invented' (Hobsbawm & Ranger, 1983) and projected onto specific spaces and people, creating 'imagined communities' (Anderson, 1991) such as the nation-state and distinct ethnocultural groups.

Perhaps it is in modern nation-building that the 'ethno' layer of making heritage through the counterpart Other finds its most poignant expression. There, heritage is deployed as an instrument for the conceiving of nationhood and national identity in which groups of ethnocultural minorities are created – often from the perspective of the majority groups and set off against them, representing the alterity while also being an indispensable part of a (supposedly) shared memory and history – so as to rationalize and legitimatize the hegemony of the majorities and to promote the nationalist course of unity, cohesion and homogeneity from within. The effect of such processes is not only the invention of ethnicities, what Roosens (1989) terms 'ethnogenesis', but necessarily the minorization and marginalization of these groups on the basis of geography, economic power, cultural pattern, language, etc., enunciated in set descriptors such as the 'remote, local, agrarian, primordial, outdated, and subordinate', which are in turn circulated as historical truths.

The way in which ethnocultural heritage works as a political instrument and (controlled) knowledge basis of ethnotaxonomy for forging and maintaining nation-states and multicultural societies manifests itself in various geopolitical contexts.[4] China is a case in point, wherein the state ideology and discourse of a 'unified, multinational country' has resulted in the official classification of fifty-six ethnic nationalities (with the Han being the majority and constituting more than ninety percent of the Chinese population) shortly after the founding of the People's Republic in 1949 (Mullaney, 2011). This self-imagined diversity is managed through the duality of political regulation and acculturation of the 'barbaric' minorities by the 'advanced' Han majority (Ma, 2016), and state-sponsored multiculturalism is such that the ethnocultural identity and diversity are routinely represented in the juxtaposition of 56 equal but – with the exception of the Han – uniquely and exotically dressed individuals (Wang, 2015). Together, in their ethnicized and semiotized physical appearances, these individuals symbolize and embody *at once* the 56 different ethnic groups *and* one harmonious whole. Such an image arguably belongs to the kind of compartmentalized multiculturalism in which particular(ized) clothing and body becomes the essential(ized) emblematic token of ethnocultural diversity and heritage. It resonates with Gladney's (1994; see also Blum, 2001) exposition of the construction of subaltern subjects and peripheral citizens by virtue of the exoticization of the minorities in China's ethnicity politics. Hence, heritage in Chinese multiculturalism, comparable to elsewhere, is a politically loaded construct that seeks out the (exotic, dissembling, marked) *minority* from the (normative, homogeneous, invisible) *majority* from within the nation, in order to sustain and authenticate its core political economy. Its logic of using cultural items, be it clothing, language, or something else, to mark out social positions and differences, closely resembles Bourdieu's (1984) notion of 'distinction', thus, is fraught with hegemony, inequality and peripherality.

In the context of globalization, the need for articulating and promoting heritage seems heightened. On the one hand, the deterritorialization, displacement and cultural disjunctures and differences (Appadurai, 1996) have made it all the more important to rediscover and re-establish local attachment and identity through the preservation and rejuvenation of history and heritage, both tangible and intangible. On the other hand, the emergence of heritage tourism as part of the globalized new economy has created niche markets for the production and consumption of heritage (and its associated artifacts and experiences). As demonstrated by Heller (e.g. 2003, 2014), the rise of the new economy in late capitalism rests largely on the commodification of the periphery and the transaction of the added value of symbolic distinctions between the periphery and the center, typified in the form of identity tourism. Driven by this new economic pattern, heritage tourism becomes a primary stage on which discourses, images and objects of such center-periphery distinctions – framed as *heritage* – are produced, performed, circulated and consumed. This form of globalization is crucial for the disenfranchised ethnic and small-culture groups in terms of both 'profit' and 'pride' (Duchêne & Heller, 2012), which explains the surge in heritage-based tourism activities in the ethnocultural peripheries of China.

The conceptualization of heritage in relation to the conditions of modernity and globalization reveals the systemic peripherality heritage indexes and the globalized economic, political and cultural motifs in which it operates. Given that authenticity is pivotal to both *heritage as identity making* and *heritage as tourism commodification*, we must also address the extent to which heritage authenticity such as that of Enshi, engages with the global and local regimes of meaning making and enables for itself a tenable position in both the tourism market and the cultural politics of recognition. In other words, we need to examine how the Tujia in Enshi may, through heritage tourism as a new opportunity, be considered authentic simultaneously in relation to existing state multiculturalism, the new tourist market and the place itself: authenticity as a polycentric challenge. It is to these aspects we now turn to.

Heritage Authenticity and Chronotopic Identities

The way authenticity is sociolinguistically materialized, indexed, negotiated and performed has been examined in the works of Coupland (2003, 2010, 2014) and others (e.g. Blommaert & Varis, 2013; Lacoste *et al.*, 2014; Wilce & Fenigsen, 2014). We take the converging arguments in these works as follows (see Coupland, 2014 for an overview): (1) authenticity is always expressed through the deployment of linguistic, discursive and/or semiotic resources; (2) in globalization, meanings of authenticity are increasingly embedded in both local and translocal frames of reference; (3) authenticity is better understood as the effect of 'authentication', that is, the tensions and dynamics between normative constraints and agentive production – with the goal to establish and reach a benchmark of (often multi-layered) 'enoughness'; (4) the emphasis on de-essentializing authenticity and on its performative dimension points us towards new potentials of interpreting (seemingly 'inauthentic') cultural and identity behaviors.

In particular, we draw attention to authenticity with regard to heritage tourism and peripheral globalization. As said, heritage emerges as a modernist construct, with its normative parameters – 'orders of authenticity' (Wang, 2012) – centering on geopolitical and sociocultural peripherality and serving to sustain the political economy of the nation-state. In Chinese multiculturalism, this can be seen in the essentialized othering through exoticitization of ethnocultural heritage, largely based on the state-prescribed ethnotaxonomy from the perspective of the Han majority. Heritage tourism capitalizes on exactly the kind of asymmetrical distinction created by dichotomizing the majority versus the minority, the advanced versus the barbaric, the urban versus the rural, the modern versus the traditional, the global versus the local, etc. Its core business is both the semiotization and the commodification of authenticity (Jaworski & Pritchard, 2005), which, on the part of the periphery-supplier, involves selecting *specific* cultural resources and communicating them in highly *specific* ways for *specific* audiences on *specific* occasions. Such processes, necessarily 'inauthentic' due to modification and commodification, generate alternative revenues of 'inauthentic authenticity' (Wang, 2015). As Heller (2014: 154) asserts, in understanding authenticity in the periphery, '[c]ommodification affords us a window into ongoing change, allowing us to link up individual subjectivity, interactional processes, and the conditions of the symbolic market'.

How, then, can we study the actual forms taken by this sociolinguistic process of commodification, caught in the polycentric challenge of authenticity described earlier? How can we, in answering this question, also account for the inevitable 'inauthenticity' connoted in the act of commodification (and associated performativity), and the way the paradoxical inauthentic authenticity is organized as a sustainable and coherent part into a shared lifeworld? Here, Bakhtin's seminal idea of 'chronotope' and its recent sociolinguistic uptakes (e.g. Agha, 2007; Blommaert & De Fina, 2017; Lampert & Perrino, 2007; Woolard, 2013) offer a great source of inspiration.

In Bakhtin's literary analysis, chronotope was used for addressing 'the intrinsic connectedness of temporal and spatial relationships that are artistically expressed' in novels (Bakhtin, 1981: 84), namely, the *timespace specificity* from which discourse of plot, history and identity emerges.

For Bakhtin, *time and space* are inseparable in constructing narratives and characters; they function as a fused, concrete whole – identifiable as chronotope – which is structured and encoded in specific ways, generating historical and semiotic conditions of meaning making. This conceptualization makes it possible to dissect and describe the multiple timespace configurations that co-occur, not only in literary (en)textuality, in terms of *novelistic* chronotopes through which readers can extract and connect multiple social meanings and agencies represented in a story, but more generally, as *cultural* chronotopes: 'depiction of place-time-and-personhood to which social interactants orient when they engage each other through discursive signs of any kind' (Agha, 2007: 320).

The cultural potential of chronotopes is formulated as 'invokable histories' in Blommaert's (2015: 110) attempt to bring together the notion of chronotope and of context and scale for addressing the complexity of language in society. Drawing on the central argument of discourse *in* history, Blommaert considers chronotope as an important aspect of contextualization in which 'meaning as value effects [is] derived from local enactments of historically loaded semiotic resources' (2015: 108; see also Gumperz, 2003). From this perspective, all interactive events can be seen as chronotopically organized: situated in timespace, occurring as here-and-now while indexing a myriad of 'historically configured and ordered tropes' (Blommaert, 2015: 111). These tropes, or culturally recognizable systems of meanings and values, are applied and made understandable through *genres*, by means of ideologized, normative and enregistered features and styles that index and codify specific timespace relations. Each chronotope installs its own discursive frames and orders of indexicality as well as orders of authenticity. Each invocation of timespace also constitutes ascription of specific genres, registers, indexicals and other chronotopically relevant norms, and, as such, enactment of specific intentions, behaviors and effects.

Building on this interpretation, chronotope can be fruitfully combined with 'scale', another timespace metaphor that illustrates social stratification (Blommaert, 2007, 2010; Carr & Lempert, 2016; Collins *et al.*, 2009), i.e. the ways in which language resources are unevenly distributed, and acts of communication are unequally materialized and evaluated against normative complexes and orders of indexicality, with hierarchically attributed meanings and values. Through the notion of scale, argues Blommaert (2015: 111), we can critically examine the chronotopic organizations of language resources in terms of 'the degrees of availability and accessibility of adequate contexts creatively invoked in discourse' as well as 'the scalar effects of recognizability'. Scale points us towards 'the scope of understandability (... and) scope of creativity' (Blommaert, 2015: 11) of the discursive enactment of timespace, and, we may add, the interrelations of co-occurring chronotopes within that enactment (distinguished by Bakhtin as 'major' and 'minor') that keep different orders of authenticity in balance. The issues at stake in chronotopes, thus, are about distinctions in power, authority, agency and voice – issues that are part and parcel of the sociolinguistic critique on language and inequalities in the works of Bourdieu (1991), Hymes (1996) and others.

Blommaert's intervention on chronotope by connecting it with the notions of context and scale, is aimed at a less reductive approach to the complexity presented in 'the total linguistic fact' (Silverstein, 1985), a challenge faced by sociolinguistics on how to account for 'a complex construction of multiple historicities compressed into one synchronized act of performance, projecting different forms of factuality and truth, all of them ideologically configured and thus indexically deployed and all of them determined by the concrete sociolinguistic conditions of their production and uptake, endowing them with a scaled communicability at each moment of enactment' (Blommaert, 2015: 113–114).

To this end, it may well be feasible to suggest that all communicative behaviors can be examined as chronotopically organized cultural practices in which the timespace configurations reveal not only the nano politics of identity at the personal level, but also more far-reaching sociocultural changes in cultural globalization (Blommaert & De Fina, 2017). On this potential, we are reminded of Agha's argument for the scope of generalizability by defining chronotope as 'a semiotic representation of time and space *peopled* by certain social types' (Agha, 2007: 321, our emphasis). The agentive dimension of chronotope is made translucent, as Agha (2007: 321) states further: 'The act of producing or construing a chronotopic representation itself has a chronotopic organization (of time, space and personhood) which may be transformed by that act'. The capacity to actualize recognizable meaning, personhood and social reality through chronotope points to its performative dimension – by orienting toward multiple, polycentric timespace frames and scaled normativities specified therein (Baynham, 2015). Such timespace orientations are essentially acts of identity and realizations of 'recombinant selves' (Agha, 2007: 324), which in return may generate new meanings and changes, thus, pushing the boundaries of authenticity.

Returning to our earlier discussion on heritage authenticity, we see that the concept of chronotope has much to offer to heritage tourism and identity construction in peripheral globalization at both descriptive and analytical levels. *Heritage* itself is a chronotopic notion, located in a particular(ized) image of an eternalized past, attached to a certain place and group. The use of the term activates a whole package of associated frames and ways of thinking, talking, signing, dressing and behaving. In globalization, the chronotope of heritage, with its orders of authenticity centering on peripherality, maps onto that of the global center-periphery distinction amplified by late capitalism; while it also merges with the chronotope of tourism driven by the commodification of authenticity. All these are organized into the chronotope of locality: Enshi as a geopolitical and sociocultural periphery in China. Within this is nested yet another chronotope, that of the state multiculturalism in China emerged from its nation-building process, in which the Tujia as yet another chronotope is situated. The (multi-)chronotopic nature of our object of study is prominent and consequential. But, how are these different chronotopes semiotically combined and materialized? How might the 'invokable histories' be configured into a 'recombinant' new act of self? To what extent is the chronotopic organization understood as 'authentic', and to whom? Let us now bring these questions into the empirical field of observation, or the chronotopic setting, that we have opened in the beginning.

Dissecting Chronotopes of Authenticity

That chronotopic setting is 19 August 2013, Enshi. The 30th anniversary of Enshi as the last officially recognized minority prefecture in China punctuates a crucial and sociolinguistically dense moment of identity making. It serves as a memorial of the local ethnic minority status given by the state. It opens a stage for performing and reiterating the heritage assumed by that status for the local people. It also inserts a need to promote the local heritage tourism. To put in the terms developed above, the setting is constituted into a combination of chronotopes that are called into play on a locally contrived occasion. We will now home in on the complex details and dynamics in the chronotopic configuration of the setting through a sustained look at one example.

Chronotopic organization in heritage performance

The example is one of the many events and activities organized locally in different parts of Enshi during the fortnight preceding the actual anniversary day. Our ethnographic attention, access and selection of data here are necessarily reflexively shaped by our personal and subjective encounter and experience in the field, be it sometimes 'incidental' (Pinsky,

2015). In this case, this led us (through local acquaintances) to the small village of Shuitian Ba, on 17 August 2013, two days before the official festival date. Shuitian Ba village was, until that moment, a remote and little known hamlet in Xuan'en, the poorest county in Enshi. On that day, however, this peripheral village was turned into the center of an open air culture festival. Several heritage-related activities were taking place from dawn to dusk, including an outdoor stage performance of ethnic art, a national mountain bike tournament, and the opening of a local Tujia folk museum, attracting thousands of participants and visitors from near and far (such as Europe). A précis of the event and its multiplex timespace composition is captured in the following image (see Figure 7.1).

What we see is part of the outdoor stage performance in the heart of the village. Two major chronotopic units are readily identifiable: one of the stage, and one of the village surroundings in which the stage is set. Each unit entails several more chronotopes that are brought in and materialized semiotically, driven by a certain ideology of heritage authenticity.

We turn first to the stage as a chronotopic unit, focusing on the semiotic framing in the stage background design. While being a chronotopic

Figure 7.1 A chronotopic organization of 'authentic' Tujia in Enshi (© Xuan Wang 2013)

semiotization in itself, the stage background design also defines the overall chronotope of the event by announcing its thematic title in red characters: *Prefectural Day Celebration – Walk into A Thousand Tujia Households*. Underneath in yellow color and smaller size, are the four sub-thematic titles: (1) A Thousand Tujia Households country leisure and tourism opening ceremony; (2) the first national mountain bike invitation tournament; (3) intangible cultural heritage show; (4) A Thousand Tujia Households Ecological Beauty photography competition. These are followed by a signature of time and space – Xuan'en, Hubei, 19 August 2013 – and completed with names of the main organizers, participant groups, and sponsors.

The core message delivered here is about *Prefectural Day Celebration*, the official anniversary of the local minority status received from the state. This is converted and combined into the new agenda engendered by and in turn reinforcing that status: heritage tourism, developed locally as the project of *A Thousand Tujia Households* (more about this project below). The expression 'walk into' is a public invitation, paraphrasing 'welcome' and indexing a tourism marketing discourse. The centrality of this double message, of the locally implemented but state-directed political, economic and cultural priority, is indexed in the (red) color and (large) size of the writing, even in its font: with the thematic title mostly written in the font *Fang Zheng* (literally 'clear and square'), a print font with a serious and meticulous appearance indicating formality, only leaving out the name of the local project, *A Thousand Tujia Households,* which adopts a calligraphy font, a more flowy handwriting style that sets the name off against the rest of the line, perhaps to imply a degree of possibility for maneuvering and creativity.

Several sub chronotopes can be also observed, pointing to distinct yet interrelated elements of the heritage tourism project implemented in Shuitian Ba and opening for interpretation and consumption on the day. These elements correspond with the sub-thematic titles mentioned above, and chronotopically reorganize the place as a destination (1) of rural tourism, represented in its ethnicized primordial, idyllic lifestyle; (2) of extreme tourism, explorable as a remote and dangerous place through the modern adventure sport of mountain biking; (3) of cultural tourism, inhabited by the ethnic Other, crystallized and exhibited in certain (intangible) forms of tradition; and (4) of ecotourism, as a space undisturbed by modern living, with uncontaminated natural beauty. Taken together, these strands index and put into practice the logic of heritage tourism and its tropes (multilayered and revolving around peripherality), co-constructing an 'authentic' local through the commodification of its profound peripherality.

The intertwining of these chronotopes sanctions and 'orders' the deployment of more semiotic indexicals into that same stage background design, in the form of a collage of different images on which all the aforementioned thematic titles are inscribed. In this collage, Shuitian Ba village is seen lying peacefully in the gentle cradle of beautiful mountains (which until recently were iconic of Enshi's remoteness and poverty). The center of the panoramic view is occupied by a stretch of lushly green tea fields (tea has been a well-known produce of Xuan'en for two centuries). On both sides of the fields, along the foot of the mountains, sit small, tidy clusters of 'traditional' farm houses (which were in fact newly built under the local *A Thousand Tujia Households* project). In the bottom right corner of the collage, we also find a superimposed image of professional-looking road cyclists in action (an image associated with modern sports originated from Western Europe). Undoubtedly, these images are carefully selected and chronotopically reorganized into the stage background design. The aesthetic depiction of the village echoes and complements the (rural, adventure, cultural, and eco-) forms of heritage tourism inscribed in the thematic titles listed above. They also reaffirm ideologically the local multiple orientations to the translocal (heritage) authenticity simultaneously invoked in these titles – we are observing what Blommaert (2005: 126) called 'layered simultaneity' here. Shuitian Ba village is authentic, as it seems, because of the confluence of all of these elements in that historical-synchronic moment of enactment and observation. The chronotopically invoked words, images and ideas of *heritage-as-tourism*, as evidenced so far, all point to authenticity as a romanticized, exoticized and commodified version of peripherality. This version of peripherality, as we will see next, is embedded in and mobilized in support of the overall heritage project of Enshi: the construction of an authentic minority identity of the Tujia.

Let us now look at the second aspect of the stage, the actual show unfolding within that chronotope. What is being performed is a dramatized dance called Ten Sisters, which reenacts the Tujia tradition of 'wedding lament'. This performance is yet another chronotopic organization, richly semiotized through music, singing, costumes, body movements and storytelling. We see that all dancers are dressed in supposedly Tujia-style costumes (the 'authentic' Tujia costumes are hard to identify, see Wang, 2015). The bride and the groom are wearing matching red. With head covered under a red veil, the bride is being carried away by the groom on his back. The bridesmaids, the other nine of the ten sisters, are in identical pink dresses. They line up behind the couple, crying and waving farewell to the bride with red handkerchiefs. One of them seems to find it difficult to see off the bride: she stands by the couple, holding a red umbrella over the bride to shelter her from the sun. The music is sad and grieving, and the lyrics speak about the bride's reluctance to leave home and her gratitude to her parents.

The 'invokable histories' of this chronotopic organization, taking the form of dance show, are indexical of China's state ideology of multiculturalism and its imperative perception and representation of ethnic minorities. As discussed earlier, this ideology derives from an ethnotaxonomy, claiming certain (sometimes imagined or caricatured) aspects of the past or distinctions as traditions and ethnically 'unique' heritage, and circulating these as knowledge and truth that transcend timespace. This order of authenticity overarches the heritage making in Enshi. Although the wedding lament is a dated custom once practiced in many Han and other ethnic communities in China (and elsewhere), it has been officially attached to the Tujia and assumed as part of the group's timeless, unique feature and cultural heritage. The ritual is reenacted and chronotopically incorporated into various identity moments to indicate authenticity, such as here on the stage in Shuitian Ba village for the 30th anniversary of Enshi. In fact, wedding lament has become a Tujia 'classic'; the ritual – or, rather, the idea of it – has been enregistered as part of the local identity repertoire even though the vast majority in Enshi have not even seen it in its 'authentic' form themselves.

The dance performance of Ten Sisters in Shuitian Ba is one of the numerous reinterpretations of the Tujia wedding lament ritual. Within its own timespace frame as a dance, it artistically and intertextually recycles the official discourse of the 'authentic' Tujia. Meanwhile, the dance serves as a focal point of the chronotope generated on the stage: it ties in with the theme 'intangible cultural heritage show' written in the stage background design; it delivers that theme through selected multimodal semiosis and, via the stage, opens its semiotization of authenticity to multiple audiences and interpretations. The dancers on this stage are what we might call the 'heritagized' body. By being members of the local communities, wearing the Tujia-style clothing, and doing the ritual of wedding lament through dancing, the dancers themselves have become the most 'authentic' embodiment of Tujia authenticity. The bodies *per se* and what they can do and represent, in this sense, are called upon as an elemental form of chronotopic resource for achieving that authenticity, thus, an elemental part of the Tujia heritage. This insertion of the 'heritagized' body onto the stage is the semiotic axis to all the chronotopic work, i.e. *heritage-as-ethnicity*, unfolding in that moment of celebration in Shuitian Ba.

This brings us to the village as a chronotopic unit in which the celebration event takes place. We see the mountains iconic of Shuitian Ba being a central part of this chronotope. They frame the stage celebration as both the natural landscape of the village and the stage background design. This creates an authenticating effect to what is happening on the stage and, by extension, to the Tujia heritage projected from that stage. The same can be said about the corporeal and semiotic juxtaposition of the tea fields, the traditional farm houses and the cyclists. The village provides the locality and a foundational timespace framework. However, locality is not merely the backdrop outside of things that are happening, it is also designed and brought in as a key chronotopic resource.

A Thousand Tujia Households is a local heritage project that has turned Shuitian Ba village into the ideal(ized) locality for the celebration. The project, funded by the county government of Xuan'en, was to make a model village out of Shuitian Ba showcasing the natural beauty of the mountainous region, the idyllic agrarian lifestyle, and the unique Tujia way of life, focusing on housing – all in all, an 'authentic' package of heritage features under the umbrella term of Tujia, which feeds directly into the heritage tourism market and its commodification of Tujia authenticity. We have seen all of these semiotically represented on the stage. Not as immediately visible in that synchronicity, is the process of (chronotopic) design of the village. To achieve the goal, the village has been transformed. The previous paddy fields (origin of the village name) were replaced with tea fields, concentrated in the primary location of the village center. New roads and paths were built, featuring a Dong[5] style footbridge over the brook running through the village. The location and size of the local farm houses were also reorganized so that they would look tidier and more uniformly recognizable. More interestingly, a proportion of the project funding was spent on revamping these houses to give them an ethnically 'authentic' appearance. This involved replastering the external walls of many houses to hide their originally tiled facades (the latter was an urban trend in Enshi at the time), replacing the aluminum window frames with carved wooden ones, and adding artistic features to the roofs and eaves of the houses. All these efforts have contributed to the 'authentic' locality and are visually connected to other 'authentic' products and performances found in the village.

One may ask whether the production of locality here has paradoxically triggered 'artificial authenticity', therefore, inauthenticity. However, what counts as the original? Is the original the authentic? At what point does an intentional adjustment turn its object into something inauthentic? Answers to such questions are contentious and complex. We prefer to consider the *A Thousand Tujia Households* project as an example in which the semiotic modification of a chronotopic setting is part of the wider process of striving for a sense of authenticity at different scale-levels; it therefore belongs to the production of authenticity.

To summarize, the example from Shuitian Ba village illustrates complex chronotopic organizations of different aspects of the Tujia heritage in action. In the format of a stage performance, different timespace frames are mobilized to represent the 'authentic' Tujia for political and economic purposes. The stage and the village become multi-chronotopic, in the sense that they generate a nexus of chronotopes, with the Tujia dance performance being the focal point, and the stage background design semiotically mirroring the corporeal surroundings and activities of the occasion. Each chronotope brings along its own historical meanings, with different configurations and meanings merging into a fused whole through the stage setting on which the Tujia heritage is performed – in a double sense of the word: as a theatrical performance, and as an agentive process of semiotization. This performative aspect, as we have seen, involves notable efforts of 'semiotic design' (Wang, 2015). Chronotopes examined here are necessarily part of the larger chronotopes of heritage in Enshi, in China and in globalization. They show that the performance of heritage authenticity, or any identity claim, is organized in relation to multiple timespace frames of meaning making.

Chronotopic scaling and authenticity

We have suggested earlier that scale is a notion that can describe the scope of communicability of chronotopically organized and semiotized behaviors (Blommaert, 2015). If heritage can be observed as such a phenomenon, following our discussion so far, tourism offers a scale at which heritage can be articulated, negotiated and understood. The scale of tourism mobilizes specific norms, genres and expectations toward which communication on heritage and authenticity orients – we have seen these in the case of Enshi being 'translated' into the globalized formats of rural, adventure, ethnic and eco-tourism and respective spatiotemporal configurations of local engagements. There are other scales that are prevalent, such as the state ethnopolitics of multiculturalism, or the local histories and conditions. All these scales inform and shape the way heritage can be performed and developed in an 'authentic' way. This suggests that heritage is a profoundly multi-scalar and polycentric process, in which different scales interact with one another, but not on equal footings. They may come into play at a semiotic, ideological or discursive level. They may work in parallel, conjoint, competing or conflicting relations with one another, and in turn involve different contributors and evaluators. The outcome is heteroglossic, a package of multiple meanings and voices. Thus, such dynamics and the opportunities, tensions and transactions they instigate qualify 'heritage' as a verb (to echo Street, 1993).

From this perspective, heritage can be understood as a scaled collective process of meaning making in a given timespace. 'Heritaging', we might say, is a matter of scaling: maneuvering with the dialectic interplays of the relevant scales to arrive at a sense of authenticity through chronotopically organized 'synchronized' activities. This understanding may go some way to explaining our remaining questions on the issue of heritage authenticity we have encountered in Enshi, an issue that appears to be largely about responding to the orders of authenticity at the scale of globalized heritage tourism and that of state heritage politics. Through the example illustrated above, we have gained insight into the intricate chronotopic organizations of heritage authenticity and understood that it is within a complex regime of normativities that a range of chronotopes are brought together to explore an important identity opportunity for Enshi. The questions we are left with are: In what way can we actually interpret the local uptake of heritage tourism under these conditions still as an agentive process of heritaging and, in the end, self-realized authenticity for the community itself? In what way can we keep a balanced view between the conformative and the performative, the staged and the everyday, the authentic and the inauthentic, in order to better account for meaning making in the periphery? To answer these questions, we have to start somewhere else, with the genesis of Enshi Tujia and Miao Autonomous Prefecture.

The establishment of Enshi's minority status through its ethnic population of the Tujia was a convoluted story. In the process of nation building after 1949, the Chinese government implemented ethnic classification in order to give recognition to minority groups and to integrate them into a 'unified, multinational country'. A large number of the 55 minority groups we now know in China were officially identified in the 1950s. Each ethnic group, called *minzu*, (supposedly) has its own territory, common history, unique language, culture and tradition. However, as Mullaney (2011) shows in his account of this part of Chinese history, the ethnotaxonomy applied at the time had its epistemological, ontological and methodological foundations in Western modernist social scientific beliefs in disciplines such as linguistics and ethnology (and, we could add, its political conversion into a 'model state', the Soviet Union). It was unable to clearly define all ethnic groups according to pre-assumed, fixed categories such as language or specific cultural traits. The Tujia group was not recognized until 1957 because the group had been mixing and living together with other groups; they lacked the obvious cultural features that would make them visibly different from the other groups. Its classification was prompted accidentally when a representative of the Miao from a town bordering Hunan and Hubei provinces pleaded with the central government to 'reclassify' her and her people in Hunan as the Tujia, since their language differed from that of the Miao (Tan & Hu, 2009).

However, whereas areas in Western Hunan were officially recognized in 1957 as Tujia territories, based on the local communities' self-identification and fieldwork conducted by Chinese ethnologists, their neighbors in Enshi, Western Hubei, did not receive the same recognition. The ethnic classification was soon brought to a halt with the change of political climate in China prefiguring the Great Proletarian Cultural Revolution, when claiming any different identity risked being seen as counter-revolutionary factionism. It was not until after the Cultural Revolution that the ethnic classification was resumed, to address some of the issues left over from two decades ago. Enshi's case reopened.

Brown (2002) records that when the status reclassification and restoration of the Tujia started in Enshi in the early 1980s, many local people were unwilling to 'become' Tujia since they 'did not have Tujia consciousness' (2002: 375) and preferred to consider themselves Han. Brown argues that the categories of ethnic boundary and distinction created by the local government – mainly by genealogical information and history of residence – did not reflect the actual cultural practice and sociopolitical experience of the individuals; it was a 'manipulation' of population statistics based on an artificial dichotomy between the Tujia and the Han, a tactic of authentication by the local government that was 'both economically beneficial and politically safe' for the local populace as a whole (2002: 389). The disjunction between the state recognition and the local sense of self observed here illustrates the sensitivity and power dynamics of authenticity in relation to ethnic identity in China – particularly so for Enshi – in which the influence of the state prevails.

In the light of this historical trajectory, we may understand that for Enshi, what heritaging initially invokes is perhaps an uncomfortable sense of inauthenticity rather than authenticity and, consequently, anxiety about how to *become* authentic. This question is hardly meaningful in terms of daily life at the local scale, since being a Tujia, a Miao or else was an abstract political status largely detached from the local personal realities in which nearly all the features and evidence of 'authenticity', such as ethnic language, clothing and customs, are absent, including people's own ethnic consciousness. The question until recently has only been relevant and important at the national scale: how to *be seen as authentic* in the eyes of the state, of the majorities and of the other minorities. The chronotopes of the local group identity were separated and confined in two disjointed scales of meaning making in terms of heritage. When called upon by the state as minority, people shift into a 'heritage' mode or chronotope of communication, deploying 'authentic' heritage-related semiotic resources. The moment this duty is done, they shift out of it, picking up a different, 'inauthentic' set of resources to continue with life at the local level. The contrast and disjunction and the essentializing accusation of inauthenticity these often produce only accentuate the peripheral status of Enshi.

This predicament, however, is now brought in a different light, with globalization and heritage tourism opening up new economic, political and cultural opportunities for Enshi. Tourism began to take shape in Enshi in the late 1980s, after its reintegration and recognition as a minority region, but only came into full swing less than a decade ago. The old question of 'how to play the *minzu* [ethnic minority] card' began to merge with the new economic demand, leading to the local strategizing of heritage tourism, with the Tujia (now the largest minority group of Enshi) being positioned as its spearhead. The entrée of a new heritage discourse from the global scale begins to reshape the meaning of authenticity in Enshi. Its natural scenery of steep mountains and local culture have been politically reframed and economically repackaged, turning from an image of wilderness and underdevelopment into one of rare beauty, ecological privilege, nostalgic leisure and bucolic life. This indicates a symbolic shift in the order of authenticity that has historically stigmatized Enshi. The global template of heritage tourism simultaneously authenticates and de-authenticates heritage. On the one hand, it seeks the 'real' local in order to commodify it; on the other hand, it disrupts and 'contaminates' the local way of life through translocal encounters and involvements – tourists are by definition not local, 'not from here'. This creates scaled chronotopic patterns that reorganize heritage into the (authentic) 'timeless-here' in mixture and coordination with the (inauthentic) commodification and rescrambling of timespace and resources, as we have seen in the example of Shuitian Ba in Enshi. There, it seems, the new order of authenticity at the global scale-level offers scope and chronotopic opportunities to simultaneously articulate heritage authenticity at the national and the local scale-levels: people can fit their previously disjointed 'on' and 'off' modes of heritage within the one chronotope of heritage tourism. By moving up and mixing scales, they manage to obtain a degree of coherence and sustainability in their dilemma of inauthentic authenticity – heritage is now chronotopically niched.

More important to our understanding about Enshi is the emerging agency involved in this reorganization. The absorption into globalization processes through heritage tourism is subtly transforming the identity making processes for Enshi. The opportunities put forward to the local communities have enabled them to engage with their 'given' heritage and the question of 'how to become authentic' in a more autonomously active way. This is evidenced in Enshi's full orientation toward tourism as a heritage strategy and the political and economic investments it makes accordingly. It is also evidenced in the local commitment to identity opportunities like the one we discussed, through the detailed, layered semiotic maneuvers so as to better perform Tujia authenticity; and it is evidenced in the scaling of heritage practices accumulated from such opportunities toward authenticity of optimal potential of recognizability. The efforts are about appropriating these opportunities, as much as about developing an order of authenticity that is locally enacted and translocally meaningful, both stimulate and rely on active semiotic design. It is in these facts that we begin to see an inception of ethnic consciousness in Enshi. In this sense, what we are also witnessing is a contemporary process of ethnogenesis, that is, the invention of the Tujia and their heritage.

Conclusion

Meaning making in the global periphery is infused with complexity. To adequately address that complexity is one of the main challenges we are faced with in sociolinguistic studies. Through the case of the Tujia in Enshi, it is clear that any critical understanding about the complexity cannot disengage with the structural conditions of peripherality and inequality in which accessibility, communicability and validity of language resources and their use are embedded. For ethnic minorities such as the Tujia, heritage is a compelling identity discourse with historically loaded and regimented meanings and values. It came with the minority status that was 'given' by the state to people in Enshi, marking out their (invented) cultural alterity and geopolitical peripherality. Therefore, what their 'own' heritage invokes is not only an unfamiliar (sometimes even absent) set of semiotic norms and resources, but also the perpetual ambivalence of (in)authenticity.

This ambivalence reemerges through heritage tourism as the Tujia engage in processes of globalization. Heritage tourism opens for Enshi an opportunity to commodify their peripherality – which has now become a resource – while addressing the issue of authenticity. By incorporating the notion of chronotope, we are able to ethnographically contextualize and dissect the local identity acts demanded by heritage tourism, but performed simultaneously at multiple scale-levels. It transpires that these acts entail careful semiotization of timespace in which heritage authenticity is communicated in a spatially and temporally reorganized, re-rationalized order. In this new order of authenticity, the Tujia are able to design and deliver what may be considered authentic for different audiences while gaining economic and political purchase. They are heritaging in ways that, previously were mainly meaningful to others, but now are also meaningful for themselves. In this sense, they are *becoming* Tujia, and their heritaging is 'producing authenticity' (Cavanaugh & Shankar, 2014).

Furthermore, heritage in a globalizing era is better understood as something chronotopically niched. The assumption of heritage as a singular chronotope of 'timeless-here' (in crystallized forms of language, clothing and other cultural traits) can no longer sufficiently explain what counts as authentic or inauthentic (see also Woolard, 2013). The binary view is under challenge in an increasingly polycentric environment in which heritaging now operates. The authenticity claims it can make are not simply against the essentialized norm imposed from one center, but through a complex process that involves semiotic maneuvering targeting recognizability for multiple centers and scales. Through chronotopic maneuvering, 'fake' acts (which are often produced for audiences who are in the position to evaluate them as such), such as stage performing, designing and commodification, are able to find their own place and validity in heritaging, making themselves a coherent and sustainable part of a co-constructed lifeworld. In this way, heritage is renewed, revised and reinserted in contemporary life – as part of the ongoing 'invention of tradition' in human society (Hobsbawm & Ranger, 1983).

This, to some extent, makes authenticity a politically more viable course for those in the periphery. As shown in the case of the Tujia, through their agency, peripheral groups are able to – even if symbolically – reclaim authenticity in specific chronotopes over certain ground, thus, a degree of autonomy over their own identity making. In minute semiotic details of performing heritage authenticity, we detect that the center-periphery relation is being locally contested and reworked, from which cultural change is emerging. However, we must also avoid the over-generalization that those in the periphery are free from the structural inequality that circumscribes their authenticity. As our study suggests, the production of a new order of authenticity is still largely situated in a peripheral cultural and political economy, based on patterns and resources defined by the center. Its own authenticity, therefore, has not escaped 'the cunning of recognition' (Povinelli, 2002) within globalization.

Notes

(1) An earlier version of this chapter was published in *AILA Review 30*. It is included here with the kind permission of the publisher. Our gratitude goes to Long Jianghua, Wang Mian, Xie Hongyan, Zhang Ting and Zhang Xiuju in Enshi, who generously provided crucial inside knowledge and logistic assistance without which the fieldwork that has inspired this chapter would have simply been impossible.
(2) This study is part of our ongoing ethnographic observation of Enshi as a periphery of sociolinguistic globalization, both online and offline (see e.g. Wang, 2012, 2015; Wang *et al.*, 2014 for background and details). The data on heritage tourism in Enshi presented here were collected by Xuan Wang in the summer 2013.
(3) Heritage tourism became an opportunity for Enshi very recently. It emerged in the 1980s, after China's economic reform of 1979 and Enshi's recognition as an ethnic minority region in 1983. In 2000, when Enshi was absorbed into the national Great Western Development Plan, heritage tourism was adopted officially as a development strategy at the levels of the local, provincial and central government, with 'strengthening the cultural foundations' and 'combining *minzu* culture and tourism' represented by the Tujia being the top of the local development agenda (Wang, 2015).
(4) Povinelli (2002) offers a cogent example in what she terms 'the cunning of recognition' in the context of Australia, where the indigenous groups have to prove their 'aboriginality' based on non-indigenous knowledge, discourse and systems of recognition that serve to reinforce liberal regimes of nationalism and multiculturalism.
(5) Another ethnic minority group found in Enshi.

References

Agha, A. (2007) Recombinant selves in mass mediated spacetime. *Language & Communication* 27, 320–335.
Anderson, B. (1991) *Imagined Communities: Reflections on the Origin and Spread of Nationalism*. London: Verso.
Appadurai, A. (1996) *Modernity at Large: Cultural Dimensions of Globalization*. Minneapolis/London: University of Minnesota Press.
Bakhtin, M.M. (1981) Forms of time and of the chronotope in the novel. In M. Holquist (ed.) *The Dialogic Imagination* (pp. 84–258). Austin: University of Texas Press.
Bauman, R. and Briggs, C. (2003) *Voices of Modernity: Language Ideologies and the Politics of Inequality*. Cambridge: Cambridge University Press.
Baynham, M. (2015) Narrative and space/time. In A. De Fina and A. Georgakopoulou (eds) *The Handbook of Narrative Analysis*. Chichester: John Wiley & Sons.
Blommaert, J. (2005) *Discourse*. Cambridge: Cambridge University Press.
Blommaert, J. (2007) Sociolinguistic scales. *Intercultural Pragmatics* 4 (1), 1–19.
Blommaert, J. (2010) *The Sociolinguistics of Globalization*. Cambridge: Cambridge University Press.

Blommaert, J. (2015) Chronotopes, scales, and complexity in the study of language in society. *Annual Review of Anthropology* 44, 105–116.

Blommaert, J. and De Fina, A. (2017) Chronotopic identities: On the timespace organization of who we are. In A. De Fina, J. Wenger and D. Ikizoglu (eds) *Diversity and Super-Diversity: Sociocultural Linguistics Perspectives* (pp. 1–15). Washington DC: Georgetown University Press.

Blommaert, J. and Varis, P. (2013) Enough is enough: The heuristics of authenticity in superdiversity. In J. Duarte and I. Gogolin (eds) *Linguistic Superdiversity in Urban Areas: Research Approaches* (pp. 143–159). Amsterdam: John Benjamins.

Blum, S.D. (2001) *Portraits of Primitives: Ordering Human Kinds in the Chinese Nation*. Lanham: Rowman & Littlefield.

Bourdieu, P. (1984) *Distinction: A Social Critique of the Judgement of Taste*. London: Routledge.

Bourdieu, P. (1991) *Language and Symbolic Power*. Cambridge, MA: Harvard University Press.

Brown, M. (2002) Local government agency: Manipulating Tujia identity. *Modern China* 28 (3), 362–395.

Carr, E. S. and Lempert, M. (eds) (2016) *Scale: Discourse and Dimensions of Social Life*. Oakland, California: University of California Press.

Cavanaugh, J.R. and Shankar, S. (2014) Producing authenticity in global capitalism: Language, materiality, and value. *American Anthropologist* 116 (1), 51–64.

Ch'en, J. (1992) *The Highlanders of Central China: A History, 1893-1937*. Armonk & London: M.E. Sharpe.

Collins, J., Slembrouck, J. and Baynham, M. (eds) (2009) *Globalization and Languages in Contact: Scale, Migration, and Communicative Practices*. London: Continuum.

Coupland, N. (2003) Sociolinguistic authenticities. *Journal of Sociolinguistics* 7 (3), 417–431.

Coupland, N. (2010) The authentic speaker and the speech community. In C. Llamas and D. Watts (eds) *Language and Identities* (pp. 99–112). Edinburgh: Edinburgh University Press.

Coupland, N. (2014) Language, society and authenticity: Themes and perspectives. In V. Lacoste, J. Leimgruber and T. Breyer (eds) *Indexing Authenticity: Sociolinguistic Perspectives* (pp. 14–42). Berlin: Walter de Gruyter.

Duchêne, A. and Heller, M. (eds) (2012) *Language in Later Capitalism: Pride and Profit*. New York and London: Routledge.

Gladney, D. (1994) Representing nationality in China: Refiguring majority/minority identities. *Journal of Asian Studies* 53 (1), 92–123.

Gumperz, J. (2003) Response essay. In S. Eerdmans, C. Previgniano and P. Thibault (eds) *Language and Interaction: Discussion with John J. Gumperz* (pp. 105–126). Amsterdam: John Benjamins.

Heller, M. (2003) Globalization, the new economy, and the commodification of language and identity. *Journal of Sociolinguistics* 7, 473–498.

Heller, M. (2014) The commodification of authenticity. In V. Lacoste, J. Leimgruber and T. Breyer (eds) *Indexing Authenticity: Sociolinguistic Perspectives* (pp. 112–136). Berlin: Walter de Gruyter.

Hobsbawm, E. and Ranger, T. (eds) (1983) *The Invention of Tradition*. Cambridge: Cambridge University Press.

Hymes, D. (1996) *Ethnography, Linguistics, Narrative Inequality: Toward an Understanding of Voice*. London: Taylor and Francis.

Jaffe, A. (2015) Staging language on Corsica: Stance, improvisation, play, and heteroglossia. *Language in Society* 44, 161–186.

Jaffe, A. (2019) Poeticizing the economy: The Corsican language in a nexus of pride and profit. *Multilingua* 38 (1), 9–27.

Jaworski, A. and Pritchard, A. (eds) (2005) *Discourse, Communication and Tourism*. Clevedon: Channel View Publications.

Lacoste, V., Leimgruber, J. and Breyer, T. (eds) (2014) *Indexing Authenticity: Sociolinguistic Perspectives*. Berlin: Walter de Gruyter.

Lampert, M. and Perrino, S. (eds) (2007) Entextualization and Temperality. Special Issue, *Language & Communication* 27, 205–335.

Ma, R. (2016) 'Culturalism' and 'nationalism' in Modern China. In M. Guibernau and J. Rex (eds) *The Ethnic Reader: Nationalism, Multiculturalism and Migration* (pp. 299–307). Cambridge: Polity Press.

Mullaney, T.S. (2011) *Coming to Terms with the Nation: Ethnic Classification in Modern China*. Berkeley: University of California Press.

Pietikäinen, S. and Kelly-Holmes, H. (eds) (2013) *Multilingualism and the Periphery*. Oxford: Oxford University Press.

Pietikäinen, S., Kelly-Holmes, H., Jaffe, A., and Coupland, N. (2016) *Sociolinguistics from the Periphery: Small Languages in New Circumstances*. Cambridge: Cambridge University Press.

Pinsky, D. (2015) The sustained snapshot: Incidental ethnographic encounters in qualitative interview studies. *Qualitative Research* 15 (3), 281–295.

Povinelli, E.A. (2002) *The Cunning of Recognition: Indigenous Alterities and the Making of Australia Multiculturalism*. Durham and London: Duke University Press.

Pujolar, J. (2013) Tourism and gender in linguistic minority communities. In S. Pietikäinen and H. Kelly-Holmes (eds) *Multilingualism and the Periphery* (pp. 55–76). Oxford: Oxford University Press.

Roosens, E. (1989) *Creating Ethnicity: The Process of Ethnogenesis*. London: Sage.

Silverstein, M. (1985) Language and the culture of gender. In E. Mertz and R. Parmentier (eds) *Semiotic Mediation* (pp. 210–259). New York: Academic Press.

Street, B. (1993) Culture is a verb: Anthropological aspects of language and cultural process. In D. Graddol, L. Thompson and M. Byram (eds) *Language and Culture* (pp. 23–43). Clevedon: British Association for Applied Linguistics in association with Multilingual Matters.

Tan, H.Z. and Hu, X.H. (2009) *The Tujia Daughter Tian Xin Tao* (土家女儿田心桃). Beijing: Publishing House of Minority Nationalities.

Wang, X. (2012) 'I am not a qualified dialect rapper': Constructing hip-hop authenticity in China. *Sociolinguistic Studies* 6 (2), 153–191.

Wang, X. (2015) Inauthentic authenticity: Semiotic design and globalization in the margins of China. *Semiotica* 203, 227–248.

Wang, X., Spotti, M., Juffermans, K., Cornips, L., Kroon, S. and Blommaert, J. (2014) Globalization in the margins: Toward a re-evaluation of language and mobility. *Applied Linguistics Review* 5 (1), 23–44.

Wilce, J. and Fenigsen, J. (eds) (2014) De-essentializing authenticity: A semiotic approach. Special Issue, *Semiotica* 203, 137–248.

Woolard, K. (2013) Is the personal political? Chronotopes and changing stances toward Catalan language and identity. *International Journal of Bilingual Education and Bilingualism* 16 (2), 210–224.

8 Languages and Regimes of Communication: Students' Struggles with Norms and Identities through Chronotopic Work

Martha Sif Karrebæk and Janus Spindler Møller

Introduction

Regardless of the fact that the Danish educational system comprises a relatively heterogeneous population of students, it predominantly favors a monolingual, (standard) Danish dominant linguistic regime (Horst & Gitz-Johansen, 2010; Karrebæk, 2013; Møller, 2016; Padovan-Özdemir & Moldenhawer, 2016). This institutional preference for Danish as a standard and for standard Danish has a number of reasons. Traditionally the educational system plays an important part in the process of nation-building in which the national language is also a central element (Anderson, 2006; Bourdieu, 1991; Østergård, 2018). In fact, in Denmark, as in other Western countries, this perception of the national language seems to be growing, and Danish educational policies and guidelines underline the tendency (e.g. Kristjánsdóttir, 2018). Furthermore, (standard) Danish is generally regarded as a ticket to societal success (Hyttel-Sørensen, 2011), probably partly because of its dominant societal status and the lack of linguistic pluralism in the public sphere. But the strong orientation to the Danish language presents schools with a challenge. They need to live up to curricular norms established by policy makers, which leaves little space for maneuvering when it comes to the formulation of more inclusive educational strategies. At the same time, they wish linguistic and ethnic minority students to feel as privileged and welcome as majority students. Yet, Danish schools are generally unaccustomed to thinking about linguistic diversity as a potential and an asset, and they are not necessarily well-equipped to formulate new strategies (but see Daugaard, 2018 for a rare example of a different stance towards linguistic pluralism). Altogether, regardless of the fact that diversity rather than homogeneity is a general experience among teachers and students in Danish schools, this is not reflected in educational goals and practices. Many languages are regarded as incompatible with an academic curriculum and with the national educational system as such, and many children are left alone with the challenge of *both* navigating an official communicative regime *and* of integrating it with different regimes, of smaller or different scope, with which they are acquainted.

Occasionally situations emerge where the different aims, needs and expectations in classrooms are at odds. We will focus on examples of such situations from two classrooms in a Copenhagen school and use the Bakhtinian notion of chronotope to investigate how linguistic resources affiliated with minority languages are employed and reacted upon in the – for the participants – well-known activity of classroom presentations. During our fieldwork the researchers, including ourselves, found Danish to be the legitimate and dominant means of instruction, and other linguistic resources (except for those attributed to English and a few other European languages) were generally not regarded as educationally relevant or appropriate (Karrebæk, 2013, 2016). The principal of the school did not install any explicit language policies but he clearly disfavored the use of minority languages (Karrebæk, 2013). Also, he told some of the researchers that he aimed for 'color-blindness' among the teachers. We think that he meant that teachers should have the same (high) academic demands of all students regardless of the students' background, and that they needed to find strategies that erased *ethno-linguistic* identities in order to focus on *academic* identities and achievements. This stance was generally reflected in classroom interaction. Given the predominant societal understanding of the Danish language in relation to the educational system we understand the motivation for the principal's focus. Yet, we maintain that it also had negative consequences. For instance, on the rare occasions where students introduced registers of language associated with non-Danish-ness in official classroom activities, their teachers faced a difficult task in finding adequate responses. In addition, many students were uncomfortable with or unsure of how to handle such linguistic resources (Karrebæk, 2013, 2016).

In the following, we will analyze two situations which emerged during everyday classroom life and which illustrate dilemmas in relation to the handling of linguistic resources associated with non-Danish identities and not regarded as standard Danish. Both situations involve a platform event (Goffman, 1983) in which young girls of ethnic minority backgrounds perform for their peers and teachers. In one of them, the performing girls have planned to play a recording where Arabic and Somali linguistic resources are used in conjunction with Danish. As the recording does not work, the girls are invited by the teachers to perform unrehearsed in these languages. They are very reluctant to do so, and this leads to long and uncomfortable negotiations. In the other situation, a girl of Turkish background stylizes the (Turkish) Immigrant Other. In both situations, metapragmatic characterizations offer us evidence for some of the participants' chronotopic understandings, and we also consider how what is not said or what is said reluctantly compares to what is articulated and received with much enthusiasm. We find that regardless of the audible applauses received by the performing girls, the situations highlight the charged position of minority students in the regular school system in Denmark, and they possibly even contribute to processes of marginalization. The institutional setting seems to allow readily for certain indexicalities (Blommaert & De Fina, 2017) – only certain interpretations came about – and these indexicalities include specific and problematic understandings of minority identities. Linguistic features and ethnolinguistic labels activated such problematic meanings in our cases

Overall, in this chapter we aim to tackle two questions which we agree with Blommaert (2015: 17) are central for a multi-dimensional and social approach to language and meaning, namely: '(a) *what* do we understand? And (b) how come we understand it *as such*?' These questions can be responded to in a variety of ways, depending on what our object of analysis is taken to be, and who we refer to with 'we'. 'We' could be the participants performing on the recordings, their audiences, ourselves, (other) citizens of Danish society, or the readers of this contribution. And the object of analysis could be some specific children in a couple of classrooms at a specific time and day in a specific activity. It could be a (historically embedded) practice, perhaps even in a type of school, or even a type of children (those of ethnic and linguistic minority) in Denmark. In other words, the object and the addressee change according to the scale that we choose, in the sense of Carr and Lempert (2016). And although we are interested in the specific children, and in doing an emic analysis, of the situations located in time and space, we believe that it is also worthwhile to take the step beyond the speech event (Wortham & Reyes, 2015), which of course is an unavailable choice for the participants themselves. Analytically we include considerations of form (linguistic features), usage (use and avoidance of language, forms of participation) and ideological perceptions (implicitly or explicitly activated) (cf. Silverstein, 1985), and we discuss the participants' different available and performed identities. We consider these situations as types (i.e. platform events in school), what the performing students aim to present, the audience's response, and the larger embedding of the situations. In both situations, non-Danish ethnicities, identities and stereotypes are also made relevant, and although the racialization is not equally clear, explicit and institutionally sanctioned, both point to unequal social structures and to understandings of what is seen as non-Danish ethnicities which disfavor academic achievement. This becomes visible through the observation of what is possible to articulate (and what isn't), through the stereotypes enacted or refused, and through the meanings and values attributed to occurring (and absent) linguistic features. Using the chronotope (Bakhtin, 1981) as an analytical lens thereby, among other things, helps us draw forward the cross-situational aspect of the analyses, and accomplish multi-dimensional analyses of meaning.

Chronotopes of School and Performance in Platform Events

The Bakhtinian chronotope, or timespace, is a type of frame, which assumes an intrinsic time-space relation where particular characters move, and particular activities take place. Silverstein (2005) suitably talks about chronotopes as '*envelopes of understanding*' which solicit certain presuppositions and inferences within a delimited frame. Furthermore, the chronotope encompasses generic aspects of (expectations to) types of texts. We experience similarity across events as we compare them to the generic chronotopic structure or even to other events interpreted through the same chronotope (Silverstein, 2005). Situations are thereby connected to other situations, as participants draw on (or presuppose) situations experienced as similar or comparable in some way, and as they act according to their experiences and expectations. Two types of generic chronotopic structures are relevant to our study: the platform event and the student presentation. In the student presentation, the structure includes a presenter, the class as audience and the teacher as an evaluator. The content is academic, and it leads to a final academic assessment. There are many other expectations, some on an individual level, and some more conventional. In the platform event the expected social identities are performer(s) and audience (Goffman, 1983: 7). In such events, which include staged performance, performers use language which 'tend[s] to be linguistically stylized, pushing the limits of language' while at the same time 'building on the foundation of existing social meanings' (Bell & Gibson, 2011: 555).

Platform events and student presentations involve a delimited interpretive frame, within which the performer displays certain skills, is accountable to an audience, and is aware that this is the case. Following the same logic, the heightened focus on form and on the performance itself may lead to avoidance of certain ways of speaking which are seen as incompatible with the event type. Also, when a platform event occurs in class, it is embedded in the timespace of school, and thus two generic types affect expectations, behavior and interpretations simultaneously. Students participate repeatedly in both types of events and they use prior experiences when they interpret others' performances or when they themselves perform. The type, and the keying necessary to make others understand, is learned throughout the school career. In other words, chronotopes (here platform events and student presentations) are enacted locally, but our interpretations build on translocal experiences. We therefore need to be careful: despite participants' many shared experiences, all life trajectories and histories of socialization are unique, and this makes participants differ in their interpretations. In Blommaert's words:

> What is 'brought about' as a joint collaborative activity such as a conversation may obscure deep differences in what is being 'brought along' by different participants, and consequently in what is 'taken along' by these participants after the activity. (Blommaert, 2015: 4)

So, when Selda performs as a Turkish clown (as we shall see), she draws on prior performance experiences, her experience in school at large and a wealth of other things (what it means to be Turkish, etc.). Some of the effects (e.g. the indexical associations created) of her local performance are intended, and others are probably not. Some of these effects may be due to the fact that Selda has little insight into the life experiences of her classmates, whereas others have to do with her position in society at large. This means that what is enacted within a chronotope is connected to prior and future events, and it is a way for participants to create future value (Munn, 1986). Types of situations have different potential for producing value. For students, exams and graded presentations may add to a grade point average, which in turn defines where a young person can go later in life. Grade point average is a simple and formalized type of value. Other values comprise the understanding of a young person as talented/(un)engaged/humorous/cooperative, etc.

As Bakhtin was well-aware, and as others (notably Agha, 2007) have underlined, all language-in-use (literary work, platform events, and mundane conversation) orient towards its own internal and genre-based organization, towards the addressees, and towards the conditions of performance. The analyses presented here focus on specific interpersonal semiotic encounters where identities are situated in one timespace but refer to a different timespace (Agha, 2007). Despite the fact that we can analyze the situations as involving different chronotopes (e.g. the situation in which the performance and performers are embedded vs. the performed situation in which the performer inserts herself), it is also important that these chronotopes are evoked simultaneously, embedded within each other, or cross-referring to one another. Thereby they and the enacted persona within them may seem to approach each other, perhaps even merging (Karrebæk & Ghandchi, 2017; Perrino, 2011). At least, if no work is done to avoid this. We will later argue that this is potentially significant for what is and is not embraced by the students.

Field Site and Data

Our examples come from an extensive collaborative empirical project carried out in Copenhagen, Denmark, from 2009 and still ongoing at the time of writing. The setting was a culturally and linguistically diverse urban school in a former traditional working class area where a group of senior and junior researchers have done sociolinguistic ethnographic fieldwork among students from school entry (5–6 years) to school exit (age 15–16). The school setting was pivotal and we occasionally followed students outside of classrooms, to mother tongue classes in Turkish and Arabic, at home, to the youth clubs, after school center, or just on the streets. Our main types of data cover: field diaries, self-, group- and home-recordings, video-data, ethnographic interviews with teachers and parents, written texts, CMC, etc. (Madsen *et al.*, 2016). All participants are anonymized. In this contribution we present data from a well-researched group of 8th graders (see e.g. Ag, 2010; Madsen, 2013; Stæhr, 2010, 2014) who left the school in 2011 and a younger cohort whom we are still engaging with (see also Karrebæk, 2016; Nassri, 2016; Nørreby, 2017).

Chronotopic Work in the Use and Avoidance of Linguistic Resources

The Turkish magician-clown

In this section, we will discuss a situation in which Selda, a 3rd grade (10 years old) girl of Turkish background, parodied a – or perhaps *the* – Turkish immigrant in a platform performance in class. Selda was born in

Turkey from Turkish parents, and she arrived in Denmark at a very young age. She repeated kindergarten class in her current school after a year in another public school. Selda attended Turkish mother tongue classes (although with very little enthusiasm according to our observations) and her Turkish teacher described her as fluent in Turkish. Her spoken Danish showed few traces of her migration background, and her Danish teacher characterized her as a good student who wished to be orderly and live up to expectations, an impression shared by us. In terms of the peer group, Selda did not have any close friends in class, at least not at this time in 3rd grade year. Yet, she sought the company of a group of girls with ethnic minority backgrounds, two of whom of Turkish descent. These girls spoke in a way we recognize as urban youth language, where linguistic resources from minority languages such as Arabic are frequent; Selda's way of speaking was more in line with a modern (standard) Copenhagen register. The relation between the girls was conflict-ridden and Selda often came out the loser. More on this below where we focus on Selda's use of linguistic features, the indexical values of such features, and the motivation for and effects of her performance.[1]

Selda's performance was part of a show arranged by the teachers. The students were free to choose their own act or if they did not want to perform. They had time to rehearse in class. The event was relatively informal, with no formal evaluation, although the teachers provided spontaneous feedback upon their return to class. There were 12 acts in total – a riddle, a joke, a skit about a strict mother, a song about friendship, a fable written by two of the boys, etc. Selda's act was number seven and she was introduced as doing a magic trick. Although the situation was informal, staged performances are inherently objects of evaluation, and they are generally demonstrations of strategic and reflexive language use. In this case, Selda made use of 'strategic inauthenticity' (Coupland, 2001), or (linguistic) stylization, as often seen in performance (Bell & Gibson, 2011: 555; Coupland, 2001). It is strategic because self-aware, and it may be described as inauthentic when the linguistic features used are not associated with the speaker's ordinary linguistic repertoire (Rampton, 2009). Although the relation between authenticity and inauthenticity is not so straightforward, performers (and here Selda) often distance from the *persona* associated with the style used, and they often use this as a strategy to comment on social issues. Thereby social and ideological understandings are made salient, and the performance can have both immediate effects – entertainment – and more long-term sociolinguistic effects – in terms of the validation of a stereotype. Also, the successful performance presupposes an audience who recognizes the semiotic value associated with the performance – or the chronotope that it is enacted within – and it is therefore tied to the normative expectations which it may mirror (Coupland, 2001: 350). Last, Coupland (2001: 350) suggests that stylizations dislocate a speaker and utterance from the immediate speaking context, and in relation to the present study, we could see this as a speaker's introduction of a new chronotope.

On this particular day, none of the authors of this contribution were present along with the students. It was recorded by some of the other members of the research team. Yet, Karrebæk did fieldwork among the 3rd graders, and knew Selda from both regular classrooms and Turkish mother tongue classes. We enter the situation at the moment of introduction. The entire act lasts approximately four minutes. Non-standard pronunciation and other types of deviation are marked in the transcript.

Transcript 1

Spring 2014; audio-recording

Participants: Selda (Turkish descent), Aud = audience, comprising all other 3rd graders, their teachers, three researchers, SM = stage master, Kate (girl from 3rd grade), Adam (boy from 3rd grade), Unk = Unknown speaker

Legend

*	= creaky voice
♪	= sing-song intonation
°	= absence of glottal stop where expected
↑	= prosodic rise to high
↓	= prosodic fall to low
⁻xxx⁻	= very high pitch
bold	= different types of non-standard pronunciation

		Original	Translation
01	SM:	det næste er Selda der skal vise os (si/e)n tryllekunst	the next is Selda who is going to show us her/a magic trick
02	Aud:	((applause))	
03	Selda:	ui jeg kom fra Tjyrki°↑et (0.7) de:t må jeg lige sige tje ↑jer (1.2)	I came from Turkey (0.7) I must just tell you that (1.2)
04		og nu skal jeg vise jer en tjrylle↓kun̊st (3.3)	and now I am going to show you a magic trick (3.3.)

05	nej° det er ik ↓den° (2.7) slet ik ↓den (2.0) slet ↓ik (1.3) nat↓tjøj	no it isn't that (2.7) not that at all (2.0) not at all (1.3) pajamas
06	((sounds surprised))	
07 Aud:	((laughing))	

...

28 Selda:	jeg må nø:dt tje at prøve en gang tje fordi hun var lidt ⁻dum⁻	I have to try once more because she was a little stupid
29 Aud:	((laughing))	
30	(0.8)	

...

35 Selda:	ø:h jeg vil gerne ha: dig med bonushår (1.8) undskyld (3.8)	e:h I would like to ha:ve you with bonus hair (1.8) sorry (3.8)
36	jeg ka ik finde ud af dan°sk så: jeg tjaler lidt mærke↓ligt (1.3)	I don't know Danish so: I speak a little strange (1.3)
37	du må kun prøve det ȇn ↑gang (0.7) _ellers så dræber jeg	you can only try it once (0.7) or else I'll kill
38	↓dig lissom hende der_	you like her
39 Aud:	((laughing))	
40 Selda:	han der	he there

...

44 Selda:	sådan der så har du prøvet ((applause)) NE:J ven°t (.) ven°t ven°t (.)	like that then you have tried (applause) NO: wait (.) wait wait wait
45	ven°t vi skal lige vente (1.3) sætter vi den lige her og så	wait we just have to wait (1.3) just put this one here and then
46	venter ↓vi (5.7) jeg ringer lige tje min sø↓ster	we wait (5.7) I'll just call my sister
47	(1.2)	
48 Aud:	((laughing))	
49 Selda:	hvorfor har du tjaget min ø:h legetjøj med (0.9) okay farvel	why did you bring my toy (0.9) okay goodbye

50	har du ⁻**fødselsdag**° i dag°⁻	is it your birthday today
51 Aud:	((laughing))	
52 Selda:	okay jeg sender ba:re en: gulerod tje dig farvel	okay I am just going to send you a: carrot goodbye
53 Aud:	((laughing))	
54 (1.3)		

Although the announcement focuses on this as a magic trick, the linguistic aspects take center stage in the performance. Whereas ordinarily Selda speaks a modern Copenhagen Danish,[2] here her linguistic performance includes a range of non-standard features, features which appear exaggerated and act as contextualization cues. They run the gamut from segmental phonetics to speech acts. We present an overview in Table 8.1.

The features listed in Table 8.1 differ both in terms of frequency, saliency, and (perhaps) metapragmatic transparency. Most generalized is [ç] rather than standard [tˢ]) for /t/ in syllable initial position. Other studies (e.g. Hyttel-Sørensen, 2017; Møller, 2009) have demonstrated how this feature is associated with two different, yet related, registers of speech today (Agha, 2007), both primarily associated with immigrant Danish: an urban youth register and the Danish spoken by (adult) learners of Danish (here labeled learner Danish), although it has also been attested earlier in non-ethnically marked Copenhagen speech (Maegaard, 2007: 87). The urban youth style is widely used and well-known in the school in general and in Selda's 3rd grade class specifically (Karrebæk, 2016). It is also used in the peer group that Selda aspires to, in particular by one of the girls; in fact, this girl is a relatively rare example of a female user of this register (Nørreby, 2017). In contrast, we never encountered students who used a register of learner Danish during our fieldwork. Indexically the urban youth register is associated with urban, assertive, masculine youngsters and with having a non-Danish background (Madsen, 2013). At the same time, it is becoming increasingly mainstream because of its use by popular rap artists, and thereby it gets less tied to counter-culture, and the stereotype of the societally marginalized, educationally weak, aggressive gangster of immigrant background (Hyttel-Sørensen, 2017; Stæhr & Madsen, 2016; Nørreby, 2017). Accented Danish is generally associated with incompetence, in particular if the accent is understood as belonging to a person from Africa, Asia or the Middle-East (Kirilova, 2006). We find it important that Selda does not discriminate between the two registers in her enactment regardless of the sociolinguistic argument that they differ. This suggests that there are still wide-spread negative associations of the

Table 8.1 Overview of linguistic features that index non-standardness used by Selda

Category	Type	Example	Frequency
Pronunciation	t as [ç] instead of [tʰ]	Jeg kom fra Tjyrkiet (line 03)	Almost generalized
	l as [ɭ] instead of [l]	Slet ik (line 05)	Perhaps lexically dependent
	vowel quality	Lægge [lɛg] dem her (lines 09–10)	Few instances
	absence of glottal stop	Gå° (line 25)	Almost generalized
	t as [d] instead of [ð]	Tjyrkiet (line 03)	Once
	/r/ = [ɾ]	Jeg ringer lige (line 46)	Once
Prosody	Rising final intonation	Du må kun prøve det en gang (line 37)	Relatively many instances
	Creaky voice / low pitch	Ellers så dræber jeg dig (lines 37–38)	Few instances
Grammar	Grammatical gender	*Min* legetøj (instead of *mit* legetøj) (line 49)	Once
	Sexus	Han der (instead of hende der) (line 40)	Once
	Case	Han der (instead of ham der) (line 40)	Once
Lexis		Bonushår	Once
Deviant and absurd action	Confrontational language	Ellers så dræber jeg dig (lines 37–38)	Few instances
	Demonstrations of incompetence	Nej ik den slet ik den slet ik nattjøj (line 05)	Few instances
	Inconsiderateness / un-empathic behavior	Har du fødselsdag i dag? Okay så sender jeg bare en gulerod tje dig (lines 50–52)	Few instances

urban youth register, and in particular that it is associated with an unflattering version of the immigrant Other, as also noticed by Nørreby (2017). The generalized feature [ç] is probably the shibboleth that activates a negatively valued immigrant stereotype; other features strengthen this stereotype. For instance, the un-empathetic attitude, confrontational language, creaky voice and low pitch all call up the image of an aggressive gangster, and the failure in locating props, the non-standard use of gender (grammatical and sex), lexis (and perhaps prosody) all point to an understanding of incompetence. Yet, Selda does not include other emblematic features of these registers. A typical (and often parodied) feature of learner Danish is to place the finite verb as the third constituent in declarative main clauses; in standard Danish it is the second constituent. And urban youth language is often identified through its use of lexicon from immigrant languages, notably *koran* and *wallah* (Karrebæk, 2016). We find none of this here.

Selda's performance suggests that the stereotypical associations between certain language features, ways of behaving and cultural stereotypes are well-known among the 9–11 year old students. Those that may be unaware are enlightened by Selda in her first turn: 'I came from Turkey'. The metapragmatic understanding of the ways she speaks is clarified (to some extent) when she characterizes this as not proper Danish ('I can't figure out Danish') and (therefore) 'a little strange' (line 36). Her explicit characterization follows an odd expression. She describes one of the boys' hair as *bonus hair*, probably a direct translation from Turkish *bonus saçlı*, referring to particularly wild, unruly, messy, curly hair (which describes very well the hair of the boy she addresses). It is questionable whether the example of transfer is intentional, and whether its fit with the other linguistic features is comprehended by her audience. But it seems likely that the 'strange language' is to be taken as an overall evaluation of her linguistic performance, rather than of the use of the single expression, and this language use is certainly recognized at least by some of her audience.[3]

The immediate reception and evaluation of Selda's performance is positive: her classmates laugh and applaud repeatedly. We cannot know for certain why, and their enthusiasm probably has different reasons, but a trivial observation is that Selda introduces apparent incongruences and perhaps taboo into the school context; this is often associated with humorous effects (Glenn, 2003). The incongruences and taboos are connected to Selda's use of features which differ from what is expected from a good and appropriate school-child in Denmark. They are erased (Irvine & Gal, 2000), suppressed, ignored or reproached if they turn up, as we have already mentioned. Thus, Selda enacts a *persona* who is unruly, aggressive, impolite, inconsiderate, not focused on learning – and who does not speak standard Danish. Selda is able to do this, and still be recognized as a good student, exactly because she creates a timespace envelope – a chronotope – in which she inserts a Turkish/immigrant *persona*. She brackets out the timespace associated with school – in that timespace she lives up to mainstream norms and teacher expectations. She is now the Turkish immigrant who fails on all the measures normally applied. This is funny because her performance is good, because she is confronting norms, breaking taboos by speaking in erased or unsanctioned ways, and making fun of people, but it is also funny – or so we suggest – because this *persona* is both her and not her. It is no secret that Selda has a Turkish background, and this is probably also the reason why it is a permissible performance in the eyes of the others, including the school authorities. At the same time, she makes a clear line of demarcation between the timespace of school in which her school identity is situated and the performed *persona*. Notice that she is not employing all the features that could have been incorporated in the performance, and she undoubtedly knows of *wallah* and *koran* and their relation to the immigrant stereotype. This is so widespread in the school, even among her peers, that she can hardly have missed it. We suggest that Selda is doing double-voicing. She is performing somebody who *could* have been her, and in order to underline that this is performance – and strategic inauthenticity – she distances herself by avoiding some features.

Some questions remain. Why is Selda drawing on her own background to create a parody of the immigrant? Why here, why now in front of these people, and with what right (cf. Rampton, 2009)? We suggest that Selda is accomplishing several things at once during her performance. First of all, by demonstrating the difference between her usual self and her performed self, she makes it clear that she is aware of other possible selves and she demonstrates her understanding that they belong in other timespaces than school. This re-affirms her identity as a good school-child, rather than as one of the unruly immigrant kids; she creates a contrast to the 'newly arrived/linguistically incompetent' persons; and she claims belonging, rather than just residence, in Denmark (cf. Blommaert & De Fina, 2017). Second, rather trivially, Selda wants to entertain her peers. Through successful entertainment she gets recognition and popularity, and her use of language is a way to accomplish this. And as so often, humor illuminates local social norms (Glenn, 2003). Third, both immediate goals are ways to create future value. It is an educational investment – making teachers realize that she is a model minority (Shankar, 2008), by accentuating the fact that she usually observes the monolingual and other behavioral norms prescribed; at the same time, it is an investment in peer group value. Fourth, as part of a more personal agenda, Selda may be making a comment to the group of girls which she is aspiring to. These girls use the urban youth style, they are assertive and confrontational, and they are often belittling her, exploiting her norm-observing behavior. In this performance, Selda may vindicate herself for such humiliation, and she does it in a school-sanctioned way through generalized ridicule.

The effects of the performance are both long-term and short-term. In the situation, Selda appears to be happy with her success, and she comments on it several times when they return to class. In terms of the investment in her identity as a model student, it is more complicated. School-careers run over many years, and Selda had some six years of obligatory school left. There are signs that the performance may pay off for her in the long run. In the follow-up session the math and the Danish teachers praise her; the math teacher asks how she got the idea of this 'story' and he mentions her ability to both follow a script and improvise. Another possible long-term effect – perhaps with wider implications, and at least orienting to a different scale – concerns that Selda's performance validates an already circulating stereotype of the incompetent immigrant identified through the particular and deviant use of Danish. When asked by the teacher how she got the idea, Selda replies that she saw a man who could not speak Danish, and then she thought of doing that, too. Notice, that in her formulation of the experience, the linguistic performance does not even qualify as speaking Danish. It is only partly confirmed by Selda's other teacher who praises her 'clear voice'. The response follows one of her classmates who praises and quotes her, using highly accented speech. The teacher then adds 'You had such a clear voice Selda ... even though you were supposed to sound (.) as if you spoke (.) poor Danish'. None of the teachers mention that there may be something problematic about parodying an already stigmatized group. Nor do they ask about her reasons for choosing the Turk, a category with which she is also affiliated. The chronotope in which mainstream Danish education unfolds is validated, as is the understanding that it is not appropriate to speak this type of Danish, which then again is affirmed as deviant.

From trilingual poetry to the 'language tone of Somali'

The next case unfolded in 8th grade among another cohort of students. In this group, 80% of the students reported to have a minority linguistic background. A number of studies have documented how these students exploited the linguistic richness accessible to them in peer group settings. For example, they engaged in practices that involved combining linguistic features associated with a range of different languages (see e.g. Madsen, 2013) or displayed an interest in what things were called in 'each other's languages' and accordingly exploited this knowledge to form in-group slang (Møller, 2017). However, we found such behavior to be almost non-existing in the mainstream classroom interaction. To our knowledge, the teachers did not bring minority languages into the daily activities of teaching, and the students only did so extremely rarely. Again, we argue that looking at how the interaction unfolded in the rare occasions where it actually happened may help explain why they are rare. In the example we are about to see the participants' displays of chronotopic understanding of the situation changed radically when minority languages more or less against the will of the students became part of their classroom presentation.

Instances where language resources associated with minority languages were brought in typically occurred when the students were relatively free to choose themes. So-called 'project weeks' provided such an opportunity. During project weeks, the students worked in groups with self-selected topics. As a compulsory part of these weeks' activities, the groups presented their projects in front of peers and teachers. The groups were encouraged to include a creative element in the presentation, and these creative elements in particular drew on resources associated with linguistic and/or ethnic backgrounds (see Møller, 2016). One example is a group of boys who chose to work with 'The multicultural society' and as their creative element served a specific type of Arabic cake. Another example is a group of girls who dressed up as well-known politicians and used this to discuss through the politicians political discourses concerning state-enforced removal of children with a migration background. In addition to making the presentations entertaining, the creative elements should disseminate and nuance the work of the project groups. In this way, they should (and did) not contradict the serious academic framing, and this is an academic element which constitutes an important difference from the magician performance described in the above. In fact, in general there was an increasing focus on grades as the students reached the final years. Students and teachers treated the presentations during project weeks seriously as the groups were graded for their work.

The incident we now turn to unfolded during a project week presentation (see also Møller, 2015). The presenting group consisted of three girls: Fartun (Somali background), Israh (Arabic background) and Mathilde (Danish majority background). While several other students spoke Arabic, Fartun was the only Somali speaker. The girls' topic was terrorism, their presentation mainly circulated around Islamic terrorism, and in conclusion they suggested a global unified strategy as a way to reduce terrorism. Present in the classroom were 20 students, two teachers (Inger and Janne), and two researchers (Jens Normann Jørgensen and Janus Spindler Møller). Inger, their class teacher, spent many hours weekly with the class and had done so for many years. Israh and Fartun wore radio microphones and another recorder captured the interaction going on between teachers and students. Our analysis is based on these recordings, field notes, and the slideshow presented by the group.

As the creative element in the presentation, the group had made a poem, which among other things consisted in an appeal to stop terrorism and increase intercultural respect. The girls had made a pre-recording of the poem where they performed it in three successive versions: in Arabic (Israh), in Somali (Fartun), and in Danish (Mathilde). Their idea was to play this recording during the presentation, and to prepare for this they had placed the sound file on the classroom computer. However, when they tried to locate the file during the presentation, they were unable to locate it. We will now address in detail what took place.

While the girls searched the classroom computer for the file, they conducted a whispered negotiation of an alternative plan, and they finally suggested to the teachers that they just read the Danish version aloud. The teachers, who did not seem to know about the poem before, now started asking clarifying questions. After a while the teachers suggested that the group members performed it on the spot, including the Arabic and Somali versions. Israh and Fartun in particular were very reluctant to do this. About four minutes after the girls discovered they could not find the sound file, the other students and the teachers started getting impatient however. Then Inger (the class teacher) decided to move the increasingly chaotic situation forward. The exchange below followed just after the other teacher (Janne) seemed to have accepted to get only the Danish version:

Transcript 2

Winter 2010; audio-recording

Participants: Inger (class teacher), Janne (helping teacher), Israh (student, group member), Fartun (student, group member)

Legend

(1.0)	pauses in seconds
(.)	pauses shorter than 0.5 second
[bla]	overlapping speech
(bla)	our comments
xxx	inaudible
(*bla bla*)	translation to English

	Original	*Translation*
01 Janne:	men så må Mathilde læse den danske version op	but then Mathilde has to read the Danish version
02 Inger:	jeg synes godt nok det er ærgeligt	I think it's such a shame
03 Janne:	ja det er rigtig	yes that's right
04 Inger:	det er rigtig rigtig ærgeligt	it's really really a shame
05 Israh:	vi havde brugt tid på det	we had spent time on it

06 Inger:	ja men (.) hvad med og øh og prøve at gøre det så godt I kan alligevel (.)	yes but (.) how about eh doing it as well as you can anyway (.)
07	øh det gør ikke noget der er pauser	eh it doesn't matter if there are breaks
08 Israh:	mm det tog	but it took
09 Inger:	prøv at læse det op tag digtet og [så prøv at oversætte det til] arabisk og somalisk	try to read it aloud take the poem and [then try to translate it to] Arabic and Somali
10 Fartun:	[nej det gider vi ikke] (whispered)	[no we don't want to]

As a reaction to the other teacher's suggestion, Inger states twice (in line 02 and 04) that it would be 'a shame' to not present the trilingual version of the poem. Inger never explicitly formulates why it is a shame but moves on to setting the course of the activity in line 06-07 and 09. Here she urges Fartun and Israh to perform the poem in Arabic and Somali, respectively. Thereby she turns the planned activity of playing a sound file prepared in advance into an activity of staged performance. Fartun (in line 10) instantly shows resistance and in the following exchanges both Fartun and Israh display discomfort. In what follows, we ask why and argue that the discomfort is related to a change of chronotopical understanding of the situation which the performance of minority languages in the classroom leads to.

Following the decision to make the girls perform individually, Inger starts putting pressure on Israh and Fartun and asks Israh to go first. The following two minutes, Israh states repeatedly that she does not want to. Now supported by Janne, Inger uses different persuasion strategies. For example, both teachers state that this is not an exam so therefore there is no reason to be nervous. While this is probably an attempt to calm Israh down, this argument also moves the situation away from the serious and exam-like atmosphere that otherwise characterizes the classroom activities on that day and into another chronotope (we will return to this). Israh keeps declining. Eventually several of the other students show signs of impatience, and this may be why Israh finally gives in. She delivers a detailed and fluent translation in Arabic, which indicates that her reluctance was not caused by insufficient language skills. Her presentation is followed by a loud applause.

After the applause, Inger calls for silence and gives the floor to Fartun. Fartun simply stays silent and ignores Inger's invitations. But Inger continues the persuasion attempts. In the following extract Fartun is finally pushed to perform the poem in Somali. The extract follows 13 seconds of silence:

Transcript 3

Winter 2010; audio-recording

Participants: Inger (class teacher), Israh (student, group member), Fartun (student, group member), Student (a classmate in the audience)

		Original	*Translation*
01	Inger:	altså Fartun du kan bilde mig hvad som helst ind fordi jeg kan ikke somalisk så ved du hvad bare nogle lyde på somalisk (.) det ville være helt fint	you know what Fartun you can make me believe anything because I don't know Somali so you know what just some sounds in Somali that would be just fine
		(giggling in the background)	
02	Israh:	[Fartun]	[Fartun]
03	Inger:	[kom i gang] (.) så tag den derfra (.) og hvis du ikke ved et ord (.)	[get started] (.) take it from there (.) and if you don't know a word (.)
04		så opfinder du det bare	you just make it up
05	Fartun:	okay (giggling)	okay
06	Student:	hun kan ikke forstå det	she can't understand it
07	Inger:	vi vil bare have den tone vi vil bare have sprogtonen (.) okay	we just want that tone we just want the language tone (.) okay
08	Fartun:	okay	okay
09	Inger:	du kan kalde det hvad det vil du kan sige det er en slikpind eller et eller	you can call it anything you want you can say that it is a lollipop or something that is in
10		andet altså på somalisk jeg ved det ikke (.) lad os så høre	Somali I don't know (.) let's hear it then
11	Israh:	hold din [kæft] (in low voice, giggling)	you [must be kidding me]

12 Inger:	[ssh]	[shush]
13 Israh:	det er [pinligt] (in low voice, giggling)	this is [embarrassing]
14 Fartun:	[okay]	[okay]
15 Inger:	ssh	shush

(Fartun performs the poem in Somali)

While trying to persuade Fartun to perform the poem, Inger spells out what she expects to get out of the presentation, this for the first time. Inger states that Fartun can actually say anything since Inger is unable to understand it anyway (line 01). Again this is probably an attempt to make Fartun relax (and then perform), but at the same time it constructs Somali as only of aesthetic value in the situation. Inger elaborates on her line of argumentation (line 03, 07) by explicating that Fartun may just invent words and that all they want is the 'language tone'. She even increases the pressure by using 'we' instead of 'I' (line 07), thereby representing a larger group than herself (though we do not know exactly who the 'we' refers to – the teachers or the entire class). Inger finally illustrates Fartun's possibility of saying anything she wants in Somali – even just 'lollipop' (lines 9-10); this adds a comical component to the line of persuasion. Again, the jocular contribution is most likely an attempt to relieve the tense atmosphere, but again it renders Somali denotationally meaningless and with no relation to the academic content of the group's presentation.

Now the situation has moved quite far away from a serious poem about suicide bombers and intercultural understanding. Inger has – probably unintentionally – constructed the Somali as exotic entertainment with comical undertones rather than as part of an academic endeavor. Seen in this light it is not surprising that Israh (standing next to Fartun) whisperingly indicates that she is embarrassed (line 11–13). However, the final outcome is that Fartun performs. She presents a very competent translation of the written Danish text, and again it is likely that her embarrassment has to do with something else than her Somali language skills. Just after Fartun's presentation, the classmates deliver loud applause. Then Mathilde reads the Danish version. There is no hesitation before and the classmates' reaction is a more hesitant applause. This version is treated as neither embarrassing nor worthy of special attention. In contrast, the loud applause from the audience following the Arabic and the Somali version could indicate appreciation of the use of minority languages in the classroom or perhaps recognition of the effort it takes for Israh and

Fartun to overcome themselves. What remains is the question of why both girls resented so vehemently performing the poem in Arabic and Somali.

To the extent that Inger's argumentation expresses a more general ideology concerning minority languages in the classroom, the extract provides a potential answer to our question. Minority language use is to a large degree treated as incompatible with the identity potential offered by the chronotope of classroom presentation. Speaking Arabic or Somali does not index being an academically successful student, and does not point to school contexts (or educationally relevant content). Listening to Somali is treated as an aesthetic experience rather than as part of rational and serious activities. This demonstrates how minority languages invoke a chronotopical understanding of the classroom space as now a room for exotic and comical entertainment. In this way, the combination of staged classroom performance and minority languages ends up offering Israh and Fartun identities similar to 'The Turkish magician-clown' in case 1, with the important difference that Fartun and Israh did not opt for this identity nor do they try to exploit the potentials in it. At first the result is that Fartun and Israh try to opt out of the chronotopic frame of classroom presentation and the teachers' description of the outcome as academically unimportant, but entertaining, does not at all improve the students' motivation to perform. Only massive pressure from especially the teacher Inger gets Israh and Fartun to continue.

At this point, we want to stress that Inger had good reason for what she did, and that she was well-liked by both researchers and students. Inger's first priority seemed to be to get the presentation back on track. It is likely that she tried to get the girls to complete their initial idea and perhaps even wished to demonstrate a welcoming attitude towards the linguistic diversity among the students. Unfortunately, the outcome was somehow the opposite. The attempt to involve minority languages ended up displaying their lack of legitimacy in classroom interaction – apart from a certain entertainment potential and aesthetic value. On this basis, it is not difficult to understand Fartun and Israh's reluctance toward using Somali and Arabic. From being a streamlined presentation, the situation entered into a vicious circle. The girls' reluctance related to performing the poem in Somali and Arabic made the teachers spell out the frivolous, but potentially comical entertaining value associated with the use of minority languages. The metacommentary whispered by Israh and Fartun displayed their aversions and increasing discomfort. In the end Inger won the struggle, but this probably had more to do with the distribution of power in the classroom than with a change in Israh and Fartun's understanding and attitudes toward bringing Arabic and Somali into a serious project presentation.

This raises two additional questions: Why did the girls choose to introduce minority languages in their presentation in the first place? And what is the difference between playing Arabic and Somali on a recording and presenting (or performing) them 'live'? To us, the trilingual version of the poem symbolically unites the three voices into one. The juxtaposition of the three languages provides the same message as the propositional content of intercultural understanding and peace. There is thus an iconic relation between form and content. Of course we do not know to what degree the girls had these types of reflections, but what we do know is that this line of interpretation was not offered in class. When the teachers were discussing the presentation with the girls afterwards, the poem was not mentioned at all, neither in terms of content nor just the performance. With regard to the second question, we see the pre-recording as allowing the girls to avoid live, classroom performance. This had the potential to make the poem more generic, less personal, and it could be a strategy to avoid a chronotope that links use of minority languages to mere entertainment, and the girls to the identities of entertainers rather than academically-oriented students in the timespace of the classroom.

Concluding Remarks

Blommaert (2015: 14) argues that ethnic labels and linguistic resources associated with minorities are among tropic emblems that can lead directly to chronotopic interpretations, not least in the educational setting. This seems to us to apply almost perfectly to the cases we have analyzed in this chapter. In our analyses, we have paid particular attention to the interaction between the platform event and the school presentation as chronotopes. We have argued that both invite heightened awareness concerning linguistic form. We discussed the intrinsic relationship between situationally available identities, linguistic resources and activity types as they unfold in time and space. In the first case, Selda created a comical *persona* who came from Turkey, used 'street language' and 'learner Danish', made rude comments to members of the audience, and performed unsuccessful magic tricks. This *persona* was well received by the audience. In the second case, Fartun and Israh only reluctantly performed in Somali and Arabic in class when their original plan to play a poem recorded in advance needed adjustment. The more Israh and Fartun expressed their reluctance (or simply kept quiet), the more detailed the teacher outlined her idea of the role of the languages (especially Somali). As a result, the trilingual poem in the presentation ended up as 'the language tone of Somali' where Fartun for that matter could replace any word with 'lollipop' without anybody noticing as long as it was 'in Somali'. The two cases both point to the association of linguistic resources associated with ethnic minorities (whether minority languages or accented Danish) with comical entertainment and, as a result, lack of seriousness in an academic setting. In both cases, these chronotopic understandings were revealed in the metacommentaries – of course with the important difference that in one case the student Selda exploited the chronotope to her own advantage and in the other, the chronotopic understanding was laid out by the teacher leading to Israh and Fartun's expressions of reluctance and embarrassment. Together we think that the cases illustrate how the presence of language associated with ethnic minority backgrounds may invoke a chronotope of non-academic, potentially comical entertainment. The links between language, value, stereotypes, etc., were not problematized in the discussions that followed (at least not those discussions we have had access to). This suggests that in the longer run, from a distance or at a different *scale*, both cases may end up supporting a chronotopic structure in which language resources associated with ethnic minorities are detached from the perception of what counts as legitimate and valuable language use in mainstream education.

Taking a more applied perspective, our use of the theoretical lens of chronotopes points to ways of engaging with the instances of language associated with minorities. The 'Turkish magician' case could easily lead to a discussion of relations between language use and stereotypes and to expectations regarding language use in school. Concerning the trilingual poem, this could (as already suggested) be discussed in the light of the project it occurred in, and furthermore be used for discussions of linguistic and cultural diversity and challenges in connection to translation. These approaches presuppose that language resources associated with minority speakers may be seen as potentially valuable contributions in mainstream education. Yet, this is not the case at present. It is important that it is not our goal to criticize individual teachers. The teachers did their best to teach the children skills and competences valued by larger society, and they had never been encouraged to engage academically with linguistic diversity in the classrooms. Our point is that there was little room to imagine how to accommodate other semiotic resources than those connected to mainstream Danish-ness in educational activities. The unfortunate links made between language and stereotypes in class were not problematized in the discussions that followed. This illustrates the charged position of minority students in general and it suggests that on a longer run both cases may end up supporting the chronotopic organization that detaches language resources associated with ethnic minorities from the perception of what counts as valuable language use in mainstream education. So in conclusion, mainstream Danish education may not ridicule the immigrant Other intentionally. Yet, it creates him or her as an Other, and neglects the possibility of discussing ways of being a good school-child which do not involve speaking standard Danish, or speaking standard Danish all the time. Linguistic resources associated with the minority speaker become emblems of deviant behavior, they become shibboleths of a chronotope which stands in opposition to mainstream education.

Notes

(1) This performance has also been analyzed by Nørreby (2017). We agree with Nørreby on most of his observations and conclusions, but our aim is different. We are interested in relating this performance to a chronotopic understanding and the effects of introducing language associated with immigrants in mainstream classes. Nørreby is studying the multiple meanings of the register used by Selda as well as a child in a different school.
(2) Selda may have slightly fewer glottal stops than would be expected from a contemporary Copenhagen raised child, but it is very hard to determine for sure. Overall her language is indistinguishable from what one would expect from a native speaker of Danish.
(3) In the post-performance session, Selda's performance receives two comments by her class-mates who mention elements that they found 'funny'. One says: 'I think it is funny when Selda she says oh (.) it's your birthday oh well okay I will just send you a carrot'. All of this pronounced by the child in a way that recalls 'circus Danish', or adult learner Danish. The other classmate mentions the 'or else I will kill you', which is done in a way that evokes a gangster register. This means that each of the classmates has recognized a different sociolinguistic aspect of her performance. In addition, it shows that her way of speaking has been noticed and taken up by her classmates, and that they are able to recognize the registers or styles that she is drawing on.

References

Ag, A. (2010) *Sprogbrug og identitetsarbejde hos senmoderne storbypiger. Københavnerstudier i tosprogethed* 53. København: Københavns Universitet.
Agha, A. (2007) Recombinant selves in mass mediated spacetime. *Language & Communication* 27 (3), 320–335.
Anderson, B. (2006) *Imagined Communities: Reflections on the Origin and Spread of Nationalism* (Revised edition). London: Verso (original work published 1983).
Bakhtin, M. (1981) *The Dialogic Imagination: Four Essays* (edited by M. Holquist; translated by C. Emerson and M. Holquist). Austin: University of Texas Press.
Bell, A. and Gibson, A. (2011) Staging language: An introduction to the sociolinguistics of performance. *Journal of Sociolinguistics* 15 (5), 555–572.
Blommaert, J. (2015) Chronotopes, scales and complexity in the study of language in society. *Annual Review of Anthropology* 44, 105–116.
Blommaert, J. and De Fina, A. (2017) Chronotopic identities: On the timespace organization of who we are. In A. De Fina, D. Ikizoglu and J. Wegner (eds) *Diversity and Superdiversity: Sociocultural Linguistic Perspectives* (pp. 1–15). Washington: Georgetown University Press.
Bourdieu, P. (1991) *Language & Symbolic Power*. Harvard: Harvard University Press.

Carr, E.S. and Lempert, M. (2016) Introduction: The pragmatics of scale. In E.S. Carr and M. Lempert (eds) *Scale: Discourse and dimensions of social life* (pp. 1–21). Oakland: University of California Press.

Coupland, N. (2001) Dialect stylization in radio talk. *Language in Society* 30 (3), 345–375.

Daugaard, L.M. (2018) Fleksibel flersprogethed i modtagelsesklassen. In L.M. Daugaard, N. Hauge Jensen and K. Søndergård Kristensen (eds) *Nyankomne elever i skolen. Sprogpædagogiske perspektiver på basisundervisning i dansk som andetsprog* (pp. 58–77). Aarhus: KVaN.

Glenn, P.J. (2003) *Laughter in Interaction*. Cambridge: Cambridge University Press.

Goffman, E. (1983) The interaction order: American Sociological Association, 1982 Presidential Address. *American Sociological Review* 48 (1), 1–17.

Horst, C. and Gitz-Johansen, T. (2010) Education of ethnic minority children in Denmark: Monocultural hegemony and counterpositions. *Intercultural Education* 21 (1), 137–151.

Hyttel-Sørensen, L. (2011) Children and language attitudes: A study of language attitudes among eight year old children in Denmark. In J.S. Møller and J.N. Jørgensen (eds) *Language Enregisterment and Attitudes* 63 (pp. 10–26). Copenhagen: University of Copenhagen.

Hyttel-Sørensen, L. (2017) 'Gangster' or 'wannabe'. Experimental and ethnographic approaches to a contemporary urban vernacular in Copenhagen. PhD thesis, University of Copenhagen.

Irvine, J.T. and Gal, S. (2000) Language ideology and linguistic differentiation. In P.V. Kroskrity (ed.) *Regimes of Language: Ideologies, Polities, and Identities* (pp. 35–84). Santa Fe, New Mexico: School of American Research Press.

Karrebæk, M.S. (2013) 'Don't speak like that to her!' Linguistic minority children's socialization into an ideology of monolingualism. *Journal of Sociolinguistics* 17 (3), 355–375.

Karrebæk, M.S. (2016) 'I am lucky I can speak Arabic': The use of Arabic in the linguistic hegemony in Copenhagen. In D. Duncker and B. Perregaard (eds) *Creativity and Continuity: Perspectives on the Dynamics of Language Conventionalisation* (pp. 281–306). Copenhagen: UPress.

Karrebæk, M.S. and Ghandchi, N. (2017) The very sensitive question: Chronotopes, insecurities and Farsi heritage language classrooms. *Pragmatics & Society* 8 (1), 38–60.

Kirilova, M. (2006) Han er en fra Amager, men også lidt fra Afrika, b. 40: holdninger til accent: en empirisk baseret undersøgelse af indfødte danskeres holdninger til dansk sprog med forskellige accenter. Københavnerstudier i tosprogethed 40. København: Københavns Universitet.

Kristjánsdóttir, B. (2018) *Uddannelsespolitik i nationalismens tegn*. Aarhus: Universitetsforlag.

Madsen, L.M. (2013) 'High' and 'low' in urban Danish speech styles. *Language in Society* 42, 115–138.

Madsen, L.M., Karrebæk, M.S. and Møller, J.S. (eds) (2016) *Everyday Languaging: Collaborative Research on the Language Use of Children and Youth*. Berlin: Mouton de Gruyter.

Maegaard, M. (2007) Udtalevariation og – forandring i københavnsk, en etnografisk undersøgelse af sprogbrug, sociale kategorier og social praksis blandt unge på en københavnsk folkeskole. Det Humanistiske Fakultet: Københavns Universitet.

Møller, J.S. (2009) Poly-lingual interaction across childhood, youth and adulthood. PhD thesis, University of Copenhagen.

Møller, J.S. (2015) The enregisterment of minority languages in a Danish classroom. In A. Agha and Frog (eds) *Registers of Communication* (Studia Fennica Linguistica 18) (pp. 107–123). Helsinki: Finnish Litterature Society.

Møller, J.S. (2016) Discursive reactions to nationalism among adolescents in Copenhagen. In L.M. Madsen, M.S. Karrebæk and J.S. Møller (eds) *Everyday Languaging: Collaborative Research on the Language Use of Children and Youth* (pp. 219–242). Berlin: Mouton de Gruyter.

Møller, J.S. (2017) 'You Black Black': Polycentric norms for the use of terms associated with ethnicity. In K. Arnaut, M.S. Karrebæk, M. Spotti and J. Blommaert (eds) *Engaging Superdiversity: Recombining Spaces, Times and Language Practices* (pp. 123–146). Bristol: Multilingual Matters.

Munn, N. (1986) *The Fame of Gawa: A Symbolic Study of Value Transformation in a Massim (Papua New Guinea) Society*. Cambridge: Cambridge University Press

Nassri, L. (2016) 'Well, because we are the One Direction girls' – Popular culture, friendship and social status in a peer group. In L.M. Madsen, M.S. Karrebæk and J.S. Møller (eds) *Everyday Languaging: Collaborative Research on the Language Use of Children and Youth* (pp. 145–166). Berlin: Mouton de Gruyter.

Nørreby, T.R. (2017) Language and social status differences in two urban schools. PhD thesis, University of Copenhagen.

Østergård, U. (2018) Homo nationalis: det nationale menneske. In D. Budtz Pedersen, F. Collin and F. Stjernfelt (eds) *Kampen om mennesket: Forskellige menneskebilleder og deres grænsestrid* (pp. 93–132). København: Hans Reitzels Forlag.

Padovan-Özdemir, M. and Moldenhawer, B. (2016) Making precarious migrant families and weaving the well-fare nation-state fabric 1970-2010. *Race, Ethnicity and Education* 20 (6), 723–736.

Perrino, S. (2011) Chronotopes of story and storytelling event in interviews. *Language in Society* 40 (1), 91–103.

Rampton, B. (2009) Interaction ritual and not just artful performance in crossing and stylization. *Language in Society* 38 (2), 149–176.

Shankar, S. (2008) Speaking like a model minority: 'FOB' styles, gender, and racial meanings among Desi teens in Silicon Valley. *Journal of Linguistic Anthropology* 18 (2), 268–289.

Silverstein, M. (1985) Language and the culture of gender: At the intersection of structure, usage, and ideology. In E. Mertz and R. Parmentier (eds) *Semiotic Mediation: Sociocultural and Psychological Perspectives* (pp. 219–259). New York: Academic Press.

Silverstein, M. (2005) Axes of evals: Token versus type interdiscursivity. *Journal of Linguistic Anthropology* 15 (1), 6–22.

Stæhr, A. (2010) '*Rappen reddede os*' – *et studie af senmoderne storbydrenges identitetsarbejde i fritids- og skolemiljøer*. Københavnerstudier i tosprogethed 54. København: Københavns Universitet.

Stæhr, A. (2014) Social media and everyday language use among Copenhagen youth. PhD thesis, University of Copenhagen.

Stæhr, A. and Madsen, L.M. (2016) Ghetto language in Danish mainstream rap. *Language & Communication* 52, 60–72.

Wortham, S. and Reyes, A. (2015) *Discourse Analysis beyond the Speech Event*. London & New York: Routledge.

9 Out of Order: Authenticity and Normativity in Communication at School

Jos Swanenberg

Introduction

In present day society, due to globalization and digitalization cultural and linguistic change is more important than ever before. Change is omnipresent and it results in both an increase of diversity and new forms of diversity, leading to superdiversity, i.e. 'the diversification of diversity' (Blommaert, 2010; Vertovec, 2007). Although until recently scholarly attention has predominantly focused on areas where these processes and phenomena of cultural and linguistic change are most visible, such as large urban centers and the contemporary metropolis, they also affect the margins. By margins or peripheries we mean for instance the outskirts of big cities, smaller nations in the global south, or border regions of nations in the global north (Kroon & Swanenberg, 2019). This massive change also has linguistic, cultural and discursive consequences for pre-eminently linguistic institutions such as schools. Children come from very different home situations and bring their highly diverse linguistic and cultural backgrounds and skills into school, where they meet with a strongly normative context, also language-wise: the standard language is the main means of communication in class situations. As a consequence, children from very diverse linguistic and cultural backgrounds have to learn how to relate to the normative context of the standard language.

As children of school age learn to relate to the standard language, some will find this difficult and therefore show marked or deviant language behavior. They will have to learn to deal with different language varieties and repertoires in different contexts of time and place. They are confronted with different expectations as it comes to the choice of register: what school expects from them may differ from what their peers expect during lunch breaks and also from what their family at home expects. This requires children to learn how to use various linguistic repertoires: standard language, colloquial talk (e.g. street language), home language (e.g. dialect) etc. The question this leads to is how they do this and how they learn to do this or, in other words, how they acquire knowledge and awareness of the connectedness of repertoires and registers with the context of space and time?

In practice, people never learn 'a language' totally, but rather 'specific and specialized bits of language, sufficient to grant them "voice" and to make themselves understood by others' (Blommaert, 2005: 255). People thus gather the necessary linguistic elements and structures in order to have a voice in specific contexts, in specific time frames and with specific interlocutors. Language learning processes 'develop in a variety of learning environments and through a variety of learning modes, ranging from regimented and uniform learning modes characterizing schools and other formal learning environments, to fleeting and ephemeral "encounters" with language in informal learning environments' (Blommaert & Velghe, 2014: 138). Moreover, not only language is learned in those various ways, but also the necessary metalinguistic and metapragmatic knowledge about distinct languages and language varieties and the situations where and when they can be used.

The data presented in this chapter are partly from the countryside of the Dutch province of Limburg, where local dialect as a mother tongue is still not unusual, and partly from the neighboring province of Noord-Brabant, where local dialect as the mother tongue for small children has become already rather unusual nowadays. In Noord-Brabant, dialects are rapidly changing, they have lost their position to Dutch as a mother tongue, and they are in a process of convergence and levelling. This means that the language system for many people no longer is diglossic but has become diaglossic (Auer, 2005). In diaglossia, a language system with the dialect as a mother tongue for informal domains and the standard language for formal domains, has changed into a continuum system that allows for context driven shifts within, i.e. somewhere in between dialect and standard language. There is no clear-cut linguistic distinction anymore between the dialect (or vernacular) and the standard language, but there is an entire continuum of intermediate variations. Diaglossia does not lead to a stable system of intermediate variants (cf. Auer, 2011: 491), but represents a language repertoire with language features that may be associated with sociocultural categories. Then, dialect often is learned not as a separate language system but as a set of linguistic features that can be applied in colloquial language. Although dialect may be losing ground, colloquial language still has abundant regional features in vocabulary, phonology and syntax.

Shifts in language use however are still perceived as shifts from one language variety to another. Dialect and standard are associated with different contexts, domains and identities. People tend to regard language variation in terms of dichotomous concepts such as standard versus non-standard – in the Netherlands *Algemeen Beschaafd Nederlands* (common civilized Dutch) versus *plat, straattaal, dialect* (vernacular, street language, dialect). Such representations of languages as distinct categories, with ascribed systems and authenticities, is quite usual in the public domain. It is built on ideologies of language as a fact. In concrete interaction however, language is more like an act, as in '(polylingual) languaging' (Jørgensen, 2008; Jørgensen *et al.*, 2016). We use language for communication and for identification; language is something we do and identities are made of how we behave. Languaging leads to diverse and dynamic language utterances; language varieties are no more than sets of linguistic features that share a specific distribution in a given society. In what follows I will use the term 'repertoire' to refer to the linguistic resources an interlocutor will use within a particular context, and 'standard' and 'vernacular' to distinguish between more standard-like utterances, expected in more formal situations, and non-standard utterances, expected in informal situations. I will use terms like 'dialect' and 'standard Dutch', when referring to ideological categories of language, when for instance discussed by students or their teachers.

In the first part of this chapter, I will show transcripts of conversations from several case studies at schools for secondary education that tell us about the awareness of and dealing with the connectedness between context and choice of repertoire. The participants, adolescents in the Dutch province of Noord-Brabant, engage in interactions with their peers during school breaks. In such events, we see how shifts of repertoire tell us how language choice is connected to the specific framework in which an event takes place.

In the second part, we first look at how children in their first years at school in the province of Limburg, learn to deal with different language varieties and repertoires in different contexts. In doing so the question will be addressed how knowledge and awareness of the connectedness of repertoires with events emerge. Finally, we will look at the meaning different language varieties have for older students in primary school (in Tilburg, Noord-Brabant) and what metapragmatic knowledge they display about different varieties of speech. Together, these transcripts tell a story on what it means to 'know' a language and how to learn to fit in the community of its users.

Chronotopes and Identities

When learning the connectedness between repertoires and registers and the context of time and space, awareness of norms and values regarding language behavior is imperative. A school is an environment that imposes external top-down norms for behavior. It represents a certain structure of time and space where linguistic norms are standard, in much the same way as Bakhtin (1981) theorized the ensemble of time and space in his analysis of the novel. He coined the term chronotope to point towards the inseparability of time and space in human social action. In Bakhtin's work a chronotope is an intrinsic time-space relation where characters move and activities take place that fit a certain (situation in a) narrative. Chronotopes call for certain premises to meet the conditions of fitting a certain framework. As Bakhtin developed the concept of chronotope to describe the expectations to various types of texts, we can also describe and analyze the expectations to various events and situations (Silverstein, 2005). The chronotope not only implies the inseparability of time and space in human social action but also the effects of this inseparability on social action. Language behavior functioning as a means of communication and identification is prototypical for such social action.

In what follows, I will deal with language use in specific contexts of time and space and repertoire shifts during conversations at school. I will analyze such repertoire shifts as instances of breaking the norms of the chronotope of an educational institution, in the classroom as well as in peer interaction (e.g. during breaks). Where language use in the classroom has to fulfil certain expectations, namely the institutional norms of speaking the standard language, language use in interactions with peers may well have to fulfil other expectations, e.g. speaking vernacular and by doing so, showing that you know how to behave within a group of peers.

These shifts of repertoire are indexical of identity work. The specific time and place of an event influence the choices children make in, for instance, using vernacular or standard language in daily practices. Because language choice has cultural and social meaning, the specific time and place of an event trigger children's active and passive knowledge of languages and language varieties.

When children grow older and become adolescents, the diversity of their language use increases, because their social and cultural environment and behavior changes. Especially in conversations outside the classroom, their vernacular is very diverse and contains dialect features, language innovations, and features from distinct minority and majority languages. Interlocutors may use language in a way that may be declined in other contexts as inauthentic and incorrect. Furthermore, their language practices are reflected upon, mocked, ridiculed and used for teasing, through which the 'order' can be changed. Recent studies in youth language show the intertwining of local and foreign features, due to urbanization and globalization. The studies that Jaspers (2005) carried out at a secondary school in Antwerp show that, in contrast with general stereotypes about their supposed incompetence in Dutch, Moroccan boys deliberately and skillfully style several Dutch varieties to wrong-foot the people in authority, their teachers. Jaspers links these moments of 'linguistic sabotage' to 'ritually sensitive moments', i.e. 'moments at which actual or potential rips show up in the routine fabric of social life' (Jaspers, 2005: 290). A crucial element of this practice is 'doing ridiculous' by mixing all kinds of linguistic varieties (e.g. exaggerated forms of Antwerp dialect, standard Dutch, Dutch as if incompletely acquired, quasi ethnolect), in order to fake enthusiasm and an eagerness to learn, to stimulate ignorance and to create other kinds of ambiguity and inauthenticity. All of this is done for the sake of causing delay, confusion and unauthorized pleasure, especially in the context of boring activities:

> zie, zeker als Marokkaan hé, als ge, snapte, als ge me- Belgen begint te praten me- zo'n taaltje van pam-pam dan zeggen die, dan denken die [Antwerps:] *amai joeng die Makak die kan geen Nederlands* maar, maar als ge gelijk ons zé dan z- dan denken die [Antwerps:] *amai joenge! die kennen beter Nederlands dan ons potverdoeme hoe komt da?*
>
> (look, especially as a Moroccan, if you, you see, if you start talking to Belgians with a language like pam-pam then they'll say then they'll think [Antwerp dialect:] *man, this wog doesn't know any Dutch* but, but when you're like us then – then they'll think [Antwerp dialect:] *freakin' hell! they speak better Dutch than us dash it how's this possible?*) (Jaspers, 2005: 290)

This extract shows how the speaker is aware of different repertoires and different types of normativity. This type of 'deviant' language use is not merely a matter of shifting between repertoires or registers. It is constantly changing and it draws upon a great variety of repertoires, some of which the students may not even be conscious of and some of which they will hardly be proficient in (Blommaert & Backus, 2013). On the other hand they will correct each other when speaking the 'wrong' language variety in a certain timespace context. In other words, there is an awareness of norms and values regarding language behavior.

This awareness indicates that authenticity and normativity are not abandoned altogether in youth language. It is not a matter of 'anything goes'. Authenticity and normativity are differently and flexibly applied, according to concrete contexts, defined by time and space. Style shift situations reconfirm chronotopes, the contexts that are given indexical meaning. In these contexts, place and time are consubstantial, since usually everything that happens at a certain moment must happen somewhere (cf. Basso, 1996). Talking about events that happened once and somewhere, takes a storyteller and his interlocutors back to that specific moment in that specific place. Furthermore, it often takes them back to language behavior that fits this specific chronotope, which may well be another register than the register that fits the context at the moment the memory is shared. Place and time are not just a stage for the event that is reflected upon, but they matter, they are actively taking part in the story. The sharing of such narratives and memories makes experiences and evaluations collectively available, and as such they are the building blocks of collective identity work. As said, chronotopes ask for specific, appropriate choices of culture and language; they are connected to a behavioral script (Blommaert, 2017). A behavioral script is a sequence of behaviors that fits a certain chronotope. When specific patterns of social behavior belong to particular chronotopic configurations, they 'fit', while when they don't they are 'out of place' or 'out of order' (Blommaert, 2015). Therefore, children run the risk of being out of order when they deviate from the standard norms in school (see also Karrebæk & Møller, in this volume) or when they deviate from the norms their peers apply to informal situations such as school breaks.

In Time and Place, Still Out of Order

The dominant language in most school situations of course is the standard language. In primary and secondary education in the Netherlands one of the most important school subjects is the Dutch language, and in almost every school Dutch is also the language of instruction for all other school subjects, except for the modern foreign languages which are ideally taught through those languages. On the other hand we know that the student population is highly diverse, also regarding their various home languages or mother tongues. Young people are very creative language users; for good reason we speak of youth language, street talk, etc. Moreover, secondary schools are hothouses for the construction of identities.

Eckert (2003: 382) describes the specific context youngsters find themselves in at school as follows:

> What is commonly ignored is the fact that adolescents are not simply left to develop into adults, but are put into institutions that isolate them from adults. This situation produces a social hothouse, in which a social order emerges that solidifies the gender hierarchy as well as class, racial, and ethnic hierarchies. Adolescence slows time for the age group as, rather than focusing on getting to adulthood, adolescents enter into a kind of time warp – or a cultural sink – in which adolescence is not something to pass through, but something to achieve. And in the process, people become not more adult, but more adolescent, as the ultimate adolescent is the oldest: the high school senior. 'Adolescent culture', in other words, is very much the product of the place given to adolescents in our society.

When talking and thinking about the chronotopicity of language behavior, secondary school is a highly interesting research setting, because it is there where we see behavioral scripts at work. Adolescents show they know how to behave in certain events, they adapt their language use to the top-down norms of an educational institution, as school expects them to, and to that of their peers during lunch breaks, as these peers expect them to. In the transcripts of conversations below, we witness small disruptions when shifts of repertoire violate the framework of the behavioral scripts. This leads to one of the interlocutor's behavior being regarded as out of order. Furthermore, shifts of repertoire can be used to correct on behavior out of order.

The following four transcripts are from video recordings in various secondary schools, all situated in the Province of Noord-Brabant in the south of the Netherlands. Data were gathered in several case studies. The researchers were not present during the recordings the adolescents, on our request, made of the conversations they were having during lunch breaks. We simply asked them to share or discuss things they experienced recently, offered soft drinks and cake, put on the recording device (with their own and the schools' consent) and left the room. This way, we tried to gather data on spontaneous conversations with as little influence of the research setup as possible. Afterwards we spoke with them about their social, educational and linguistic background, their hobbies, sports, online activities etc. using a short list of questions. The names of all participants have been changed to protect their privacy.

The first transcript is from recordings in Roosendaal, where three students (aged 14, 15 and 16) are discussing living in the nearby hamlet of Kruisland, where the grandparents of one of the girls live.

Transcript 1

	Original	Translation
Anne:	Die wonen wel in dat kutdorp.	They do live in that shit hole [lit. cunt-village].
Fleur:	Nee, klein gehucht.	No, small hamlet.
Laurens:	Dat is geen kutdorp. Echt serieus, als jullie daar wonen dan is dat voor jullie echt leuk. Wedden, als jullie daar wonen vind je het leuk.	It is not a shit hole. Seriously, when you live there, you would enjoy it, really. Want to bet, when you live there, you enjoy it.
Anne:	Ik heb er gewoond.	I used to live there.
Laurens:	(...) dat je weg wilde. Nee da's leuk.	(...) that you wanted to leave. No, that's fun.
Anne:	Ja, toen was het nog wel leuk. Dat was in mijn jongere jaren.	Yes, back then it was fun. That was in my younger years.
Fleur:	Ach, meske toch.	Ah, poor girl

Living in a hamlet like Kruisland is considered boring, but then Anne admits she used to live there herself. Laurens, who still lives in Kruisland, replies 'that you wanted to leave' indicating she did not enjoy it. Anne says she *did* enjoy it, in her younger years. Then Fleur reacts, suddenly shifting from a hardly regionally colored conversation towards the local dialect, saying 'Ah, poor girl'.

Fleur reported in the interview afterwards not to speak dialect; she indeed hardly has a regional accent, not even the typical soft /g/ from this region. Still she suddenly uses the catchphrase *Ach, meske toch*, with a soft /g/ in *Ach*. She does this for the purpose of irony: showing compassion, but in a ridiculing manner, through a shift towards the dialect. By using this sort of vernacular, Fleur tells Anne to shape up: 'do not even think about such a boring hamlet as a fun place' (Dekkers, 2012: 32–33). The shift of repertoire functions as a corrective measure, telling Anne she is out of order when mentioning that living in a hamlet was fun. By shifting towards vernacular, Fleur aims for a correction through ridicule. This shows how a shift of repertoire can be used to address a fellow student who does not follow the behavioral script (one should regard living in a hamlet as boring). The shift then functions as a measure against behavior that is considered out of order.

In another sample from video recordings made in a secondary school in the city of 's-Hertogenbosch, a 15-year-old boy who is born and raised in that same city, and whose parents are Turkish, shares the table with three girls. The conversation does not go too well, awkward silence falls, and the boy decides to call a friend. He does this using a mobile phone he borrows from one of the girls, so that this friend, who is also from Turkish descent, does not know who is calling him (we obviously have no recordings of the answers, marked with [GSM]).

Transcript 2

	Original	*Translation*
Boy:	*Ewa koelie.*	Hey koelie.
[GSM]		
Boy:	*Ewa dreri hoe izzie?*	Hey boy, how is it [going]?
[GSM]		
Boy:	*Oh god, jonguh.*	Oh god, boy.
[GSM]		
Boy:	*Eeh gabbuh, hoe izzie jonguh, dreri? Rade, raad, raad wie ik ben.*	Hey mate, how is it [going] boy, boy? Guess, guess, guess who I am.

The boy does not tell his friend his name, leaving him in doubt about the identity of the caller. The speaker uses features that originate from immigrant languages, but not from his own Turkish home language. He uses the term *ewa dreri* (Arabic for 'hey kids', although he addresses a singular person here), and *koelie* – a Malay term that was used to address wage slaves in former British India and the former Dutch East Indies. However, *koelie* became a derogatory term for immigrants from India and Pakistan and it is currently used by Surinamese creoles to ridicule Surinamese Hindustanis (De Coster, 2007; Van Donselaar, 1989), referring to their Indian descent. Arabic and Malay are not his nor his interlocutor's home languages. Thus, he mixes different features from different linguistic registers, in a very specific context, addressing a friend, teasing him and fooling around. There is no one-to-one correspondence between ethnic background and the use of features from matching immigrant languages. These features simply come up when needed and are playfully applied in conversation. However, they are not simply used as part of a sociolect, excluding or including potential group members, but for special purposes in joking, insulting, and fooling around (Mutsaers & Swanenberg, 2012; see also Jaspers, 2005). The Arabic and Surinam-connected lexis appears in the playful mobile phone conversation, whereas some vernacular words that are considered as part of the city dialect come up when talking to the girls who were like the boy also born and raised in 's-Hertogenbosch.

Language shifts into this mingled type of 'street talk' as soon as the conversation at the phone starts. Talking to his friend on the phone gives the situation a new interlocutor and a new context: it evokes language that fits 'hanging out with friends on the streets after school', a chronotope quite distinct from the school situation that requires proper Dutch in the classroom or Dutch vernacular coloured with local features when sitting at a table with three girls from the same city. Shifts of repertoire are tied to behavioural scripts, meeting the expectations of various interlocutors and fitting these different chronotopes. The speech sample presented is not or hardly comprehensible for other people than the peers, making it a fine example of adolescent culture (see Eckert, 2003).

In the next transcript two boys in the village of Uden are discussing a Turkish word. Peter is from the Dutch Caribbean, Erol is born in the Netherlands, and his parents are Turkish immigrants.

Transcript 3

	Original	*Translation*
Peter:	*Oh ja wat was trouwens lelijk in het Turks? Iets met sukir.*	Right, and what was ugly in Turkish again? Something with sukir.
Erol:	*Çirkin.*	Ugly.
Peter:	*Çirkin, ja, dat zei mijn broertje. Die kende, kende çirkin.*	*Çirkin*, yes, that was what my brother said. He knew, knew *çirkin*.
Erol:	*Jouw broertje is Turk?*	Your brother is a Turk?
Peter:	*Ja, hij gaat, hij gaat, hij gaat om met Turken. Leert hij allemaal van die, ja, noemen ze straattaal, maar ik noem het Turks, dus ja.*	Well, yes, he associates with Turks. He learns all these, well, they call it street talk but I call it Turkish, so yes.

Erol and Peter discuss Peter's brother, who knows the Turkish word *çirkin*. Peter explains his brother associates with boys from Turkish descent and learns Turkish words, which by them is defined as 'street talk'. Erol asks Peter ironically 'so your brother is a Turk?', thus questioning his identity by addressing the authenticity of his speech, as if the brother is a wannabee Turk. We are used to connect language to identity, but just as in Transcript 2, language, authenticity and identity are played with, exchanged and questioned by these youngsters in their everyday conversations. This shows how a specific repertoire is part of the behavioral script of adolescent culture, with its street talk and associations of ethnic groups, in this case Turks. Yet, someone who is part of that ethnic group and thus a connoisseur of the language, will question the authenticity of the chronotopic identity the brother, who is not a Turk, tries to assume by using *çirkin*.

A conversation between three boys in another school in the small village of Mill, in the northeast of Noord-Brabant, shows their loyalty to a vernacular that contains features from the regional countryside dialect. Consistent with their preferences for motocross, mechanic engineering, fishing, and 'farmer's music' (a type of rock music that appeals to life in the countryside), it is beyond dispute that deviations of the conversation in vernacular are sanctioned.

Transcript 4

	Original	*Translation*
Tom:	Hé mar hoe ist eik met die meid van jouw?	Hey, how is it [going] with your girl.
Paul:	Is goed. Ik zal ze trouwens is ekkes essemmesse.	All right. By the way, I will send her a text message.
Tom:	Oh das een bietje asociaal hè.	Oh, that would be a bit antisocial, wouldn't it?
Paul:	Da zal ik dan wel us nie doen.	Then I won't do that.
Tom:	En Nick, en jouw meid?	So, Nick, and your girl?
Nick:	Ach jonge, die heb ik geen.	Ah, boy, I don't have one.
Tom:	Die hiete Maud.	She was called Maud.
Nick:	Wa? Tjonge gij praot echt raar. Die ken ik nog nie enses.	What? Boy, you're talking funny; I don't even know her.
Paul:	Hoe laat is het eigenlijk want daar ben ik wel benieuwd na; ik zit hier een half uur met jullie te praten.	What time is it, because I'm curious about that, I have been talking here with you for half an hour.

Nick: *Kwart over de helluf van de zeikpot.*	Quarter past half of the piss pot.
Paul: *Nee ekkes kieke.*	No, just have a look.
Nick: *Net zo laot als gister om dezelfde tied.*	Just as late as yesterday at the same time.

In this extract, Paul interrupts a discussion on the supposed girlfriend of Nick asking what time it is in a more standard variety. Nick reacts by using a corker, a nonsense answer with a vulgar wording that does not tell his fellow student what time it is, but tells him he is out of order. The vernacular wording *zeikpot*, is vulgar because the common Dutch word for a chamber-pot would be *pot* or *po*, and the dialect term would be *pispot* (piss pot); *zeik* is more rude than *pis*. The line 'quarter past half of the piss pot' would be comparable to the saying 'it is a freckle past a hair' as an answer to 'what time is it'. When Paul does not get an adequate answer, he rapidly shifts back towards the vernacular: *ekkes kieke,* requesting a serious answer to his question. Nick decides to tease him a bit more by giving him another corker, '(it is) just as late as yesterday at the same time'.

By changing the theme and style of the conversation, Paul has caused a disruption of the chronotope, because now the harmony of theme, time, space and repertoire is in danger. Obviously, talking about girlfriends and supposed girlfriends is an important issue in adolescent culture. This example displays the circulation of the sociolinguistic norm. Since vernacular fits the chronotope of talking about girlfriends, it functions as the standard for peer interaction. Corrective measures are taken when deviations from that sociolinguistic norm occur. In this case, corkers are used for those corrections.

Paul's attention might be distracted because Tom tells him not to behave antisocial, when Paul wants to send his girlfriend a text message, and then shifts his attention to Nick. Then, Paul accidentally challenges the perceptual harmony, 'the tacit agreement between interlocutors on which indexical elements are interpretable, and how much socially meaningful variability is admissible in a specific interaction' (Grondelaers & Van Hout, 2015: 69). Disharmony is a diagnostic which detects variants that do not belong in a specific linguistic context. Harmony however locally and temporarily overrides the low prestige of prescriptively wrong, but socially meaningful variants, and renders them 'fitting' in a certain interaction (Grondelaers *et al.*, 2016). In this case the vernacular is the language in which the narrative about the supposed girlfriend develops. Perceptual harmony is challenged when the chronotopicity of this conversation is violated. By asking the time Paul not only changes the topic of conversation, but also changes repertoire, and corrective measures are taken through corkers in vernacular, the language that fits the topic that should be addressed according to Nick and Tom. Here the vernacular functions as a normative language amongst peers and the interlocutor who does not adhere to this is corrected because that puts him out of order.

This gives us an insight into small-scale chronotopic identity work. Vernacular, be it associated with local dialect or street talk, is tied to the conceptual context of stories and the accompanying chronotope, for instance 'with my friends last weekend', 'hanging out with friends at the street corner', 'about that girlfriend of yours', or 'back when I used to live in a small hamlet'; exactly that is the chronotope that defines the interlocutors' language choice in these cases. Chronotopes thus determine the values, emotions and norms that count during the sharing of the stories (Bakhtin, 1981: 243).

Metapragmatic Awareness of Chronotopes

In this section, we will explore how teachers and students behave language-wise in a primary school class in order to observe how children learn to become aware of the importance of time and space in the norms and rules of behavior. We will start with the first years of primary school, when some of the young children are confronted with Dutch as the language that is normatively expected in the classroom. Whether standard Dutch is a new language to them depends of course on their home language situation. The transcripts presented here, are from data gathered by Anke Meevissen who conducted ethnographic fieldwork in primary schools in Horn and Kelpen-Oler in the Province of Limburg in the southeast of the Netherlands (Meevissen, 2012). In these villages, many of the children grow up speaking the local dialect at home. The children are aged 4 or 5. We will focus here on the language behavior children with a Limburg dialect background show in the classroom and the response to their behavior by teachers who also have a Limburg dialect background. Below is a transcript from the audio recordings made in Horn.

Transcript 5

	Original	Translation
	Original	*Translation*
Linda:	*Ich haaj nuuje schoene gekrege.*	I got new shoes.
Teacher:	*Wauw.*	Wow.
Linda:	*En Petra haaj een oorworm opgegaete.*	And Petra, she ate an earwig.
Teacher:	*Oma?*	Grandma?

Original	Translation
Linda: *Nae Petra.*	No, Petra.
Teacher: *Petra? Och god dan kriebelt die nu in de buik.*	O God, than it [the insect] now tickles inside her belly.
Linda: *En een vogeltje haaj een eitje gelag in miene bloomebak.*	Also, a little bird laid an egg in my flower box.
Teacher: *Ooh. En zit ze daar ook op? Oh wat lief. Bij jou in de bloembak voor de slaapkamer?*	Oh, and does she sit on it? Oh, how sweet. With you, in the flower box before [the window of] your bedroom?

Linda says 'I got new shoes (...) and Petra, she ate an earwig'. The teacher misunderstands the name Petra (Linda's little sister), and asks '*Oma?*' (grandma), because *peet, pet, peetje* are dialect words for 'grandmother' in this region. She than says in Dutch 'O God, than it now tickles inside her belly'. The student continues in dialect 'a little bird laid an egg in my flower box', and the teacher answers again in Dutch. This does not hinder intelligibility; although two languages are spoken, the interlocutors have a perfect conversation which can be termed as inclusive multilingualism through mutually understandable languages ('lingua receptiva'; see Backus *et al.*, 2013).

Linda tells her story about her experiences entirely in dialect. The teacher however responds in Dutch; she uses a 'move-on strategy'. There is no explicit corrective behavior, but the teacher does not answer in dialect either. She continuously answers in another language, standard Dutch. The teacher tries to set the norm for conversation in the classroom: children are expected to speak Dutch, because that is the repertoire that fits the chronotope of conversations during class.

In another classroom, in Kelpen-Oler, a different strategy is chosen: this teacher requests for a specific language. The students are talking about throwing snow balls.

Transcript 6

Original	Translation
Stefan: *En op de auto's mag je ook niet gooien.*	You may not throw at cars either.
Teacher: *Nee, maar zo ver komen we vandaag niet. We komen niet bij de auto's. Loes.*	No, but we will not go that far today. We will not reach the cars. Loes.
Loes: *Mèr waal eeh waal ...*	But we will, ehm, will ...

Teacher:	*Loes, even Nederlands praten.*	Loes, speak Dutch now.
Loes:	*Op de tegeltjes als se een bolletje maaks den ...*	On the paving stones [lit. tiles], when you make a little ball then ...
Teacher:	*Even Nederlands praten, anders kan ik je niet verstaan.*	Speak Dutch now, or else I will not understand you.
Loes:	*Op de tegeltjes.*	On the tiles.
Teacher:	*Je mag wel op de tegeltjes.*	You may go on the tiles.
Loes:	*Je kan wel een bolletje maken en den geis se op ut graas.*	You can make a little ball and then go onto the grass.

In Transcript 6, we see specific teacher requests for Dutch in lines 4 and 6: 'speak Dutch' and 'speak Dutch, otherwise I will not understand you' respectively, thus deliberately neglecting the mutual intelligibility of Limburg dialect and Dutch we saw in Transcript 5. First, Stefan says in Dutch 'you may not throw at cars'. The teacher answers in Dutch. Then Loes starts in dialect 'but we can go ...', and the teacher interrupts 'Loes, speak Dutch'. Loes goes on in Dutch 'at the paving stones', but after a few words she shifts back to dialect again 'when you make a little ball ...'. The teacher interrupts 'speak Dutch, or else I will not understand you' and Loes repeats in Dutch 'on the paving stones ...' Next, she continues in Dutch but after a few words shifts back to dialect again: '... you can make a little ball and then you go at the lawn'.

The teacher addresses the dialect speaking student in Dutch, requesting her to also speak Dutch, establishing the 'proper' language behavior fitting the chronotope (being in the company of her peers and her teacher, on or near the premises of school, during school hours). This shows how negotiations on language choice take place. Establishing this norm sets the frame for new knowledge about chronotopes, i.e. rising awareness of and sensitivity for chronotopes, behavioral scripts and choice of repertoire. Children learn where and when to choose for either Dutch or dialect. Loes is struggling, she starts her part of the conversation in dialect, but after the reprimand telling her that her language is out of order ('speak Dutch, otherwise I will not understand you'), she starts sentences in Dutch. However, she goes back to dialect again before finishing the sentence. Perhaps Loes is in doubt because the children and their teacher are not talking about a situation in the classroom but about an outside event, in the snow, an entirely different chronotope, open for fun and play. At the other hand, she could still be at the beginning of this learning process.

In Transcript 7, collected in Horn, the teacher has asked the children to list words with the vowel /iː/, in Dutch spelled as /ie/.

Transcript 7

	Original	Translation
Michiel:	*Ies.*	Ies
Teacher:	*Ies? Wat is dat?*	Ies? What is that?
Michiel:	*Dat is een soort, een ijsje.*	That is a kind of, an ice cream.
Teacher:	*Ja dat is in het Limburgs. Ies. Maar we praten hier Nederlands hè.*	Yes, it is in Limburgian. *Ies.* Yet, here, we speak Dutch, don't we.

One of the students, Michiel, responds with *ies*, a dialect word for ice cream with the vowel /ie/. Again, the norm is negotiated, the student gives an example from the dialect and is explicitly reminded he should speak Dutch 'here'. The teacher explicitly mentions the chronotopicity of language choice: here and now, we speak Dutch. This sample shows us how Michiel chooses an example, *ies*, from a repertoire that does not suit the chronotope of conversation during class. His answer is out of order, and he is explicitly told so: 'here, we speak Dutch, don't we'. The teacher thus sets the norms for the behavioral script that fits this specific chronotope: here we speak Dutch.

Language choice co-creates formality and informality of situations and the hierarchies that belong to formal situations such as classroom instruction. Exactly this metapragmatic awareness is a crucial part of our knowledge of chronotopes. Young children are socialized through the use of language and thus (begin to) learn how to interpret different behavioral scripts, and how to use different repertoires meaningfully, appropriately and effectively. They learn how to meet the expectations the different chronotopes require.

During the earlier school years teachers and their students negotiate, either explicitly or implicitly, what repertoire should be used in which situation. Standard Dutch obviously is the target language when it comes to the language for instruction, albeit regional accents and vocabulary may also be part of the interaction in class. Such dialectal repertoire can be used in specific situations, for comfort, corrective measures on undesired behavior and specific clarifications (Meevissen, 2012). But in most situations Dutch is requested, since children are confronted with the monolingual habitus and the monoglot ideology of the school, the institution considered responsible for teaching the national language.

Children are taught already in the first grades of primary education what language should be used in what situation. In this way, they develop their awareness of the connections between repertoires and chronotopes, and thus develop awareness and sensitivity for different behavioral scripts. Concurrently, children also learn about the inequality of languages and registers. Dialect does not fit the chronotope of the classroom; it is out of order in that specific formal context. School thus functions as a site for language laundering (Woolard, 2008), making children aware of the inappropriateness of the use of their mother tongue. This shows that minority languages and regional languages are marginalized, already in day care centers and playgroups. Cornips (2017) therefore argues that teachers – but also parents – cause dialects to decline through prejudiced attitudes and beliefs and a lack of knowledge of the benefits of multilingualism.

We saw some examples of how young children in primary school are learning how to choose their repertoires. How do children reflect upon these different varieties of language and the choices they make in the following years in primary school? We interviewed teachers in the city of Tilburg, Noord-Brabant, and asked if their students (age 11 or 12) would use dialect in school.

Transcript 8

	Original	*Translation*
Teacher 1:	Dat valt op. Zodra de kinderen vrijer zijn, dan vallen ze echt terug op plat Tilburgs. Zodra de kinderen mogen gaan knutselen of gaan gymmen, merk je heel snel dat die kinderen een knop omzetten.	It is striking. As soon as children are less restricted, they fall back on vernacular Tilburgish. As soon as they do arts and craft or physical education, you immediately notice those children turn the switch.
Teacher 2:	Nou. Dat ze het ook schrijven. Ze schrijven het ook echt vaak, meer als ze een opstel moeten schrijven.	Right. And they also write it. They really write it often, especially when they have to do written composition.

According to their teachers, these students speak vernacular as soon as the chronotope changes. As soon as the lessons' themes are more informal, e.g. physical education and arts and craft, 11 and 12-year old students shift to a different repertoire: vernacular. Apparently, the behavioral script of such practical lessons is different from the theoretical lessons that require another type of attention (mathematics, geography etc.).

The second teacher notes the students also write with more vernacular features when the writing genre is more narrative. So, also the change of writing genre actuates a shift of repertoire and chronotope, which gives reason for a more informal type of (writing) behavior.

One of the reasons why a local vernacular such as Tilburgish still is part of a repertoire for young people, is that is has a specific sociolinguistic function. In Transcript 9, 11 and 12-year old students of a primary school in Tilburg comment on the question why they would speak dialect instead of Dutch.

Transcript 9

	Original	Translation
Lotte:	Nou, ik denk eigenlijk dat jongens het voor de stoere praat doen.	Well, I think the boys do it for talking tough.
Ninke:	Ja, daar heeft ze wel gelijk in.	Yes, she is right I guess.
Anouk:	Ze willen bij het clubje horen.	They want to be part of the group.
Kevin:	Ja, want dadelijk ben je op straat en dan zijn er allemaal jongens die Tilburgs kunnen praten. En dan zeg ik: huh? En dan gaan ze allemaal lachen. Ja, dan sta ik kei voor schut.	Yes, because when you are out on the street and there are all these boys knowing how to speak Tilburgish. And I say 'huh?' Then they will laugh. Yes, and I will look totally foolish.

Aptly, the last three words of Kevin, *kei voor schut*, are in dialect. Speaking this type of vernacular is believed to be a helpful part of social inclusion. When you are able to speak Tilburgish, this will help you in belonging to your peer group. Otherwise one will not fit in: if you don't understand the language of your peers you will look 'totally foolish'.

The identity work being discussed here is not just about 'who you are', but about 'what you do'. Chronotopic identity work requires the knowledge of how to act: the behavioral scripts and the choice of repertoire that fit the chronotope. It comes as no surprise that we find different repertoires in present-day primary schools; repertoires are bound to chronotopes and behavioral scripts, which is in fact a matter of normativity.

When children grow up and become adolescents, the diversity of their language use increases. Especially in conversations outside the classroom, their vernacular is very diverse and may contain features from languages that may not even be part of the home languages of anyone in the classroom. Though repertoires are unique 'indexical biographies, (...) biographically assembled patchworks of functionally distributed communicative resources, constantly exhibiting variation and change' (Blommaert & Backus, 2013: 23), repertoires also follow norms and attitudes, connected to chronotopes (Schmidt & Herrgen, 2011), such as the little circles of friendship in a school.

Conclusions

In the first part of this chapter we saw how adolescents choose repertoires in a specific chronotope, as manifestations of adolescent culture (Eckert, 2003) during school breaks. The students presented in the transcripts use language in a way that may be declined in other situations as inauthentic, incorrect, or inappropriate (cf. Jaspers, 2005). Language use in these cases is not simply a matter of shifting between languages or registers. Language may constantly change and draws upon a great variety of repertoires. The repertoires that fit chronotopes related to adolescent culture typically show abundant variation.

Speakers will correct each other when drawing from the 'wrong' repertoire in a certain situation. Then, expectations connected to behavioral scripts (Blommaert, 2017) are not met, and behavior is considered out of order (Blommaert, 2015). Consequently, corrective measures can be taken by making use of repertoire shifts. In this way, a shift of repertoire can correct an utterance that is out of order, as in Transcript 1, but it can also cause a disruption of the chronotope when conversation topics are changes and simultaneously the repertoire shifts, as we saw in Transcript 4.

In the second part of this chapter we saw how children in their first years in primary school learn how to behave, culturally and linguistically, and how to belong. Conversations during class require Dutch, and the transcripts 5 to 7 show how the norms of the chronotope of a classroom are negotiated. Children speak Limburg dialect in the class room and this evokes reactions, typical for chronotopic identity work, and in their reactions different teachers use different techniques. Conversations during breaks with peers may require different repertoires. Later on in primary school, students know how to behave according to different chronotopes, and they are able to reflect on the choice of repertoire. Normativity then is not abandoned. Nor is it of lesser importance than in formal settings with top-down norms, such as the classroom. It is just differently and flexibly applied, meeting expectations following from chronotopes with bottom-up norms. Speaking vernacular may evoke a world in which a specific way of speaking is just one facet. People don't just do a language but people do a chronotope, and language is part of an ensemble of language, story, place, time and interlocutors (Johnstone, 2018). As such, chronotopes are the operating power for choices of repertoire.

If chronotopic normativities are violated, a disruption occurs in the constellation of narrative, time, place, interlocutors and language, leading to disharmony (Grondelaers & Van Hout, 2015). The tacit agreement between interlocutors on which repertoire is accepted and socially meaningful then is one of the prevailing norms, which may need reconfirmation. This can be done jokingly, by using a corker, or ironically, by insincerely showing compassion. We saw examples of both approaches where these corrective measures were taken through a shift of repertoire, which functions as a tool for chronotopic identity work. In some instances even individual identities will be questioned, 'Your brother is a Turk?' Not only language behavior but even a person may be out of order. Identity judgments are judgments of appropriateness, of the things that fit a behavioral script. Such judgments can be seen as enabling the social enactment of such behavioral scripts. When inappropriate, a person's behavior or even a person's identity will be considered out of order.

References

Auer, P. (2005) Europe's sociolinguistic unity, or: A typology of European dialect/standard constellations. In N. Delbecque, J. Van der Auwera and D. Geeraerts (eds) *Perspectives on Variation* (pp. 7–42). Berlin: Mouton de Gruyter.

Auer, P. (2011) Dialect vs. standard: A typology of scenarios in Europe. In B. Kortmann and J. Van der Auwera (eds) *The Languages and Linguistics in Europe. A Comprehensive Guide* (pp. 485–500). Berlin: De Gruyter.

Backus, A., Gorter, D., Knapp, K., Schjerve-Rindler, R., Swanenberg, J., Ten Thije, J., and Vetter, E. (2013) Inclusive multilingualism: Concept, modes and implications. *European Journal of Applied Linguistics* 1, 179–215.

Bakhtin, M. (1981) *The Dialogic Imagination. Four Essays* (edited by M. Holquist; translated by C. Emerson and M. Holquist). Austin: University of Texas Press.

Basso, K. (1996) *Wisdom Sits in Places. Landscape and Language among the Western Apache*. Albuquerque: University of New Mexico Press.

Blommaert, J. (2005) *Discourse: A Critical Introduction*. Cambridge: Cambridge University Press.

Blommaert, J. (2010) *The Sociolinguistics of Globalization*. Cambridge: Cambridge University Press.

Blommaert, J. (2015) Chronotopes, scale and complexity in the study of language in society. *Annual Review of Anthropology* 44, 105–116.

Blommaert, J. (2017) Commentary: Mobility, contexts, and the chronotope. *Language in Society*, 46 (1), 95–99.

Blommaert, J. and Backus, A. (2013) Repertoires revisited: 'Knowing language' in superdiversity. *Working Papers in Urban Language & Literacies* 67.

Blommaert J. and Velghe, F. (2014) Learning a supervernacular: Textspeak in a South African township. In A. Creese and A. Blackledge (eds) *Heteroglossia as Practice and Pedagogy* (pp.137–154). New York: Springer.

Cornips, L. (2017) *Peutertaalbeleid*. Retrieved from www.neerlandistiek.nl, 20 March 2018.

De Coster, M. (2007) *Groot scheldwoordenboek: van apenkont tot zweefteef*. Antwerpen: Standaard.

Dekkers, T. (2012) 'Ach meske, toch.' Een onderzoek naar taalgebruik, identiteit en contextualiteit op een middelbare school in Roosendaal. Master thesis, Tilburg University.

Eckert, P. (2003) Language and gender in adolescence. In J. Holmes and M. Meyerhoff (eds) *Handbook of Language and Gender* (pp. 381–400). Malden: Blackwell.

Grondelaers, S. and Van Hout, R. (2015) How (in)coherent can standard languages be? A perceptual perspective on co-variation. *Lingua. International review of General Linguistics* 172/173, 62–71.

Grondelaers, S., Van Hout, R. and Van Gent, P. (2016) Destandardization is not destandardization. Revising standardness criteria in order to revisit standard language typologies in the Netherlands. *Taal en Tongval* 68, 119–149.

Jaspers, J. (2005) Doing ridiculous: linguistic sabotage in an institutional context of monolingualism and standardisation. *Language and Communication* 25, 279–297.

Johnstone, B. (2018) Chronotopes of dialect style. Keynote presented at the *Language, Place and Periphery*-conference, Copenhagen, 18–19 January 2018.

Jørgensen, J.N. (2008) Poly-lingual languaging around and among children and adolescents. *International Journal of Multilingualism* 5 (3) 161–176.

Jørgensen, J.N., Karrebæk, M.F., Madsen, A.M. and Møller, J.S. (2016). Polylanguaging in superdiversity. In K. Arnaut, J. Blommaert, B. Rampton and M. Spotti (eds) *Language and Superdiversity* (pp. 131–148). New York: Routledge.

Kroon, S. and Swanenberg, J. (2019) *Language and Culture on the Margins. Global/Local Interactions*. New York: Routledge.

Meevissen, A. (2012) 'We praten hier Nederlands, hè?!' Een onderzoek naar taalgedrag van leerlingen in Midden-Limburg en hoe dit taalgedrag beïnvloed wordt door leerkrachten en ouders. Master thesis, Tilburg University.

Mutsaers, P. and Swanenberg, J. (2012) Super-diversity at the margins? Youth language in North Brabant, the Netherlands. *Sociolinguistic Studies* 6, 65–89.

Schmidt, J.E. and Herrgen, J. (2011) *Sprachdynamik. Eine Einführung in die moderne Regionalsprachenforschung*. Berlin: Erich Schmidt.

Silverstein, M. (2005) Axes of evals: Token versus type interdiscursivity. *Journal of Linguistic Anthropology* 15 (1), 6–22.

Van Donselaar, J. (1989) *Woordenboek van het Surinaams-Nederlands*. Muiderberg: Coutinho.

Vertovec, S. (2007) Super-diversity and its implications. *Ethnic and Racial Studies* 30, 1024–1054.

Woolard, K. (2008) Language and identity choice in Catalonia: The interplay of contrasting ideologies of linguistic authority. In K. Süselbeck, U. Mühlschlegel and P. Masson (eds) *Lengua, nación e identidad. La regulación del plurilingüismo en España y América Latina* (pp. 303–323). Frankfurt am Main: Vervuert/Madrid: Iberoamericana.

10 The Moral Economy of Chronotopic Identities: A Case Study in a Polish Community in Antwerp

Malgorzata Szabla

Identity in Superdiversity: 'Not Everything that Shines is Gold'

'Not everything that shines is gold' were the very first words I heard when starting my fieldwork in the Polish community in Berchem, Antwerp a few years ago. The warning to watch out for the Polish people – because that was what she meant – came from a middle-aged woman whom I met in the Polish delicatessen shop in Berchem. She had already lived in Belgium for a very long time and was referred to as an 'old generation Polish immigrant' by the Polish lady who ran the shop. I did not know what to think of her statement at first, but I quickly realized that it was not just an isolated incident.

Further fieldwork only strengthened my conjectures, because most Polish people whom I met in Berchem were rather suspicious of my activities and reluctant to help me in any way. Some Poles would avoid any possible contact; others would pretend not to be Polish after overhearing me speaking Polish with someone else. Polish people did not really seem to stick together and they did not display much desire to engage in contact with their fellow countrymen. It became clear to me that the 'Chinatown model', in which members of a national or ethnic group cluster together in a neighborhood and form a tight community there, did no longer apply in a superdiverse environment such as Berchem. The Poles there did not display the need to form one cohesive Polish community. The interviews that I finally managed to conduct despite all the difficulties, led to the same conclusion: the Polish community is heavily diversified and contains very different communities of practice (Lave & Wenger, 1991).

As a consequence of all of these observations, a very important identity diacritic – nationality – proved to be rather useless in Berchem. It was clear that there was not one, solid, robust and homogeneous Polish community in the neighborhood, but several different and perhaps even competing ones. I knew from that moment on that the object of my study had changed from an assumed singular Polish community tied together by strong bonds of national identity, to multiple communities organized in very different ways. The struggle to understand what happened, however, did not end there, leaving me wondering how it was possible that such an important identity diacritic seemed so conflicted in the Polish diaspora. After all, all I ever saw in the neighborhood, for instance during the European Football Championships, were Polish flags hanging from windows and attached to cars, suggesting at first sight an internally integrated and unified Polish community. The findings required a deeper investigation of the issue at hand in order to understand identity in superdiversity (Vertovec, 2007).

Introduction

The vignette above illustrates the complexity of identity in contemporary diaspora contexts, and the need for a research strategy to address it. The Polish diaspora in Berchem can be seen as a layered and non-homogeneous community (Blommaert, 2013), which makes it difficult to look at it in its totality, or in other words to look at it as a demographic community in a traditional sociological sense. This is because the community is not unified, and consequently, neither are the social norms governing its social behavior. Therefore, the Polish community, as well as the social environment in which they live, is extremely polycentric, but also profoundly polynomic, as it is not governed by one set of norms or rules, but rather by multiple sets of norms that can be operating simultaneously (Blommaert, 2018). As a consequence, individuals can easily violate particular sets of micro-hegemonies at play in the interaction with others, as every activity or interaction in a specific time and space, operates in its own nomic system (Blommaert, 2018), and can leave these individuals with a perpetual feeling of anomie (Durkheim, 2005). In practice, these nomic systems consist of a variety of different socially constructed formats, which I shall call moralized behavioral scripts, played out by acting upon them and hence shaping people's identities (Blommaert, 2015b). In other words, individuals who are not familiar with the situation in a specific 'chronotopic or timespace dimension' (Blommaert, 2015a) will most likely not fit all the required norms and as a consequence the identity of a legitimate group member will not be ascribed to them by others. What they often do not realize at that time is that they most likely fit in yet another set of norms in a different timespace constellation, which might cause the general feeling of being left out and rejected by the rest of the 'community'. This in turn can inevitably lead to tensions and misunderstandings among the members of the Polish community, which explains the animosities within the community and warnings, such as the one discussed in the vignette.

In order to understand the identity of the members of the Polish diaspora in a superdiverse neighborhood like Berchem, it is essential to view it through the lens of a complex, polycentric community, whose structure reflects the identity work performed by its members. Identity is not simply 'who and what you are' but identity is 'many things', because it depends 'on context, occasion and purpose, and it almost invariably involves a semiotic process of representation' (Blommaert, 2005: 203). Identity should therefore not be seen as something that can be owned or possessed by someone, but rather as a process of construction in which identities are 'produced, enacted and performed' (Blommaert, 2005: 205). This implies that identity is an active and non-fixed category. Its construction requires various semiotic resources for successful identity performance in one's identity repertoire and as such, inevitably connects to the issue of inequality, because not everyone has equal access to these resources (Blommaert, 2005: 207). An identity repertoire consists of a great variety of micro-hegemonies, which can only be admitted to one's repertoire if 'enough' characteristics of a specific identity are present and can be distinguished by others to regard someone as a true and authentic member of a particular identity category (Blommaert, 2010; Blommaert & Varis, 2015). Therefore, identity is inevitably context-dependent and at the same time highly normative, as different identity enactments are expected of a person within different timespaces, and hence every shift in timespace demands changes in identities (Blommaert, 2005, 2018; Blommaert & De Fina, 2017).

Identity is a process of identification, which is under constant construction. This means that different identities co-exist, shift and change frequently, and cannot be properly defined without clear reference to their chronotopic order. Therefore, following Blommaert (2018: 57), I choose to see identities as 'chronotopically organized moral behavioral scripts', as this description will be helpful in trying to explain how chronotopes impose, in actual practice, detailed moralized behavioral scripts on actual social conduct.

Moralized Behavioral Scripts

Before turning to the actual case study, let me first explain in greater detail what moral behavioral scripts actually are in connection with chronotopes and identity work. One of the first definitions conceptualizing the term explains behavioral scripts as follows:

> *Imaginable situations in marked (i.e. nonrandom) spacetime, provoking enregistered (and therefore normative, expected and presupposed) modes of behavior* ... To unpack the definition somewhat: the behavioral scripts assume the form of actual real-life situations which we can somehow imagine ..., and onto which we project normative patterns of behavior and – thence – templates of character and identity... Note that I mentioned ... spatial and temporal frame in which these behaviors are suggested to occur, or are preferred to occur: they are, in that sense, fundamentally *chronotopic*. (Blommaert, 2015b; emphasis in original)

Identity work consists of passing moral judgments about behavior, about appearances and other relevant categories (cf. Garfinkel, 2002; Goodwin, 2007). Moral behavioral scripts then are highly moralized, normative patterns of expected behavior for a specific, imaginable situation. It is expected of people to behave in a certain way in specific situations in order to fit the norm of a specific chronotopic identity. In these terms, also places can be perceived as good or bad; they can be places of happiness or places of misery. Therefore, morality refers to things that belong to what counts as acceptable in a given society or group. It is something recognized as belonging to the common repertoire of things that are done, thought and accepted as a norm in such society or group. Morality here, following Foucault (2004) revolves around the 'normal versus abnormal' axis, which people deploy within a specific chronotope. It explains why there are different moral standards and why different standards apply to different people in specific timespace dimensions. This distinction is the most powerful notion of morality within any social environment. The 'normal versus abnormal' distinction, however, is at the same time problematic, because normality can suddenly turn into abnormality if important scripts are broken. It is not a clear-cut and fixed dimension, but it is exposed to continuous change and every chronotopic change demands adjustment of norms i.e. 'a polynomic complex of moralized behavioral scripts' (Blommaert, 2018: 51).

A 'script' is an order of indexicality (Blommaert, 2010, following Silverstein, 2003), in which multiple, often very little features, need to be brought together into a form of alignment in order for them to make sense. If all these little features are indeed 'in place', they can be recognized by others as a specific script, i.e. the sequence of instructions that a person follows in order to fit the moralized behavioral script of a specific chronotope. If the attempts are successful, a person is seen as the legitimate and ratified user of a moral behavioral script and the relevant identity is ascribed to him or her (for illustrations see e.g. Roberts, 2016).

It is clear therefore that the notion of moralized behavioral scripts is strongly connected to norms and normativity, and that norms are there to make sure that people agree to certain things and act in a particular way. This implies that there is nothing objective about norms, because people who follow them are seen as morally good, and people who refuse to abide by them are morally disqualified. So, in order to highlight the actual content of norms, one could conclude that they are indispensably connected to, or even 'made out of' morality-in-practice.

The Moral Economy of Chronotopic Identity

The moral boundary of what a person accepts and what he or she does not accept is the boundary of identity. This is the point in time where a person needs to present him or herself 'against' the other. It is, for instance, a choice of joining a community that shares the same moral script, or rejecting it. However, identity is always two-sided. It is about how a person wants to be perceived, but also about how a person is actually perceived by others. In these terms a person needs to not only 'subscribe' to a specific identity, but also needs to be 'ascribed' to it, which can only succeed if enough identity characteristics are displayed by an individual for others to be recognized.

The actually performed identity is therefore an outcome of the moral behavioral scripts deployed in specific chronotopes. Different chronotopes trigger different identity enactments, because they are subjected to different moral behavioral scripts. It is however possible that a specific chronotope consists of multiple moral behavioral scripts and consequently a particular moral behavioral script can be active in various chronotopes. For instance, a person can perform the identity of a student and a friend while at school (one chronotope, two moral behavioral scripts), but in an outside school setting the same person can still be a friend of his or her classmate. Hence, in the latter case, the chronotope changes but the moral behavioral script remains the same in both chronotopes. It is a complex process, because identity is subject to habitualization, moralization and normatization.

Before illustrating the usefulness of the concepts in my particular case study, let me first go back to the fieldwork vignette in the beginning of this chapter and explain it on the basis of the same principle. In a way, the warning I received from a lady in a Polish delicatessen shop could be compared to a narrative of her life events. Often unstructured forms of storytelling emphasize the complex structure of identity. It is not monolithic, nor idiosyncratic or fixed. Identity is never a clear-cut phenomenon, but rather an assemblage (Latour, 2005) of identity diacritics, both large ones and micro-hegemonies at different but connected levels at the same time. Therefore, people never refer to large diacritics alone, because they never occur in isolation. People can say that they are Polish, or that they believe in God, but even then, these notions are moralized and never occur alone. By observing the actual, detailed and precise way in which they occur, it becomes clear that moralization processes are inevitable, because people make moral judgments all the time.

Even from a simple description of a person, it is quite easy to notice whether or not he or she is liked by the narrator of the story. The process of moralization is a very powerful one and these descriptions are never neutral, because people constantly make moral judgments. These judgments are the identity diacritics or boundaries, because if a person states that he or she likes somebody, or a particular form of behavior, he or she immediately inscribes him or herself into it. This means that one's expression of approval or preference with regard to particular behaviors immediately inscribes him or her to a category of people who do a certain thing, simply because if one approves others' behavior, it means that he or she would be able to do it as well. When a person disapproves of something, he or she also makes an identity statement, in the sense that this is not what that person stands for, this is not who this individual is, or that he or she would simply not do that, because he or she would not want to be associated with people who do it.

However, the process of moralization in itself is rather flexible and relatively sanction-free, because identity can change when people shift to different timespaces. This implies that a poor student might become a 'bad' landlord in the future, even if at present he or she would disagree with the negative practices of landlords. This does not mean however that his attitude change will fit in a moral behavioral script of groups that he has been a member of during his studies, and therefore he runs the risk of not being perceived as a legitimate member of that group. Similarly, a person can hold two different and even opposing identities. A person can be an environmentally active member of a green party and at the same time drive a car with a V8 engine. Or parents might be in favor of ethnically mixed schools and still send their kids to a white school, simply because for quality reasons it feels like the best thing to do for their kids (Blommaert & Varis, 2015).

It is clear that the process of moralization is the key to the identity distinction between the good and the bad Poles, as expressed by the lady I met in the Polish delicatessen shop. Of course, ascribed identities do not always reflect reality and might not necessarily be relevant for the Poles themselves, but they are essential in order to understand how Polish people are perceived by others (in this case other Poles) in order to make larger statements about identity and their community.

Chronotopes in Paulina's Story

In the following, I will demonstrate on the basis of the life history of Paulina, a participant in my case study, how she connects moral orientations to concrete forms of behavior, located in a specific chronotope.[1] The reason for choosing the interview with this particular participant is the fact that it really stood out from all the others. While a majority of the interviewees told relatively simple stories, and focused on very limited aspects of their life, such as categories of work and home, Paulina's story is very dynamic and rich. It is based on an eight-hour interview plus a few shorter follow up interviews. Paulina was the main narrator of her life history, however at specific times during the interviews other family members were also present and contributed to the interview as well.

In order to give a better overview of this highly complex and dynamic case, the timeline of Paulina's life events with regard to her working activities and living places has been sketched in Table 10.1. The table shows how Paulina's work and living places change in different periods of time. It is clear that Paulina moved to Antwerp post the EU membership of Poland in 2004, and as part of a new wave of Polish migration to Belgium. Migration during that period was quite easy, because Polish migrants could freely enter the country, and were allowed to stay in Belgium for an unlimited time if they received the permit to stay. The socioeconomic conditions of migrants however often made it very difficult for them to achieve the necessary documents to legalize their stay, which in turn made it impossible to apply for the permit to work legally. This meant that even after the EU-accession of Poland many Polish migrants were residing in Belgium illegally, and since the opening of the labor market for Polish migrants took place in 2009, most of their working activities during this period were unofficial as well.

Table 10.1 Paulina's timeline

Year	Occupation & Activities	Residence
2004	Paulina went to Belgium to work during her school holidays. She went with her sister Eline who moved to Belgium in order to re-unite with her husband	Paulina lives with her sister and her sister's husband in a small studio in Antwerp Piotr lives in a small studio arranged for him by his aunt who lives in Belgium since 1990.
	– Housekeeper at a Jewish home – Paulina meets her husband Piotr and moves in with him – Illegal work, no permit for permanent stay in Belgium	Living in the center of Antwerp in a small studio in a tenement house
2005	– Cleaning lady at Belgian houses – Paulina marries Piotr in Poland	
2006	– Cleaning lady at Belgian houses – Piotr finds a legal job and acquires official permit to stay in Belgium together with Paulina	
2007	Cleaning lady at Belgian houses	Living together with friends in a nice house in the center of Antwerp
2008	Pregnancy break	Without any notice, Paulina's friends move out of the house two months after the birth of Sylwester. Need for a cheaper place due to financial difficulties. Renting a small apartment in the O Street in the center of Antwerp (Moroccan district).
2009	– Cleaning lady at the public hospital – Piotr opens his own building company – Paulina starts working officially	
2010–2011	Cleaning lady at the Beauty Salon	Renting a little house in W. Possibility of good schooling for their son.
	Receptionist at the Beauty Salon	
2012	Paulina opens her own company that is importing windows from Poland in order to support the growing number of projects of her husband	
2013–2014		Renting a nice, big house in R.
2015	Pregnancy break	

The interview with Paulina, at first sight, seems like a very messy case with many contradictions and difficulties that in a way question the reliability of the case. At times, her story even seems to be incoherent and her life seems to be quite conflicting. The table already minimizes these effects, because it is structured and organized with regard to time and space. However, how can the contradictions and incoherencies in her story line be explained? First and foremost, life events are not necessarily coherent in the experiences of individuals. They are, on the contrary very often disrupted. Secondly, people's lives are complex and tangled rather than linear, clear-cut and without any difficulties. Individuals often need to change direction during their life journey. They might need to turn around, speed up or slow down in order to avoid, or to deal with obstacles on their way. Living one's life does not directly lead to the destination and that is why the stories that people tell about themselves are not structured and linear during the interviews, but reflect reality as it is. Therefore, the inconsistencies in such stories should not be seen as contradictions, but as actual identity work that needs to be done, because of the changes in the social environment in which people live. This is how superdiversity operates in practice, because the understanding of the flexibility of people to adjust and re-adjust to perpetual changes around them is how superdiversity should be understood (Vertovec, 2007). In other words, identity work reflects the superdiverse ensemble of chronotopes in which actual life happens. And this is the first step to understanding identity in superdiversity. It is not about large categories and diacritics, but about being mobile by means of reassessment of all sorts of little things. A person can re-order things and attach another value to them at different points in time and for various reasons. Issues, which were very important at first, can become irrelevant, while unimportant and sometimes even trivial things can become essential in the course of time and space. Thus, people who live in superdiverse contexts also have to make meaning and create identities in that context. Therefore, superdiversity is part of a specific timespace to which people react in a moralizing way and engage with in normatively ordered forms of behavior.

The visualization of the chronotopes in Paulina's life is presented in Figure 10.1. The boxes A, B and C represent Paulina's family life. From the moment she was born in Poland, Paulina was in a family, where her family life develops. At this point in time, her entire family resides in Poland (phase A). However, when Paulina decides to move to Belgium with her sister Eline, her family life is re-chronotopicalized. It is no longer the same and therefore enters the chronotopic stage B. Another shift in the chronotope occurs when Paulina's entire family finally moves to Belgium to reunite with her (stage C). Her family life begins a new episode again and new stages may follow. This change in chronotope has both advantages and disadvantages. Advantages, because the family is finally together and all the important issues can be addressed face to face, on a daily basis. In addition, the frequency of contact is much higher and the family can actually spend time together. On the other hand, it also has disadvantages, because different space and time dimensions of this chronotope do not guarantee the same relations as in the

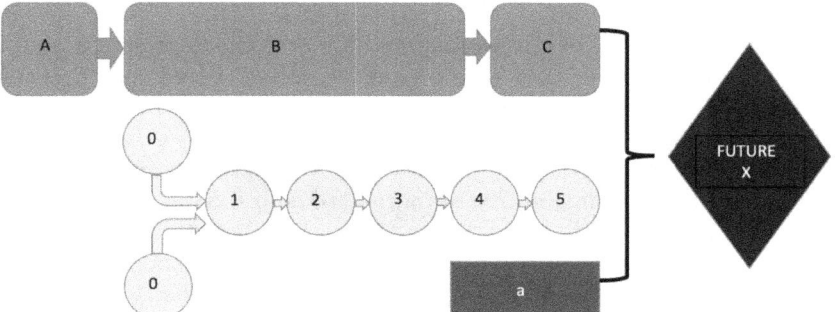

Figure 10.1 Visualization of changing chronotopes and chronotopes' co-occurences

initial stage (A). It is not possible to re-create a chronotope, because the timespace dimension has changed and consequently social norms within the family change as well. In addition, if anything would change in the family situation again (e.g. someone would get into a fight or return to Poland), the family would again enter a phase of re-chronotopicalization, bringing with itself new challenges, benefits and constraints. As Paulina states during the interview, she always dreamt about having her family all together in Belgium:

> Already from the very beginning, I dreamt of getting all my family to Belgium (…). We managed to get everyone over. (Paulina, interview 10 February 2016)

The circles numbered 0 to 5 in Figure 10.1 illustrate the neighborhoods in which Paulina has lived. It is an outstanding example of a changing chronotope, because Paulina and her husband Piotr are moving through Europe, and later through the region of Antwerp throughout their life history. Both of them first separately move from Poland to Belgium and Antwerp and start by living in very small apartments (circles 0). After they meet, they move together into a small studio in a tenement house (1), but later they rent a small house with friends in the center of Antwerp (2). Due to financial difficulties, they are forced to move to one of the cheapest districts of Antwerp (3). Finally, their financial situation gets a bit better and they manage to afford to move to another neighborhood, W. (4) in order to provide their son Sylwester with a good education. A few years later, they start their own companies, and as they prosper, they can afford a big house in an even better neighborhood (5).

Even though the family decides to move to another house R. (5), where another piece of the history and another chronotope starts, the old chronotope of the child is maintained (a-box). The parents' decision to keep Sylwester in the same school while they move to another village (5) is driven by the well-being of their child. The parents do not want to draw him away from everything he has known for the last couple of years. Paulina believes that it would be uprooting for their son, because he would not only lose his friends, but he would also lose everything that he has built in terms of his identity within that school. The decision to bring him to an inner city-school could have a negative impact on their son, because they believe that he is not tough enough to manage in a new school, especially if it would be situated in a bad neighborhood. Paulina and Piotr are concerned with the future of their son and they do not want him to go through a hard time. They are trying to be good parents and that is also why it is clear that the choice of their living and educational places is not incidental. The family decides to move to another living place, because it offers more comfort for them and the child, but their son stays in a particular chronotope nonetheless, because it is the best for him. This leads to the overlapping of the chronotopes. While some of them change into other chronotopes, specific ones, such as the one of Sylwester's schooling are maintained. It is clear that the moral orientation of Paulina, and her willingness to be a good mother and offer her child the best schooling directs her behavior in a specific timespace dimension.

> We looked for an apartment at the outskirts of the city. We absolutely did not want to live in the center, because we had Sylwester in such an age that we started looking for a school for him, and we wanted him to go to a good school. We found an apartment in W, it is a village, bigger than here, because here you have nothing, but it is irrelevant. There the village was a bit bigger, but they had a good school so that is why we moved there.
> (Paulina, interview, 10 February 2016)

Consequently, the most powerful chronotope is the future – a projected or imagined chronotope (diamond box X). Even though it is not yet in place, it is a very important and relevant concept. For example, a large part of Polish migrants come to Belgium to work, while they are at the same time building their house in Poland. Their projected chronotope implies that when they have earned enough money, and managed to finish building their house in Poland, they will finally return to their home country. And then, they will become an important, wealthy and respected person in their village.

The projected chronotope of Paulina is very powerful as well; after her maternity leave she said she would go back to school in order to find a job in a public hospital as a nurse. This, again, is a concrete form of behavior, which could be explained by the social expectations towards Paulina. In Belgium it is very common to return to work after maternity leave, and the chances of being successful increase depending on the level of education. It is clear that specific moral scripts are projected onto specific forms of behavior. It is not likely that Paulina would be perceived as having made a career if she never came back to work after her maternity leave. In the specific chronotope she is in, she can follow the moral behavioral scripts of being a good mother, but as long as she will not find a job or improve her work qualifications she will not be perceived as successful by others. Paulina is aware of this, and because she is ambitious, and wants to have a 'successful' identity, she plans to follow the script to achieve it.

Dealing with Contradiction: O Street

In a specific episode of her life, Paulina, together with her husband and Polish friends, used to live in the center of Antwerp in a nice little house (Circle 2 in Figure 10.1). However, at a certain point everything goes wrong. Their friends leave them with all the unpaid bills and Paulina's family ends up in financial difficulties. They are left with no other choice than to move to a cheaper place.

> They left us with all the bills. I was not even working at the time. Piotr still had his low salary. We had to live off the crumbs that we still had hidden from the time when I was still working illegally. They just left us, in this huge house with huge bills, with all the bills. I gave birth and they moved out. (Paulina, interview, 10 February 2016)

They move to the O Street in a neighborhood of Antwerp where a large Moroccan-origin population resides (Circle 3 in Figure 10.1). The Moroccans who live there create the environment in which Paulina and Piotr can survive, even though they are in a bad financial situation. The place itself is not perceived positively, it is not a good neighborhood. If given a choice, Paulina would never choose to live there.

> And so we moved, we somehow managed, to the center of Antwerp, next to the well-known street, O Street. It is a well-known street for Poles, because you can buy there very cheap things for 2 euro, for 5 euro. Moroccans are selling them. So, that's where we lived. The apartment was great, but the neighborhood was terrible. (Paulina, interview, 10 February 2016)

The neighborhood has a specific type of infrastructure. The supplies are very cheap, and accommodation is nice and reasonably priced, which attracts people with all kinds of backgrounds. Paulina and Piotr settle for a bad neighborhood, because it offers good things. It is a moralized place. Piotr and Paulina live in a 'bad' place, and they are there, because they have to and not because they choose to be there. It is the only place in which they can manage in this situation. If they will do a bit better financially, they will not stay there, they will move out immediately to a better neighborhood. Paulina follows the moral behavioral scripts of this projected chronotope, because she wants to change her current situation in the future in order to be perceived as more successful by herself and others.[2]

Before moving to this neighborhood, Paulina had rather negative ideas of the place, as it is a cheap neighborhood with a poor reputation. Quite a number of Polish females living in the neighborhood reside there with their Moroccan partners. These ladies do not have the best reputation in the Polish community-at-large. They are often rejected and condemned within the Polish community. Some of my participants, who are in the situation of being married to Turkish or Moroccan-origin men, explained their situation as follow:

> I was here with a Turk for twelve years. In the beginning, I met a lot of Polish people. But my situation was not viewed positively. They excluded me from their group because I was living with a Turk. Polish people managed to completely exclude me from their Polish group. (Asia, interview, 8 November 2015)

> There are many situations in which they showed me that I am not one of them. It has not been once or twice that I have been rejected and pushed away by other Polish people. There were various situations, more or less drastic, always hurtful, which made it very clear that we Polish people are huge racists. I am not Polish among Poles, because I did not marry a Pole. It disqualifies me. And every interaction with them is the same. (Sonia, email interview, 12 October 2015)

When Paulina moved to the Moroccan neighborhood, she needed to learn the moral economy of the place, the new chronotope. The easiest way to achieve this was through Polish ladies who had already acquired an insider's perspective in how the neighborhood functions, but could still speak the Polish language – women who live with Moroccan-origin men, in short. Despite the negative perceptions that are circulating within the Polish community with regard to these ladies, when entering this particular chronotope, their insider knowledge becomes essential. A person who in another chronotope is perceived as 'bad' can become a very important resource person and teacher. Their knowledge, which at first was seen as the key to their marginality, now becomes very important for Paulina's integration in this chronotope. In other words, from the perspective of Paulina's earlier chronotope, in which only Paulina and her family were present, Polish ladies who marry Moroccan-origin men would be seen in a negative way; but in the current chronotope, where Paulina's family and Polish ladies married to Moroccan-origin men cohabit, the 'bad' Polish lady would be perceived in a positive way. In the Moroccan neighborhood a mixed marriage is common and 'normal'; Paulina has to acquire this normative code and finds it normal and profitable for better adjusting to her new environment.

So what has actually happened? Is Paulina inconsistent? I would rather say she had to change her moral economy in order to survive there. Paulina's situation changes, the chronotope shifts, and so her identity work adapts to her new surroundings with different chronotopic behavioral norms.

This contradiction illustrates the complexity of identity work in the sense that people suddenly change moral and identity positions. They can speak differently, react very differently and even act very differently compared to the past. Suddenly what used to be a deviation becomes normalized. Chronotopes change along with the identity or the other way around, which implies that people who were first seen as bad can now be seen as useful, interesting, helpful and cooperative. This change however is not permanent and depends on specific moralized behavioral scripts that operate within particular chronotopes.

Conclusions

The above analysis shows how peoples' unspecific contextual worlds operate as moral agents to provide them with concrete sets of norms in specific chronotopes. From this perspective a moral agent constitutes an identity. When a person speaks about his/her life, he or she never speaks in a purely factual way. A person speaks about him or herself and others in a moral construction which points out the scripts of the chronotope and identity. Similarly, the analysis of Paulina's life history illustrates how moral dimensions are continuously placed onto specific behaviors in different chronotopes.

Therefore, in order to understand identity in superdiversity, it is crucial to understand the ways in which people function in densely diversified social environments and social contexts. It is essential to realize that an individual's identity repertoire consists of multiple identities, each relevant within a specific social sphere, a specific chronotope. And in that sense a person needs to perform a different identity at work and at home. It is not that a person is necessarily fragmented or conflicted, or that his or her multiple identities do not fit into a sort of general personhood. On the contrary, an individual needs to be integrated in all sorts of social spheres. And of course, he or she cannot be the same individual with his or her employer as with his or her spouse or mother. Those are three different identities and if a person will confuse them, none of them will be successful. This is the fine fiber of identity.

The notion of chronotope is a way of rephrasing the notion of context that can be seen as a broad and under-defined word and that is often used as a very generic concept. Everyone knows what context is, but nobody knows what is exactly meant by it. In order to check its validity, it is necessary to investigate its usefulness with help of other analytic vocabulary, such as 'chronotope' (Blommaert, this volume). By referring to context through chronotope, it is possible to make context much more specific, because it automatically involves the notions of space and time, agency, identity, behavior, norms, the nature of the community and rules as to who can enter the chronotope and who cannot. The context viewed through the prism of chronotope allows for far more specificity and hence generates much more precise findings. The use of general notions forces a person to generalize, while there is no room for generalizations in a superdiverse world, because it is hard to understand diversity and complexity without utmost care and precision. This does not mean that the notion of context is not useful, on the contrary, the notion of context is essential and therefore requires utmost care and specificity, when referring to it. The concept of chronotope may just offer exactly that specificity, shaping context into the chronotopic contexts that generate conditions to better understand the dynamics of the social actions in the superdiverse world.

Notes

(1) Paulina is the pseudonym of the interviewee. The first interview with her and her family took place at their house on 10 February 2016 in Belgium. The follow up interviews were conducted in the next two months of 2016 in the same place.
(2) This imagined chronotope is actually brought into reality by Paulina, as she manages to move to a better neighborhood (Circle 4 in Figure 10.1) after living for two years in a very bad one (Circle 3 in Figure 10.1). From that moment on, the chronotope is no longer projected, but it turns into an active chronotope.

References

Blommaert, J. (2005) *Discourse. A Critical Introduction*. Cambridge: Cambridge University Press.
Blommaert, J. (2010) *The Sociolinguistics of Globalization*. Cambridge: Cambridge University Press.
Blommaert, J. (2013) *Ethnography, Superdiversity and Linguistic Landscapes: Chronicles of Complexity*. Bristol: Multilingual Matters.
Blommaert, J. (2015a) Chronotopes, scales and complexity in the study of language in society. *Annual Review of Anthropology* 44, 105–116.
Blommaert, J. (2015b) Language, behavioral scripts and valuation: Comments on 'Transnationalizing Chineseness.' *Research on Alternative Democratic Life in Europe*. Retrieved from https://alternative-democracy-research.org/2015/06/04/comments-on-transnationalizing-chineseness/.
Blommaert, J. (2018) *Durkheim and the Internet: Sociolinguistics and the Sociological Imagination*. London: Bloomsbury.
Blommaert, J. and De Fina, A. (2017) Chronotopic identities: On the spacetime organization of who we are. In A. De Fina, D. Ikizoglu and J. Wegner (eds) *Diversity and Superdiversity: Sociocultural Linguistic Perspectives* (pp. 1–15). Washington: Georgetown University Press.
Blommaert, J. and Varis, P. (2015) Enoughness, accent and light communities: Essays on contemporary identities. *Tilburg Papers in Culture Studies* 139.
Durkheim, E. (2005) *Suicide: A Study in Sociology*. London: Routledge.
Foucault, M. (2004) *Abnormal: Lectures at the Collège de France, 1974–1975*. New York: Picador.
Garfinkel, H. (2002) *Ethnomethodology's Program: Working out Durkheim's Aphorism* (edited by Anne Warfield Rawls). Lanham: Rowman & Littlefield.
Goodwin, C. (2007) Participation, stance and affect in the organization of practice. *Discourse & Society* 18 (1), 53–73.
Latour, B. (2005) *Reassembling the Social: An Introduction to Actor-Network-Theory*. Oxford: Oxford University Press.
Lave, J. and Wenger, E. (1991) *Situated Learning: Legitimate Peripheral Participation*. Cambridge: Cambridge University Press.
Roberts, C. (2016) Translating global experience into institutional models of competency: Linguistic inequality in the job interview. In K. Arnaut, J. Blommaert, B. Rampton, and M. Spotti (eds) *Language and Superdiversity: Recombining Spaces, Times and Language Practices* (pp. 237–260). New York: Routledge.
Silverstein, M. (2003) Indexical order and the dialectics of sociolinguistic life. *Language and Communication* 23, 193–229.
Vertovec, S. (2007) Super-diversity and its implications. *Ethnic and Racial Studies* 30 (6), 1024–1054.

11 Insights and Challenges of Chronotopic Analysis for Sociolinguistics

Anna De Fina

Bakhtin's theory of the chronotope developed, as is well known, within the field of literary studies, therefore it has found wide and punctual applications in literature, but has been far less known and discussed, at least until this moment, in linguistics. This is probably due to the fact that its implications for the analysis of semiotic phenomena in everyday life are not readily apparent to everyone. However, Bakhtin's work in this area has drawn the attention of a relatively small group of linguistic anthropologists and sociolinguists who saw the potential of this construct and who offered a variety of interpretations of the significance of Bakhtin's ideas about the chronotope for the analysis of sociolinguistic phenomena, pointing to possible venues of development (see Agha, 2007; Blommaert, 2015; Blommaert & De Fina, 2017; Dick, 2010; Lempert & Perrino, 2007; Perrino, 2007; Woolard, 2013). This work is now starting to gain traction and recent times have seen a growing interest among socio- and anthropological linguists. The chapters collected in this volume are a testimony to that. In order to offer some thoughts on these contributions, I will first sketch what I see as the most fundamental elements of Bakhtin's theory in order to then discuss the papers collected here in terms of the kinds of applications and insights that they propose.

As I mentioned above, Bakhtin developed the construct of the chronotope in relation to his analysis of different genres of the novel, and particularly in relation to three ancient literary genres: the adventure novel of ordeal, the adventure novel of everyday life and the biographical/autobiographical novel. The most widespread definition of the chronotope – and one amply taken up in the essays collected here – is the one that the

Russian critic offers at the beginning of his essay 'Forms of time and of the chronotope in the novel':

> We will give the name chronotope (literally, 'time space') to the intrinsic connectedness of temporal and spatial relationships that are artistically expressed in literature. (...) What counts for us is the fact that it expresses the inseparability of space and time (time as the fourth dimension of space). (Bakhtin, 1981: 84)

Central to this definition is the impossibility of understanding space and time separately. And indeed, throughout his essay Bakhtin demonstrates how chronotopes are conformed by specific time dimensions (for example cyclical time or unchanging time) that are characterized by certain kinds of divisions, subdivisions, tempos and rhythms in the development of the plot and connects these temporal markers with unique types of spaces or of space organizations. Thus, he explains for example that in the ancient novel of adventure time has no development and no impact on individual characters and that space is vast and undefined as well in the sense that places can be interchangeable with each other since they also do not really affect the plot. He illustrates how there are specific spaces of encounter or dis-encounter that are basic to the actions such as for example *the road* or, in the case of classical Greek drama, *the public square*. Besides being characterized by space/time connections, chronotopes are defined in terms of motifs that underlie novels and that take on certain characteristics thanks to their insertion into the kind of chronotope that is dominant in a particular genre. In that sense, the same motifs and tropes can be found in entirely different times and genres, but they will take up a distinct form because of their connection with general chronotopes. Bakhtin also always underscores the role of language and discourse in instantiating chronotopes by pointing not only to specific linguistic indicators of space and time but also to specific discursive genres and styles as typical elements of chronotopes.

There are three aspects of this theory that, in my opinion, are important not only because they underlie the work presented in the papers collected here, but also because, as we will see, they pose specific challenges in terms of applications and analysis. The first aspect that I want to underscore is the close connection established by Bakhtin between chronotopes and the realm of ideologies. He does so by pointing to different levels: on the one hand within each chronotope we find open references to and discussions of philosophical, social, scientific issues and topics of interest at the time in which the novelistic genre examined was prevalent.

On the other hand, the ways space and time are characterized and related to each other, also respond to societal ideologies and expectations. Thus, for example, Bakhtin notes that in the ancient biographical novel there is no distinction between autobiography and biography because there is no separate consciousness of the individual, or that in Greek classical novels the most symbolic space is represented by the public square as the private and personal sphere has no significance for Greek society. Thus, ideology is present both literally as an organizing principle of the chronotope and as an element of the plot.

This leads us to a second characteristic of Bakhtin's theory: the chronotope has fractal qualities and therefore chronotopes are present and can be analyzed at different scales. Indeed, we find that the whole novel has a chronotopic structure, but also that single motifs, or single characters can be chronotopic. Each chronotopic level, however, gets its meaning and logic from its connection with the whole.

Finally, and most importantly for the chapters of this book: identities are seen as essentially chronotopic, a point that Bakhtin makes over and over again. At the beginning of his essay the Russian author states that 'the image of man is always intrinsically chronotopic' (Bakhtin, 1981: 85). Later, when talking about the portrayal of individuals in the Greek romance he argues that:

> It is nevertheless a living human being moving through space and not merely a physical body in the literal sense of the term. While it is true that his life may be completely passive – 'Fate' runs the game – he nevertheless endures the game fate plays. And he not only endures – he keeps on being the same person and emerges from this game, from all these turns of fate and chance, with his identity absolutely unchanged. This distinctive correspondence of an identity with a particular self is the organizing center of the human image in the Greek romance. (Bakthin, 1981: 105)

In sum, according to Bakhtin identities can only be seen as part of a chronotopic whole described as receiving its coherence and its historical rooting from its connections to the ideologies of a certain time which, in turn, act as a structuring element for the way literary genres are organized.

These ideas on the chronotopicity of identities have been developed in more recent times by Agha, who argues that 'entextualized projections of time cannot be isolated from those of locale and personhood' (2007: 320), and Blommaert and De Fina, who state that 'it is possible to see and describe much of what is observed as contemporary identity work as being chronotopically organized. Indeed, it is organized in, or at least with reference to, specific timespace configurations which are nonrandom and compelling as contexts' (2017: 1).

The contributions collected in this volume further advance these insights. As Kroon and Swanenberg emphasize in their introduction, it is no coincidence that this interest in chronotopes has emerged in the present time of change in sociolinguistics, as globalization and mobility challenge long held assumptions about the stability of the relationships between spaces and identities inviting us to rethink the ways in which identities are embedded into contexts and particularly their relations with spatiotemporal coordinates delimiting a variety of communicative practices. And in fact, the contributing authors demonstrate the productivity of chronotopic analysis in very different domains: from online and mass-mediated interactions (Dovchin; Li & Blommaert; Goebel), to schools (Karrebæk & Møller; Swanenberg), from tourist sites (Gao; Wang & Kroon) to superdiverse neighborhoods (Szabla). These papers contribute in different ways not only to illustrate how the construct of the chronotope can illuminate identity analysis but also to reflect on some of the challenges that this type of work presents for 21st-century linguists. Some of the themes that emerge as prominent among the chapters collected in the volume are the following:

- The mechanisms through which chronotopes emerge, develop and are circulated.
- The relationships among chronotopes and among chronotopes and scales.
- The kinds of resources that count as organized behavior in different chronotopes and the normativities associated with them.
- The validity of chronotope as a notion and a type of analysis for sociolinguistics.

The emergence and circulation of chronotopes is a dominant theme in the piece by Goebel who focuses on 'mass mediated chronotopic identities'. In particular, he analyzes the chronotope of the civil servant in Indonesia at a time characterized by the growing influence of international organizations such as the International Monetary Fund and the World Bank, and of regime change in the direction dictated by such organizations. Goebel clearly relates the emergence of chronotopes to top-down processes of enregisterment which are fostered at different scales through the circulation of documents by powerful transnational and national entities and the reprise by the press of specific themes and tropes. Goebel proposes that enregisterment is largely due to the action of 'interdiscursive hubs', i.e. discursive practices through which elements of different stories are recombined into a new story involving a particular representation of the civil servant. Goebel emphasizes the central role of reported speech, in particular the speech of powerful figures of authority at different scales and of the use of deictics in the creation of this new story. His chapter brings to light an interesting contradiction: while chronotopes are born as punctual time/space/identity connections, their fixation implies generalization and essentialization. Goebel takes up the concept of 'iconization' from Irvine and Gal as denoting 'the process whereby signs that have situation, person, and activity-specific indexical inter-relationships are transformed to be understood as an essential and enduring feature of groups, rather than of an individual involved in a specific interaction' (2000: 37). Through iconization the civil servant becomes a figure of personhood indexing fixed characteristics. Another important point made by Goebel concerns the timing of chronotopic fixation, which may be greatly accelerated or 'turbo sped' within certain social circumstances.

Goebel's piece centers on emergence, circulation and enregisterment as a top down phenomenon dominated by processes that are well beyond the control of local actors and individuals. Both the issue of the timing in the birth and enregisterment of chronotopes and of the agency of individuals or social actors in their evolution and change are important and very relevant to the analysis of different semiotic processes. Indeed, it seems to me that chronotopic representations may emerge at very different rates and through processes that may variously combine top down and bottom up modalities. These possibilities of variation are evident in the contribution by Li and Blommaert that examine the chronotope of the *baifumei*, an online 'image of personality' which has become very popular in China. Here we see a process of enregisterment that is the fruit of bottom up practices in which users of social media are the main agents, even though the logic dominating the economic transactions around the performance of feminine beauty is not controlled by them in the same way. The creation and diffusion of chronotopes through online media however, demonstrates the possibilities of agency that are afforded by mediated environments which are to a great extent controlled by users. Although chronotopes are always formed and circulated via enregisterment, first of all enregisterment itself can happen at very fast rates in online environments and secondly users have, at least potentially, the ability to negotatiate and modify them through their continuously evolving practices.

The question of agency is also openly posed in Wang and Kroon's study about the construction of authenticity in the Chinese province of

Enshi. The authors demonstrate how members of the Tujia ethnic group have found a way of projecting a chronotope of authenticity that fits their own interests and needs even though the chronotopes on which they draw are partly engendered and determined by economic and social processes dominated by alien local and transnational interests.

Another interesting phenomenon illustrated in the analysis proposed by Li and Blommaert is the coexistence of semiotic chunks that respond to different time dimensions in the constitution of new chronotopes. While the *baifumei* itself represents a relatively recent phenomenon in China, its emergence results from the combination of new elements of 'modern beauty' with stereotypical representations of the female body that have sedimented through centuries, and the mixing of traditional with very new practices of exhibition and consumption of that beauty. We are able to witness then how semiotic recombinations are often based on much that is already established and can be read and understood through the eyes of tradition together with much that has become recognizable more recently precisely via an accelerated circulation in online practices. And in fact there is a transformative power in chronotopes that is well captured by Agha, who notes:

> Although [chronotopic] depictions draw on ideas of place, time and personhood that are presupposed by current participants, they contrast with them as depictions, frequently transforming and re-ordering the presuppositions with which they contrast. (Agha, 2007: 323)

The relationships among chronotopes and among them and scales is at the center of Wang and Kroon's chapter. Wang and Kroon's careful analysis of the 'semiotic production of authenticity' in the case of the Tujia ethnic group, shows how such process rests on a multiplicity of chronotopes and that a simplistic view of binary oppositions between timeless tradition and modernity is utterly inadequate to capture the complexities involved in the dynamics between centers and peripheries that are typical of social and economic processes in the globalized world. Such complexities underlie the production and negotiation of identities as well. Thus, the authors illustrate how authenticity is projected through a variety of chronotopes such as those involved in rural life, ecotourism and adventure that are both hierarchically organized and inserted into wider chronotopes at different scales involving the global/translocal, the national and the regional/local. Authenticity is then the result of a selection of topics, figures of personhood represented in times and spaces which are recombined according to a market logic that links local and translocal interests.

Chronotopes can also be related by contrast, as discussed by Gao, in her analysis of people's reaction to change in West Street, Yangshuo, in southern China and of the different identities which they associate with chronotopes that represent diverging value systems. In their discourse, the same place can index a variety of scenarios involving different roles and images and these chronotopic representations may coexist, producing conflicting effects for identity enactments by inhabitants of the area. As Gao notes, identities may be associated with multilayered and coexisting chronotopes rather than with homogeneous and compatible ones.

A third topic that different contributors deal with in their analysis is the question of what counts as organized behavior, i.e. what resources constitute the defining elements of a chronotope and make it recognizable. An issue that Karrebæk and Møller take up explicitly by referring to Blommaert's (2015: 113) questions: '(a) what do we understand? And (b) how come we understand it as such?' Karrebæk and Møller start from participants' reactions to language use in very specific types of performance enacted in a Danish school: a student presentation and a platform event. The authors illustrate how these events are carefully organized according to certain scripts that students know very well. Such scripts involve the performance of academic competence through creative presentations. By analyzing both audience and main actors' reactions to the performances Karrebæk and Møller are able to reconstruct the emergence of different chronotopic representations associated with the use of local or ethnic languages and to illustrate how the insertion of stretches of speech that are not in Danish is sufficient to change the chronotopic understanding of an event from a serious academic performance into an amusing spectacle.

The association of chronotopes with the use of specific linguistic resources is also at the center of Dovchin's study of inverted language among young Mongolians and of Swanenberg's analysis of repertoire shifts among students in Dutch educational institutions within different kinds of language practices. Both chapters illustrate that chronotopic identities emerge and are associated with very specific time/place configurations in which linguistic resources do not correspond with identifiable languages but rather with the use of linguistic chunks that may be connected to separate languages or semiotic chinks resulting from the conscious manipulation of known languages. Participants make their judgements of adequacy about the use of linguistic resources based on the fact that in different environments chronotopic identities are enacted and defined according to criteria that take into account relationships, times and spaces both physical and virtual.

The contribution by Li and Blommaert widens the scope of chronotopic analysis beyond the simple consideration of the role of linguistic resources by demonstrating the importance of a punctual analysis of the technological affordances exploited by users for the projection of the set of features that are considered sufficient to conform the online chronotope of the *baifumei*. Indeed as the authors note, taking up Blommaert and Varis (2015: 5), identity practices are 'discursive orientations towards sets of features that are (or can be) seen as emblematic'. Thus, they discuss how besides what they call 'interactional scripts', users of online media need to have a specific kind of avatar and upload a series of doctored photographs or video-streamed pictures containing a set of fixed elements associated with the *baifumei* persona. Interactional scrips also involve specific behaviors for participants such as the offering of gifts to the *baifumei* and certain linguistic routines that gain public recognition through feedback. Li and Blommaert argue that this analysis demonstrates the specificity of identity work in online contexts, however, in my view another very important implication of their study is the need to look very carefully at the elements that constitute the 'enoughness' of any chronotopic persona for its recognizability.

All the chapters discussed above also touch upon the issue of normativity seen as a set of rules that underlie value judgments in regard to the acceptability and suitability of the use of semiotic resources as part of adequate behavior within precise time and space parameters. Metalinguistic judgements, which are interrogated in many of the chapters provide insight into the kinds of norms that regulate in the different cases analyzed the use of linguistic and semiotic resources. Issues of normativity and value judgements constitute a central topic in Szabla's study of Polish migrants' relations to place in Antwerp's neighborhoods. Szabla applies Blommaert's (2015) insight that chronotopic representations come with 'moralized behavioral scripts' to show how individuals construct the story of their own movements in time and place in relation to moral norms that are associated with those spatiotemporal configurations. Thus, their values and normative systems change and adapt to the varying chronotopic identities related to the neighborhoods in which they have moved.

The last, but not least important topic, that is at the core of all the contributions collected here but that is also explicitly dealt with by Blommaert in his chapter aptly titled 'Are chronotopes useful?' refers to the significance of this construct for sociolinguistic analysis. Blommaert points to three aspects that explain why the notion of chronotope constitutes an important development in the ways in which sociolinguists conceive of context. First, the chronotope rather than isolating ad hoc elements or aspects of context, attempts to capture the wholeness of the social occasion by relating places, times and identities with scripts and normative behaviors and values.

Second, the chronotope captures the historical dimension that characterizes every context by relating behavior to processes of sedimentation of meanings and habitus and therefore to their recognizability, while leaving open the potential for continuous reinterpretations and reconfigurations.

Third, as Blommaert underscores, the behavioral scripts indexed by specific chronotopes are always associated with value judgements through which participants assess the suitability and moral acceptability of communicative action, and therefore with general value systems that also are profoundly ideological.

The first point differentiates chronotopic analysis from notions of context based exclusively on the analysis of the local level (such as those focused on sequential implicativeness), on cognitive factors such as implicatures and relevance, or on dichotomic views of the micro and the macro. Indeed, the focus is to the infinite specificity of the 'social situation' and of the resources that participants put in play within it and therefore to the minute details of interaction and to the variability in the nature of those resources, with no a priori preeminence given to language.

The second point highlights the role of ideologies and common sense understandings in the recognizability of situations, but also draws our attention on the diverse and stratified levels of history that may coexist in chronotopes, on different velocities of creation, sedimentation and fixation, and on the various scales that may be involved in the constitution and circulation of these frames.

The third point invites us to account for the sphere encompassing the ethical and moral domain and therefore, in my view, also implies the need to take into serious consideration the range of emotions and affects that are associated with specific chronotopes. A consideration of these factors opens the door for appreciating both the ways in which emotions are related to particular personae or worlds and the reasons for the effectiveness of certain chronotopic representations versus others.

Overall, I think that the most important implication that we can draw not only from Blommaert's chapter but from all of the contributions is that there can be no chronotopic analysis without ethnography and no understanding of identities without a close analysis of the specificity of semiotic practices. Indeed, all the studies in the volume illustrate how the units of talk and associated resources that allow for the recognition of 'envelopes of understanding' (Silverstein, 2005) can only be defined through careful and painstaking ethnographic work focused on ways in which participants understand and construct social realities. Ethnography and its focus on practices constitutes the basis to determine, among other things, how participants make sense of scripts, how they interpret the use of resources, what elements constitute the enoughness among the features of a chronotope, what scales are involved in the creation of particular chronotopes, how these are defined and related, and what the relevant spatiotemporal dimensions are.

As I mentioned at the beginning of this commentary, answering these questions is no easy task and this is the challenge of doing chronotopic analysis and a challenge that contributors to the volume meet in their studies with different degrees of success. Indeed, for example, given that chronotopes can be seen as operating at different scales and have fractal qualities, it is not easy to define them at each level. There is always the risk of being too generic or too specific in the individuation of chronotopes. Ultimately there is also the problem of how to name a chronotope. Indeed, there are chronotopic identities that relate explicitly named personae to particular worlds, such as in the case of the *baifumei* or in the case of well-established historical or literary figures such as Odysseus. However, other chronotopic identities are not as evident. For example, what kind of identities are indexed by a chronotope such as the one of rural life or ecotourism? And what are the features of these chronotopic representations? Furthermore, are chronotopes always recognizable to participants in communicative interactions or can they also represent useful analytical tools for researchers? All these questions have no easy answer.

A second difficulty is that of relating in punctual ways spaces and times with identities, in order to illustrate how a chronotopic analysis may differ from a mere study of language varieties, registers and styles. Thus, an exclusive focus on linguistic resources will not do without a description of other resources and of relevant spatiotemporal parameters. However, categories of time and space can be vague, multidimensional and multiscalar, thus the specification of such parameters may present great difficulties as well.

Last but not least, even when an analyst has been able to define the characteristics of individual chronotopes, teasing out the ways in which different chronotopes connect and relate to each other may present a daunting task. As Silverstein notes,

> what actually happens is that people use language and perilinguistic semiotics on particular occasions of discursive interaction; however, such usage on any particular occasion bears a potential relationship to discourse on some other occasion or occasions in a phenomenally different spatiotemporal envelope. (2005: 6)

And indeed, chronotopic analysis involves the complex task of reconstructing interdiscursive chains represented for example in genres and styles and a host of other possible interconnections between discursive and semiotic phenomena, which again requires uncovering links between communicative acts that may have taken place in very different times and spaces.

The points made above illustrate some of the challenges that the application of the notion of chronotope to concrete communicative events presents to sociolinguists. The contributors to this volume show many ways in which ethnographically inspired analyses can meet them while at the same time bringing to light their complexities. By doing so, they also set the basis for new paths for developments in the investigation of the chronotope in sociolinguistics.

References

Agha, A. (2007) Recombinant selves in mass mediated spacetime. *Language & Communication* 27, 320–335.

Bakhtin, M. (1981) Forms of time and of the chronotope in the novel: Notes toward a historical poetics. In M. Bakhtin *The Dialogic Imagination: Four Essays* (edited by M. Holquist; translated by C. Emerson and M. Holquist) (pp. 84–258). Austin: University of Texas Press.

Blommaert, J. (2015) Chronotopes, scales, and complexity in the study of language in society. *The Annual Review of Anthropology* 44, 105–116.

Blommaert, J. and De Fina, A. (2017) Chronotopic identities: On the timespace organization of who we are. In A. De Fina, D. Ikizoglu and J. Wegner (eds) *Diversity and Super-Diversity* (pp. 1–14). Washington, DC: Georgetown University Press.

Blommaert, J. and Varis, P. (2015) Enoughness, accent and light communities: Essays on contemporary identities. *Tilburg Papers in Culture Studies* 76.

Dick, H. (2010) Imagined lives and modernist chronotopes in Mexican nonmigrant discourse. *American Ethnologist* 37, 275–290.

Irvine, J. and Gal, S. (2000) Language ideology and linguistic differentiation. In P.V. Kroskrity (ed.) *Regimes of Language: Ideologies, Polities and Identities* (pp. 35–84). Santa Fe: School of American Research Press.

Lempert, M. and Perrino, S. (2007) Editorial: Entextualization and the end of temporality. *Language & Communication* 27, 205–211.

Perrino, S. (2007) Cross-chronotope alignment in Senegalese oral narrative. *Language & Communication* 2, 227–244.

Silverstein, M. (2005) Axes of evals: Token versus type interdiscursivity. *Journal of Linguistic Anthropology* 15 (1), 6–22.

Woolard, K. (2013) Is the personal political? Chronotopes and changing stances toward Catalan language and identity. *International Journal of Bilingual Education and Bilingualism* 16, 210–224.

Index

action(s) 5, 14, 17–18, 20–23, 27–28, 30, 49, 61, 63, 87–88, 116, 119, 138, 156, 188, 191, 193, 198
  social, 5, 14, 17–18, 20–21, 27, 49, 156
agency(ies) 3, 5, 72, 83, 88–89, 111–112, 123–124, 126, 188, 194
Agha, Asif 3, 19, 21, 67–70, 81, 88–89, 100, 110–112, 132–133, 137, 190, 192, 195
Appadurai, Arjun 1, 4, 49, 90, 108
Arabic 130, 133–134, 142–144, 146–148, 151, 161–162
authenticity 3, 7, 9–10, 12–13, 15, 51–52, 63, 65, 105–107, 109–127, 134, 153, 155, 157–159, 161, 163, 165, 167, 169, 171, 173, 194–195
  commodification of 110, 113, 126
  heritage 105, 107, 109, 111–115, 117, 119–125, 127
  inauthentic 105, 110, 123, 127
  inauthenticity 10, 105–106, 110, 118, 121–122, 134, 140, 157
  order(s) of 3, 110–113, 117, 120, 122, 123–125
  production of 105, 119, 195
  semiotization of 117

baifumei (白富美) 8, 49, 51–59, 61, 63, 65–66, 194–195, 197, 199
Bakhtin, Mikhail 1, 3, 4, 19–20, 27, 68, 87–88, 110–112, 129, 131–132, 156, 165, 190–192
behavioral script(s) 13, 20–22, 56, 158–160, 163, 167–172, 175–179, 185–187, 189, 197–198
Belgium 6, 13, 25, 174, 180–185, 188
Blommaert, Jan 1–5, 7–8, 10, 13–14, 17, 20, 22, 27–30, 49–52, 56, 63, 67–69, 81–82, 88–90, 96–97, 100, 102, 109–112, 116, 119, 130, 132, 140, 148, 153–154, 157–158, 171, 175–177, 180, 188, 190, 192–198
Bourdieu, Pierre 20, 69, 108, 112, 128

Castells, Manuel 1, 4, 11, 49
China 6, 8–10, 15, 49, 51–53, 55–57, 59, 61–63, 65–66, 86–87, 89, 91–93, 95, 97, 99, 101, 103–109, 111, 113, 115, 117, 119–121, 123, 125–127, 194–196
chronotope(s) 2–3, 5, 8, 12–14, 16–17, 19–23, 25–29, 31–33, 35, 37, 39, 41–43, 45–47, 49, 51, 53, 55–59, 61, 63–65, 67–69, 72, 74, 79, 81, 83, 85, 87–91, 96–98, 100–107, 109–127, 129, 131–133, 135, 139, 141, 144, 147–152, 156, 158, 162, 164–173, 176–178, 180, 182–200
  macroscopic 25, 27–29, 31–33, 35, 37–39, 41–43, 45, 47
  mass-mediated 68, 72
  microscopic 25, 27–29, 31–33, 35, 37, 39, 41–43, 45, 47
  online 8, 61, 63, 197
Cicourel, Aaron 17, 21, 23
civil service 72, 76, 78–79
code(s) 20, 25, 28, 32, 35, 37, 45–46, 82, 90, 187
  secret 32, 35, 37, 46, 139
commodification 9, 103, 109–110, 113, 115, 118, 122, 124, 126
  of authenticity 110, 113, 126
community(ies) 4–5, 7, 10, 13, 15–16, 31, 47, 49, 63–65, 83, 88, 97–98, 100–101, 104–105, 120, 126, 156, 174–176, 178, 180, 186, 188
  imagined 107, 125, 150
  micro-communities 4, 7
complexity 3–4, 14, 23, 27, 46, 83, 89, 103, 105, 111–112, 123, 126, 150, 172, 175, 187–189, 200

Index

configuration 3, 5, 12–13, 17–18, 21, 28–29, 62, 70–71, 73, 81, 83, 88, 102, 105, 111–113, 119, 158, 193, 196–197
  timespace 3, 5, 13, 17–18, 21, 28, 62, 88, 102, 105, 111–112, 193
context 4, 6–7, 10, 12–14, 16–17, 21–23, 25–26, 28–30, 38, 40, 48, 50, 52, 56, 75, 84, 88–89, 106, 108, 111–112, 125, 135, 139, 153–159, 161–162, 164–165, 169, 173, 176, 182, 188, 197–198
contextualization 3, 23–24, 28, 45, 106, 111, 137
contrast(s) 88–89, 100, 103, 122, 140, 196
  chronotopic 88–89, 91, 96, 98, 100, 102–103
Coupland, Nicholas 105, 109, 134–135
creativity 24, 25–26, 28–30, 32, 38, 42, 45, 112, 115, 151
  linguistic 25–26, 28–29, 32, 38, 42, 45

deictics 8, 68, 70, 73, 78–80, 82, 194
Denmark 6, 128, 130, 133–134, 139–140, 151
diacritic(s) 175, 179, 182
dialect 127, 151, 154–155, 157, 160, 162–173
diaspora (Polish) 175–176
digitalization 4, 7, 14, 153
distinction 83, 108, 110, 113, 121, 126, 154, 177, 180, 192

economy 8, 26, 29, 56, 64, 66, 88, 91–92, 94, 98, 100, 102, 104, 106–110, 125–127, 174–175, 177–179, 181, 183, 185–187, 189
  moral 174–175, 179, 181, 183, 185–187, 189
  tourism 92, 94, 98, 100, 102, 106–107, 109
education 6, 11–13, 15, 23, 104, 127, 141, 149–152, 155, 158, 169, 183, 185, 200
  educational system 6, 11, 128–130
emblematic 52, 108, 138, 197
embodiment 117
ethnogenesis 108, 123, 127
ethnotaxonomy 108, 110, 117, 120
euphemism 32, 38–39, 46
exoticitization 110

Foucault, Michel 50, 66, 177, 189
frame(s) 2–3, 5, 10, 29, 38, 41, 45, 89, 105, 109, 111–113, 118–119, 154, 198

Garfinkel, Harold 19–20, 177
genre(s) 3, 6–7, 23, 27–28, 62, 111, 119, 190–192, 200
global peripheral tourism 6, 9
globalization 1–4, 7, 9–11, 13–15, 23, 26, 46–47, 65, 88–91, 101, 103, 105–110, 112–113, 119, 122–127, 153, 157, 172, 189, 193
  neoliberal 101, 103
  peripheral 106, 110, 112
  sociolinguistic 14, 106, 125
Goffman, Erving 18–23, 50, 54–56, 64, 66, 130–131, 151
Goodwin, Charles 17, 19, 22–23, 64, 66, 84, 177, 189
governance (good) 8, 67, 71–72, 79, 83–84

Han 108, 110, 117, 121, 136, 138, 151
Heller, Monica 69, 105–107, 109–110
hegemony(ies) 7, 24, 37, 107–108, 151
  micro-hegemonies 5, 175–176, 179
heritage 9–10, 37, 105–125, 127, 151
  authenticity 105, 107, 109, 111–115, 117, 119–125, 127
  tourism 10, 105–107, 109–110, 112–113, 115–116, 118, 120, 122–125
history(ies) 3, 19, 66, 75, 87–89, 91, 102, 107, 109–111, 113, 117, 119–121, 126, 132, 180, 183–184, 187, 198,
  invokable 3, 111, 113, 117
Hymes, Dell 18, 20, 22, 112

iconization 8, 67, 69–71, 73–74, 76, 81–82, 194
identity(ies) 1–15, 17–18, 20–30, 32, 34, 36–38, 40–42, 44–52, 54–56, 58, 60–110, 112–114, 116–124, 126–134, 136, 138–140, 142, 144, 146–148, 150–156, 158–166, 168, 170–189, 192–200
  ascribed 106, 155, 176, 178, 180
  diacritic(s) 175, 179, 182
  mass-mediated chonotopic 68, 69, 71–72, 81–82, 193
  politics 90, 106–107, 112

practices 25, 51–52, 83, 106, 197
prescribed 106
repertoire(s) 117, 176, 188
tourist 9
work 1, 3–14, 20, 49–50, 56, 63–64, 90, 156, 158, 165, 170–172, 176–177, 182, 187, 192, 197
imagined communities 107, 125, 150
imitation 69, 73, 77, 79–84
inauthenticity 10, 105–106, 110, 118, 121–122, 134, 140, 157
indexicality 3, 19–21, 28, 105, 111, 177
order(s) of 3, 20–21, 24, 28, 111, 177
Indonesia 6, 8, 67, 69, 71–73, 75, 77, 79, 81, 83–85, 193
inequality 9, 23, 88, 91, 108, 123–126, 169, 176, 189
inference(s) 12, 17, 131
infrastructure 50, 56, 79, 107, 186
interaction 1, 5, 11, 17–18, 20–23, 28–30, 33, 41, 43, 48, 50, 57–58, 60–64, 66, 70, 90, 103, 126, 129, 141–142, 147–148, 151–152, 155–156, 164, 168, 175, 186, 194, 198–199
interdiscursive hub(s) 68, 73, 75, 77, 81–83, 194
internet 6–8, 24, 26, 49, 51, 57, 62, 64–66, 189
invokable histories 3, 111, 113, 117

Jørgensen, Jens Normann 11, 25, 32, 142, 155

Kress, Gunther 51, 54, 64

language(s) 1–5, 7, 9, 11–16, 19–20, 23–48, 65, 68, 72, 75, 82–84, 86, 89–90, 96–98, 102–104, 107–108, 111–112, 120–135, 137–142, 144–159, 161–173, 186, 189, 191, 196, 198–200
as a pleasure 41
ideology(ies) 7, 37, 46, 84, 89, 125, 151, 200
inverted 7, 25, 27, 29–33, 35–47, 196
minority 129, 134, 141–142, 144, 146–149, 152, 157, 169
registers of 129
youth 5, 7, 25–27, 29–33, 35–39, 41, 43, 45–47, 134, 138, 157–158, 173, 196

languaging 4, 12, 15, 46, 151–152, 155, 173
linguistic creativity 26, 28–29, 32, 38, 42, 45
ludic 8, 49–51, 53, 55–57, 59, 61–65

macroscopic chronotope(s) 25, 27–29, 31–33, 35, 37–39, 41–43, 45, 47
mass-mediated chronotope(s) 68, 72
media 2, 8, 22, 24, 27, 46–49, 51, 63, 65–67, 69, 71–72, 81, 152, 194, 197
micro-communities 4, 7
micro-hegemonies 5, 175–176, 179
microscopic chronotope(s) 25, 27–29, 31–33, 35, 37, 39, 41–43, 45, 47
migration 4, 6, 10–11, 15, 26, 126–127, 134, 142, 180
minority(ies) 10, 36, 105–108, 110, 113, 115–117, 120, 122–123, 125–130, 134, 140–142, 144, 146–152, 157, 169
group(s) 10, 36, 120, 122, 125
language(s) 129, 134, 141–142, 144, 146–149, 152, 157, 169
mobility 1–2, 4, 9–11, 26, 65, 90, 104, 127, 172, 193
Mongolia 6–7, 25–27, 29–41, 43–48
moralized behavioral script(s) 13, 20–22, 175–178, 187, 197

nation-building 10, 107, 113
neoliberal globalization 101, 103
Netherlands 6, 25, 48, 155, 158–159, 162, 165, 173
normativity 11–12, 153, 155, 157–159, 161, 163, 165, 167, 169–171, 173, 178, 197

online 4–8, 11, 15, 30–32, 36, 42, 47, 49–53, 55–59, 61–66, 73, 81, 86, 125, 159, 193–195, 197
chronotope(s) 8, 61, 63, 197
online-offline nexus 6
order(s) of 3, 20–21, 28, 38, 45, 110–113, 117, 120, 122–125, 177
authenticity 3, 110–113, 117, 120, 122–125
indexicality 3, 20–21, 24, 28, 111, 177
othering 110

performance 12, 17, 19, 24, 27, 29–30, 48, 50, 52, 56, 58, 66, 83, 89, 98, 112–114,

116–117, 119, 131–135, 137, 139–142, 144, 147–148, 150, 152, 176, 194, 196
periphery(ies) 5, 8, 10, 46–48, 106–107, 109–110, 113, 120, 123–125, 127, 153, 173, 195
   peripheral globalization 106, 110, 112
   global peripheral tourism 16, 19
platform events 131–132
Poland 180–184
Polish diaspora 175–176
polycentric 109–110, 112, 119, 124, 152, 175–176
polynomic 175, 177
power 9–10, 13, 22–23, 29, 83–84, 88, 90, 104, 108, 112, 121, 126, 147, 150, 172, 195
process 119
production of authenticity 105, 119, 195

Rampton, Ben 19, 88, 134, 140
regime(s) 8, 11–12, 26–27, 67, 81, 84, 90, 98, 103, 109, 120, 125, 128–129, 131, 133, 135, 137, 139, 141, 143, 145, 147, 149, 151, 193, 200
register(s) 3, 12, 48, 69, 111, 129, 134, 137–138, 150, 152, 154, 156–158, 161, 169, 171, 199
repertoire(s) 2, 7–8, 12, 28, 30, 38, 40, 45–46, 50, 61, 117, 134, 153–157, 159–160, 162–172, 176–177, 188, 196
   identity 117, 176, 188
   language 2, 8, 12, 28, 38, 46, 134, 153–157, 159–160, 162–172, 196

scale(s) 4–6, 8, 11, 13–15, 23, 46, 67–68, 70, 81–83, 103, 105, 111–112, 119–126, 130, 141, 149–151, 165, 172, 189, 192–195, 198–200
script(s) 6, 13, 18, 20–22, 26, 34, 37, 46, 50, 56, 141, 158–159, 162–163, 167–172, 175–178, 185–187, 189, 196–199
   (moralized) behavioral 13, 20–22, 56, 158–160, 162–163, 167–172, 175–179, 185–187, 189, 197–198
secret 32–35, 37, 46, 139
code(s) 32, 35, 37, 46, 139
self-presentation 51, 64
selfie 49–53, 55, 57–59, 61, 63–65
semiotic 3, 5, 9–10, 21, 28–29, 45, 52, 62, 64, 66, 68–69, 73, 77, 79, 82, 87–89, 91, 102, 105, 107, 109, 111–112, 114, 116–119, 122–124, 127, 133–134, 149, 152, 176, 190, 194–198, 200
   design(ing) 10, 106, 119, 123, 127
   landscapes 9–10, 87
semiotization of authenticity 117
Silverstein, Michael 17–18, 20, 24, 112, 127, 131, 152, 156, 173, 177, 189, 198–200
situation 6, 11–12, 17–18, 20–23, 69, 100, 130, 133–135, 140–141, 143–144, 146–147, 156, 159, 162, 165, 167–169, 171, 175, 177, 183, 185–187, 194, 198
situated 3, 13, 20–21, 70, 106, 111, 113, 125, 133, 140, 159, 184, 189
social 2–3, 5, 7–9, 11–15, 17–30, 38, 42, 45, 47–50, 56, 61–68, 71–72, 80–91, 93, 95–103, 108, 111–112, 120, 126, 130–132, 134, 140, 151–152, 156–159, 163–164, 168, 170, 172, 175–177, 182–183, 185, 188–189, 191, 194–195, 198–199
   action 5, 14, 17–18, 20–21, 27, 49, 156
   change 13, 86–91, 93, 95–99, 101–103
   media 8, 22, 24, 47, 49, 63, 65–66, 152, 194
sociolinguistic globalization 14, 106, 125
Somali 34, 130, 141–149
stance 54, 66, 86–87, 89–90, 102–103, 127, 129, 189
state identity politics 106
student(s) 11, 18, 34, 131–132, 134, 139–140, 143, 145, 147, 149, 158, 160, 164, 166–168, 178–179, 196
   minority language 128, 130, 141, 149
superdiversity 1, 3–4, 10–11, 13–15, 23, 46–47, 65, 83, 103, 126, 150, 152–153, 172–175, 182, 187, 189, 200
system(s) 1–3, 6, 11, 15, 18–20, 28–29, 35, 45–46, 49, 58–59, 64, 74, 103, 111, 125, 128–130, 154–155, 175, 196–198
   educational 6, 11, 128–130
   language 28–29, 35, 46, 154–155
   nomic 175
   social 18, 49, 64

timespace 3–5, 11–13, 17–19, 21, 28, 46, 50, 56, 62–63, 65, 68, 81, 83, 87–90, 97–98, 102–103, 105, 110–112, 114, 117–120, 122, 124, 126, 131–133, 139, 148, 150, 158, 176–177, 182–184, 193, 200

configuration 3, 5, 13, 17–18, 21, 28, 62, 88, 102, 105, 111–112, 193
tourism 6, 9–10, 14–15, 86, 88, 91–94, 98, 100, 102–107, 109–110, 112–113, 115–116, 118–120, 122–125, 127, 195, 199
　global peripheral 6, 9
　heritage 10, 105–107, 109–110, 112–113, 115–116, 118, 120, 122–125
tourist identity 9
tropes 2–3, 66, 111, 115, 191, 193
truth(s) 19, 82, 108, 112, 117
　nomic 82
Turkish 130, 132–135, 139, 147, 149, 161–163, 186

Varis, Piia 4, 15, 31, 48, 51–52, 56, 64–65, 109, 126, 176, 180, 189, 197, 200
vernacular(s) 12, 30, 40, 151, 154–157, 160, 162–165, 169–171
Vertovec, Steven 1, 153, 175, 182

Woolard, Kathryn 89, 110, 124, 169, 190

youth 5, 7–8, 25–33, 35, 37–39, 41–43, 45–48, 69, 83, 133–134, 137–138, 140, 151–152, 157–158, 173
　language (inverted) 5, 7, 25–27, 29–33, 35–39, 41, 43, 45–47, 134, 138, 157–158, 173, 196

For Product Safety Concerns and Information please contact our EU Authorised Representative:

Easy Access System Europe

Mustamäe tee 50

10621 Tallinn

Estonia

gpsr.requests@easproject.com

www.ingramcontent.com/pod-product-compliance
Lightning Source LLC
Chambersburg PA
CBHW070607300426
44113CB00010B/1442